CREATING THE LAW

Written opinions are the primary means by which judges communicate with external actors. These sentiments include the parties to the case itself, but also more broadly journalists, public officials, lawyers, other judges, and increasingly, the mass public. In *Creating the Law*, Michael K. Romano and Todd A. Curry examine the extent to which judges tailor their language in order to avoid retribution during their retention, and how institutional variations involving intra-chamber dynamics may influence the written word of a legal opinion.

Using an extensive dataset that includes the text of all death penalty and education decisions issued by state supreme courts from 1995–2010, Romano and Curry are the first to examine the connection between retention incentives and language choices. They utilize text analysis techniques developed in the field of communications and apply them to the text of judicial decisions. In doing so, they find that judges write with their audience in mind, and emphasize duelling strategies of justification and persuasion in order to please diverse audiences that may be paying attention. Furthermore, the process of drafting a majority opinion is a team exercise, and when more individuals are involved in its crafting, the product will reflect this complexity.

This book gives students the tools for understanding how institutional variation affects judicial outcomes and shows how language relates to decision-making in the judiciary more specifically.

Michael K. Romano received his Ph.D. in 2014 from Western Michigan University and is an Assistant Professor in the Political Science Department at Shenandoah University. His research focuses on how elite actors – specifically judges in both the federal and state courts in the United States and members of Congress – craft language in order to affect policy goals and political outcomes. His work has been published in *Justice System Journal*, *Social Science Quarterly*, and *PS: Political Science & Politics*.

Todd A. Curry received his Ph.D. in political science at Western Michigan University in 2012, and is an Assistant Professor in the Political Science Department at University of Texas, El Paso. His primary area of research is State Courts of Last Resort in the United States, as well as indigenous peoples and the law and diversity in higher education. His work has been published in *Justice System Journal*, *American Review of Politics*, *PS: Political Science & Politics*, and *The Journal of Politics*.

Law, Courts and Politics

Edited by Robert M. Howard, Georgia State University

In *Democracy in America*, Alexis de Tocqueville famously noted that "scarcely any political question arises in the United States that is not resolved, sooner or later, into a judicial question." The importance of courts in settling political questions in areas ranging from health care to immigration shows the continuing astuteness of de Tocqueville's observation. To understand how courts resolve these important questions, empirical analyses of law, courts and judges, and the politics and policy influence of law and courts have never been more salient or more essential.

Law, Courts and Politics was developed to analyze these critically important questions. This series presents empirically driven manuscripts in the broad field of judicial politics and public law by scholars in law and social science. It uses the most up to date scholarship and seeks an audience of students, academics, upper division undergraduate and graduate courses in law, political science and sociology as well as anyone interested in learning more about law, courts and politics.

Judicial Review and Contemporary Democratic Theory
Power, Domination and the Courts
Scott E. Lemieux and David J. Watkins

States in American Constitutionalism
Interpretation, Authority, and Politics
Bradley D. Hays

Creating the Law
State Supreme Court Opinions and the Effect of Audiences
Michael K. Romano and Todd A. Curry

For more information about this series, please visit: www.routledge.com/Law-Courts-and-Politics/book-series/LCP

CREATING THE LAW

State Supreme Court Opinions and The Effect of Audiences

Michael K. Romano and Todd A. Curry

Routledge
Taylor & Francis Group

NEW YORK AND LONDON

First published 2020
by Routledge
52 Vanderbilt Avenue, New York, NY 10017

and by Routledge
2 Park Square, Milton Park, Abingdon, Oxon, OX14 4RN

Routledge is an imprint of the Taylor & Francis Group, an informa business

© 2020 Taylor & Francis

Library of Congress Cataloging-in-Publication Data
A catalog record for this title has been requested

ISBN: 978-1-138-61683-7 (hbk)
ISBN: 978-1-138-61684-4 (pbk)
ISBN: 978-0-429-46182-8 (ebk)

Typeset in Bembo
by Apex CoVantage, LLC

For both of our families, whom have supported us both in life
and through this project

CONTENTS

FIGURES

TABLES

ACKNOWLEDGEMENTS

This project, in its nascent form, dates back to 2010, so we have nearly a decade of individuals to recognize for supporting both of us through this project. Foremost, we need to thank the Political Science department at Western Michigan University for providing us with an environment that allowed each of to pursue specializations that were mentally stimulating and complementary. Furthermore, the amount of research and travel support that we enjoyed because of department chair and mentor, John Clark, far surpassed what we would have received at any other university.

While finishing our degrees at WMU, we also had the invaluable experience of learning from, being mentored by, and collaborating with Mark S. Hurwitz. It is difficult to quantify what Mark has done for us over the years, but with regards to this project, he introduced us to *Judges and Their Audiences*. While discussing it in class, his off-hand comment, "Now think about state judges," may officially be considered the starting point of this project.

As we both transition into our positions as assistant professors, we received significant support from each of our departments and universities. Todd would like to thank Greg Schmidt, Charles Boehmer, and Gaspare Genna for helping him balance the demands of teaching and research. A special thanks goes to William Weaver and the Patti and Paul Yetter Center for the Law at University of Texas at El Paso who provided for research assistance and the preparation of the final manuscript. A special note of thanks to Ricardo A. Romero and Tiffiny D. Stevens whom helped collect and code the majority of our data. Michael would similarly like to thank Eric Leonard, Julie Hofmann, Brett Kite and Brian Pearce-Gonzalez for helping navigate and find balance in teaching and research and providing opportunities to expand the research into the classroom setting. Michael would also like to thank Ashley Oates for her assistance in the organization, processing, and cleaning of the education data to prepare for its analysis. A special thanks goes to the Shenandoah University Summer Scholars program for helping fund under-graduate collaboration with the research developed in this text.

This project, as the culmination of nearly 10 years of work, has been before the eyes of many colleagues, and we owe much to their comments and criticisms. We would like to thank Chris W. Bonneau, Tao L. Dumas, Shane A. Gleason, Greg Goelzhauser, Melinda Gann Hall, Mark S. Hurwitz, Benjamin J, Kassow, Meghan E. Leonard, C. Scott Peters and Joseph Ross whom have all commented on drafts of these chapters. Especially notable is Michael P. Fix who read the manuscript in its entirety and made extensive comments. Any errors that remain are ours entirely.

Finally, this book would not have been possible without the amazing and continued support of our families. At every step of the process their love and understanding has been invaluable to our sanity. Todd thanks his wife Erin for her continued understanding and support through his entire academic career. He would also like to thank his daughter, Leone, for daily reminders that it is ok to take a break to read a book, play with toys, or watch TV. Your "distractions" will forever be welcome. Michael would like to thank his wife Katherine, for provid-ing him with grounding and forcing him to find a balance between professional demands and mental health. Her unending support for this project, and relentless cheerleading was instrumental in the creation, sustainment, and completion of this project.

1

INTRODUCTION

In March 2012, Rickey Alvis Bell, Jr. was convicted for the murder of Starr Harris and sentenced to death. The state of Tennessee allows for the death penalty in cases involving aggravating circumstances, and a jury panel found during the sentencing phase that despite mitigating circumstances, the nature of the crime was heinous enough to warrant a harsher punishment than is usually prescribed by the Tennessee penal code.[1] Tennessee allows for an automatic appeal of any case involving capital punishment, and in September 2015, the Tennessee Supreme Court reviewed and upheld the death sentence by a vote of 3–2. Justice Bivins, in justifying the choice of the Court, argues in the majority opinion that while the errors made during the trial phase were significant, many of them were deemed to be "harmless beyond a reasonable doubt" as they would have had no effect on the jury's final decision. Bivins would notably state in his conclusion that the death sentence was sufficiently warranted, particularly for this "brutal murder" (480 S.W.3d 486 at 47). Taken in isolation, the decision in *State v. Bell.* appears cut and dried. The justices, in reviewing the facts of the case, determined that the errors of the trial court would not have reasonably affected the outcome in the case, thus denying Bell relief from the sentence.

Tennessee, however, has an interesting and unique history with the death penalty. Mr. Bell was the only individual sentenced to death in 2012 in the state, and Tennessee regularly sentences individuals to life imprisonment rather than death according to the Department of Corrections.[2] As of 2018, it had been nine years since the state had carried out a death sentence. Thus, death penalty cases – especially when they come before the state's high court – are highly salient events.

Perhaps beyond mere coincidence, of the five justices on the Tennessee bench in the *Bell* case, three had recently successfully navigated their way through a contentious, highly negative retention campaign, barely securing their places on the court for another eight years. Justices Lee and Wade, along with Justice Cornelia Clark, had won retention in 2014 by margins as low as 5.3%, far lower than any previous election. Most retention elections margins in the state of Tennessee never drop below 10%. Justice Gary Wade, whose judicial tenure would have been secure until 2022, announced his retirement two days prior to the publication of the Court's decision in *Bell*. He dissented along with Chief Justice Sarah Lee. Justices Bivins and Kirby, both in the majority in the case, were likewise up for reelection in August of 2016, giving them little under a year before voters would decide if they would retain their seats. Writing for the majority, therefore, Justice Bivins seems to take a hard line on the viciousness of the murder, describing the facts of the case in nine exceedingly specific pages, repeatedly using the term "brutal", repeatedly reiterating the fact that the errors made by the trial court were, in fact, "harmless," and thus did not bias the jury in any meaningful fashion. Justices Bivins and Kirby would later go on to easily win retention, with approximately 77% of voters agreeing they should remain on the bench.

While a death penalty case is a highly salient event, most cases involving education stay below the public's radar. In the case of *McCleary v. State* (269 P.3d 227), the Washington high court was asked whether the state was providing "ample provisions of education" to children within the state's border. While on its face this may seem to be a banal issue, as the majority opinion points out, funding for education in K-12 schooling includes a complex set of caveats including staff compensation, special education, and other such requirements. The court was therefore required to answer several questions concerning judicial oversight of such programs. What makes this case interesting is not only the nuances of the analysis, but how Justice Debra Stephens, the majority opinion author, weaves a persuasive argument for the court's decision. Buttressed with a strong reaffirmation of the decision in *Marbury v. Madison* (1803), she argues that the state's current education plan does not provide adequate funding for education. Stephens goes so far as to quote Chief Justice Marshall's proclamation that, "it is empathetically the province and the duty of the judicial department to say what the law is." The justice, bolstered by a two-hundred-year-old precedent, lays out a plan where the legislature would revise the state's education policy with heavy judicial oversight, including judicial review of the state's plan.

Justice Bivins' majority opinion in *Bell* and Justice Stephens' opinion in *McCleary* underscore an important feature of democratic institutions. Institutional structures that exist within democracies must conform to the perception that they serve the needs of the citizenry. The method by which these institutions are evaluated for their compatibility with the electorate systematically subjects individuals serving within these institutions to the demands of representation (Dahl 1956; Pitkin 1967). The notion that judges serve as representatives within the United States is not widely excepted by the public. To a large extent, this is because the judges with whom the public are familiar – high profile judges, particularly those on the U.S. Supreme Court – actively and publicly downplay or dismiss any connection between their decision-making rationale and the public. Judges on the federal bench exist in a system designed with insulation (from both the public and the other branches of government) in mind. Particularly, provisions for life tenure and salary protections for judges have combined to make an institution that can readily claim it is "above politics."

We argue however, that judges seek approval from audiences external to the court. Specifically, since state high court judges have constituencies, judges' approval-seeking behavior will be directed at maintaining support and appeasing audience interests. As a result, judges will write their opinions with these audiences in mind. While political science certainly doesn't claim federal judges are above politics or apolitical, they also do not see them as representatives in the traditional sense (but see Curry and Romano 2018; Hall 1995; 2014, Peretti 1999). Electoral institutions, however, are not the only means by which a representational link between the electorate and the judiciary can be forged. Recent examinations of representation have turned their attention to the ability of non-elective political institutions to represent constituencies as well. Rehfeld (2006; 2009) and Saward (2012) have both reexamined representation by focusing specifically on the role of the "audience" and the ability of public actors to make "claims" to being representative of that audience. According to Rehfeld (2006), examinations of representation should take into account the audience for a particular public figure when acting in an official capacity, rather than presuming some implicit "electorate." By doing so, researchers are better able to understand how representation functions generally, even in non-elective bodies. Following this, Saward (2012) argues that public figures become "representatives," when they state claims to constituent publics, which must be accepted by these audiences in order for the representative link to be forged. In doing so, representation becomes a linguistic process, wherein the words (as well as actions) undertaken by a political actor become intrinsically linked to their ability to "stand for," a particular group. For the federal judiciary, Collins and Ringhand (2013) and Peretti (1999) provide two arguments that come closest to stating judges act as representatives. Focusing specifically on nominees for the federal bench, Collins and Ringhand (2013) argue that nominees must be representative of the current legal paradigm in order to be confirmed. Collins and Ringhand argue that the current legal paradigm is a function of the Senate and current legal precedent. The reason Robert Bork was not confirmed to the U.S. Supreme Court was that his views were outside the current legal paradigm, especially concerning the nature of privacy. A similar argument is forwarded by Peretti (1999), who uses this sort of legal representation as justification for the use of judicial review by an unaccountable judiciary.

Shifting focus from the federal judiciary to the state level, the representative link between judges and the public becomes far more explicit. This, we argue, is because the institutions used to retain judges make the audiences of the judiciary far more predictable (Curry and Romano 2018). State supreme court justices, according to the general account of representation described above, are representative agents of their state so long as the audience they make claims to (whether that be the public, elite actors, or an amalgamation of both) recognize the judge as qualified for that position. For example, Chief Judge Stephen Dillard (2017) of the Court of Appeals of Georgia confirmed this idea stating that, "Judges are public servants. They are accountable to the people and they need to be accessible to the people, so long as they do so in a manner that is consistent with their oath of office and the code of judicial conduct." To ensure they remain in power, judges must make claims to various external audiences (the legal community of the state, public officials and other branches of government, and importantly, the public) and then provide these audiences with signals that they are responding to their will. Judges recognize this requirement when making voting decisions, implicitly or explicitly (Hall 2014).

More important for us, however, is how judges use language to strike a chord with audiences. The variations in methods of retention used on state supreme courts provide the institutional nudge that changes the audiences judges should respond to. We believe this should have a substantive impact on the crafting of law within the states. So long as these judges need to be retained, the retention audience should have influence over how they behave, including how they write. There exists a fair amount of evidence that these judges do consider their audience, at least when making the choice of how to vote in specific cases. Judges in electoral systems generally decide salient cases consistent with the ideology of their constituents (Hall 1987; Canes-Wrone, Clark and Kelly 2014). Similarly, judges in elite reappointment systems are reticent to declare acts of the legislature and governor unconstitutional (Langer 2002). We know therefore, that audience representation has an effect on how judges decide cases. However, sometimes the law dictates a decision, even if it will be unpopular. When the law dictates an unpopular decision, the last defense a judge can employ is a carefully written opinion. Our explicit argument throughout this book is that judges will utilize language and craft law differently depending on features of the case and the institutions they reside in. Specifically, judges will trade off between attempting to *persuade* various audiences by integrating multiple arguments into a single, convincing decision and *justifying* their choices by using clear, simple language and in-depth analysis of a single viewpoint.

The Power of Audience and the Purpose of Judicial Opinions

Since Baum (2006), the examination of judges requires considering how their behavior is affected by who is watching, and whom the judge is trying to seek approval from. While Baum's work focuses almost exclusively on the behavior of federal judges, we believe the general theory is even more applicable to examinations of judges in the states. The theory is simple; judges, like nearly all humans, seek the approval of others. As such, they will act to please their target audience (deciding cases and writing opinions in specific ways). We feel that judges at the state level, almost all of whom must go through a mechanism of retention in order to remain on the bench, are much more likely to seek audience approval than federal judges. Furthermore, this approval seeking behavior will cause judges to behave strategically in order appease audiences external to the dispute in question; particularly retention audiences which will be responsible for providing an accountability check at the end of their term. Stated simply, we assume judges at the state level will focus greater attention on audience representation than on their own ideology, particularly when writing the majority opinion.

The most immediate audience to any judicial opinion are the other judges who sit on the collegial court (Maltzman, Spriggs, Wahlbeck 2000). This is because the opinion author needs to garner a majority of the court's judges in order to make her draft the binding opinion of the court. At the U.S. Supreme Court, there is convincing evidence that judges bargain over the content of the majority opinion before signing onto it. After this primary audience, Baum (2006) hypothesizes that judges will write for the approval of secondary audiences external to the court, which can consist of pundits, ideological groups, or different parts of the legal academy. This observation takes on increased importance when you consider that the audience a judge is writing for may vary significantly depending on the institution a judge works in (Baum 2006). While Baum primarily discusses federal judges and their inclination to write to particularized legal audiences, we believe that audiences are more likely to vary at the state level and that they will vary in a more systematic (and predictable) fashion.

We know that audience representation is important to judges at the state level. Significant evidence exists to demonstrate that judges consider how their decisions will be perceived by their retention constituency. We assume that state supreme court judges' primary audience remains the other judges on each collegial court. This audience is primary because in order to craft an opinion of the court, a judge needs support of their colleagues. However, this is not the only audience that judges should attempt to seek approval from. Judges on elected courts should also consider their retention audience, specifically their constituency, when they draft opinions. Judges who need to be reappointed by an elite body, be it the governor or legislature, should consider that retention audience when they write majority opinions. Considering both retention audiences are significantly different, both in terms of attentiveness and interest, they should write opinions on similar issues quite differently.

Why Study Opinions?

Throughout the history of the scientific study of public law, the field has had an understandable focus on votes on the merits instead of the actual content of opinions. Beginning with Pritchett (1948), continuing to Schubert (1965), and reaching a pinnacle with Segal and Spaeth (2002), quantitative work in public law has focused extensively on votes and case outcomes, with the assumption being that since judges on the U.S. Supreme Court exist in such a protected institution and occupy the top of the judicial hierarchy, they would consider nothing other than ideology when it came to vote choice in cases. Work examining strategic behavior of judges has partially shifted the focus away from votes, but the focus has largely extended to majority coalition formation rather than focusing on opinion content as the outcome (but see Maltzman, Spriggs, and Wahlbeck 2000 and Black, Owens, Wedeking and Wohlfarth 2016).

The majority opinion is a highly important tool for the court in its attempt to maintain relevance as a policymaking branch of government, as the opinion is the device responsible for the establishment of precedent, and thus, law. However, Law and Courts scholars have historically focused on votes; not disregarding the opinion but also not analyzing them in much depth: thus missing variations in content, frames, and complexity. This focus on vote outcomes and alignments obfuscates the deeper political dynamics of a court by devaluing the "multiple strategies that produce Court opinions" (Maltzman, Spriggs, and Wahlbeck 2000: 5). One of the reasons judges write opinions is that in our common law society, the interpretation of law is done in part by judges. That these opinions carry the force of law and set precedent within the boundaries of their jurisdiction should make their content worthy of study. Legal scholars often engage in doctrinal analysis of legal opinions and these have significant value, especially when examining the evolution of specific areas of law or specific statutes. We, however, seek to approach the question of variation in opinion content and style in the vein of the field of study known as Political Communications.

Political communications, in contrast to Law and Courts, focuses on the use of communications as strategic opportunities to influence news media coverage, public opinion, or other political actors. Studies of political communication have traditionally utilized sophisticated methodological techniques to assess quantitative differences between texts (Krupnikov and Searles 2018). Particularly in a world where information is more plentiful, scholarship on how such information is crafted, transmitted, and consumed is highly relevant to developing a greater understanding of the kaleidoscope of lenses through which we understand politics (Bennett and Iyengar 2008). While much of the literature focuses on how individuals consume and are affected by the presence of political information (see de Vreese and Neijens 2016; Krupnikov and Searles 2018 for review), how public officials craft communications is likewise necessary in order to fully understand what messages get transmitted and the strategy of message creation (Sellers 2010). Valenzuela, Correa and de Zúñiga (2018) find that the method of communication utilized to reach the public has a strong influence over political participation, particularly in cases of social media usage. And research on elite communications and opinion leadership has found that citizens more readily adopt issue positions of politicians when they are informed of the opinion directly from a politician (Bullock 2011; Broockman and Butler 2017).

Recently, public law scholars have begun to use tools developed in the field of political communication, to get a handle on how a court's opinion content is created. Scholars examining the Supreme Court have examined whether the lower courts, the parties to a particular case, and amici have influence on shaping the majority opinion content (Collins, Corley, and Hamner 2015, Corley, Collins, and Calvin 2011, and Corley 2008). Additionally, researchers have examined whether opinion clarity and readability increase the likelihood of lower courts to follow the U.S. Supreme Court's decisions (Corley and Wedeking 2014, Black, Owens, Wedeking, and Wohlfarth 2016). As this work focusing on judicial opinions begins to shift down the judicial hierarchy, the tools being used and the questions being asked show a mingling of work in public law and political communication (Hinkle, Martin, Shaub and Tiller 2012, Hinkle 2017, Nelson and Hinkle 2018).

Whereas the vote on the merits of a case can potentially be based on ideology, the crafting of the opinion must be measured based on the institutional and political environment a judge exists in (Fix, Kingsland, and Montgomery 2017; Maltzman, Spriggs, and Wahlbeck 2000, Nelson and Hinkle 2018). Rather than conclude that this means certain judges perform "better" or "worse," we posit that opinion clarity, argument complexity, and frame selection and salience are part of a broader conditional judicial environment. As such, we hypothesize that the institutions of the court, the environment of the state in which the court resides, and the audience to which the court is writing should all condition the language choices made by opinion authors. Thinking of judicial behavior at the state level in this way is beneficial, we argue, since it allows us to marry many of the significant considerations posited by the theories previously considered while allowing for a rich, complex judicial environment.

The Role of Strategy in Judicial Language

The majority opinion is a unique development for representative institutions and should be seen both as a requirement and an opportunity for judges, depending on which audience the author is writing for. As the audience varies because of institutional design or different issue areas, the opinion author has the ability to engage in strategic behavior, either through opinion bargaining with other members of the court, or by attempting to achieve individual goals by pleasing an external audience. While we assume that judges, regardless of institution, will engage in judicial language bargaining with their colleagues, because of the institutional variation that exists at the state level the goals of the opinion author should vary in some systematic ways.

Murphy (1973) provides us with the motivation for why judges on a collegial court should engage in opinion bargaining. If judges are truly interested in making public policy as close to their ideal point as possible, they still do so under a notable restriction on a collegial court. Their opinion must garner a majority of the court in order to be the majority decision. Because of this, the judges need to be experts in convincing other judges. The strategic nature of judicial communication through opinion writing is dependent upon two or more judges reaching agreement. From the standpoint of workload, agreement should be the modal response of any judge who is not the opinion author. If they decide they agree with the opinion author, or at a minimum are indifferent to the language employed by the opinion author, they have no further action to engage in but signing onto the opinion. Their work on that case ceases, so judges should be inclined to agree with the majority opinion, rather than writing separately in either a concurrence or dissent. A strategic opinion author, when faced with a reticent judge, someone who has an interest in conflict with the majority opinion draft, should use persuasion and bargaining to attempt to convince the judge that the majority opinion draft is worth joining. Language becomes the primary tool in this process, but opinion language is not just a discussion of specific words; it is broader, representing tone, confidence, persuasion, and logic. The tools available to the strategic opinion author is not just word choice, but how the words are put together, and what is highlighted or ignored.

As Baum (2006) highlights, judges can use their decisions (and opinions) to focus on external approval. This audience, as hypothesized by Baum, is dependent upon the individual judge, but can comprise legal academics, policy actors, and those who are required to implement the decisions. Essentially, after the internal audience, judges seek out a particularized external audience for legacy/admiration purposes. When we shift away from the federal judiciary, there is little reason to believe that judges at the state level will stop considering other judges on their court as an important, indeed primary, audience. However, the role of strategy in judicial language use should change significantly when we consider the effect of the judge's external audiences, which includes a stronger emphasis on the mass public due to their role as retention audiences in the next cycle of judicial retention.

Language Choice as a Measure of Strategy

A strong connection with the public does not mean that judges will always attempt to placate citizens when writing opinions. While judges think carefully about their language when crafting decisions, it is not necessarily the case that they attempt to write directly to the public in the same way that traditional representatives in the legislature and executive may choose to speak to the public. Judges are keenly aware that the public is an audience for their actions, however, and should be likely to keep ordinary citizens in their mind as they write and rationalize decisions. And it is unlikely that the public will be uninformed about judicial opinions that may go against their will – particularly when a judge is retained via some form of election. Thus, we contend that one role of the judicial opinion writing process is an attempt at strategic communication between judges and the various audiences. As communication is central to political knowledge and participation in democratic politics, we suspect that judges will use the opinion as a means to ensure that the various audiences will be appeased by the decisions, even if they do not directly engage with legal writing on a daily basis.

In light of this reality, we argue in this book that judges necessarily must attempt to prioritize legal writing in order to balance the need to *justify* their reason for a decision as well as attempt to *persuade* various audiences of the correctness of their choice. While justification and persuasion are often treated as synonymous in research on rhetoric and political communications, we assert that there are inherent differences in the use of language when attempting to explain a legal choice versus convincing others that this choice was the correct one for the context of the case (see Mullins 2016 for a review of this argument in the legal context). As we will explain in more depth in the chapters that follow, the language of justification is most frequently used when judges view (or wish to claim) their decision as the *only* correct legal option in order to resolve a dispute. Justification, in this matter, is specifically used to obfuscate other potential alternatives for dispute resolution, and we believe should be more likely to occur when judges and cases meet certain prerequisites – such as the inclusion of a dissent, or greater internal agreement among members of the bench. Justification is based on the assumption that there is only one distinct choice to be made in a case, and as such language should be used only to show support for why the choice made was correct. This is to say that, in cases where judges prioritize justification, the language used will indicate that there was "no other choice" in the matter under dispute, and in fact that the evidence indicates a clear, unconditional support for a judicial decision.

Contrarily, judges may also recognize that multiple arguments could be made, and contrasting decisions could result from the context of a particular case. In such situations, the available reasoning for the final decision may be multiplicitous, and judges will need to shift their language from justifying their choices toward attempting persuasion. The language of persuasion is inherently different from that of justification, as authors must recognize the existence of alternatives and present information showing how their argument has greater merit than others, or attempt to integrate several arguments into a single, coherent rationale for their decision. In the context of a legal decision, judicial persuasion is not necessarily how to apply the law consistently, but *what law to apply and why*. We argue that persuasion has a unique place in judicial decisions, and most often is tied to attempts by opinion authors to strengthen their legal arguments in light of complex, often contentious legal issues and institutional contexts.

Institutional Components that Affect Judicial Language

Functionally, because of the institutional variation at the state level, a judge's external audience should vary in systematic ways, and thus they should prioritize different types of language usage. State supreme court judges in all states minus three lack the protection of life tenure that exists at the federal level. This means judges at the state level need to be retained to the court after a period of years (term). In the same fashion that members of Congress cater to their constituency to get re-elected, we expect judges at the state level will use the tools available to them to increase their likelihood of being retained. While members of Congress are retained nationwide in the same way, the way by which judges on state supreme courts are selected and retained can be grouped into four different ways, which shift the audience dependent upon the retention constituency. We suspect, as a result, that the method of retention should modify in various ways the language used and exemplify the trade-off between justifying a choice on the one hand and attempting to persuade audiences the decision was correct on the other. Judges in the states can be retained through a variety of mechanisms: partisan and non-partisan competitive elections, elite reappointment, and retention elections. We believe these institutions will have significant influence over which audience judges will focus on when drafting their opinions. As we expect these audiences to influence how judges draft opinions, the institutions should have predictable effects on how readable and complex majority opinions are. Furthermore, judges may focus on different linguistic and topical frames if the audience is the public or an elite constituency. It is here where an analysis of opinion content can be most vital to understanding how judges perceive their place in the democratic politics of the state. The contemporary judicial opinion must be understood by a growing and diverse body of publics; including other judges, public officials, the media, and increasingly, the mass public (Aldisert; Rasch, and Bartlett 2009; Garner 2002; George 2006). Analysis of judicial opinions has documented new evidence concerning judicial performance (Choi, Gulati and Posner 2010; Clark and Carrubba 2012; Goelzhauser and Cann 2014), inter-branch and external influences over opinion content (Box-Steffensmeier, Christenson, and Hitt 2013; Corley 2008; Collins, Corley and Hamner 2015; Corley and Wedeking 2014; Corley, Collins, and Calvin 2011), as well as institutional determinants and differences in opinion writing (Owens and Wedeking 2012; Hinkle 2015; Leonard and Ross 2016). We argue that by understanding these institutional differences that exist across state courts, scholars can identify a judge's most likely audience for their opinion.

Partisan judicial elections are the closest analogue to congressional elections in that judges in these systems are retained by an electoral constituency and partisan identification appears on the ballot next to their names. Likewise, judges retained by non-partisan elections share much institutionally with partisan judges, except non-partisan judges appear on the ballot without party identification on the ballot. As party identification provides significant information to the electoral constituency, it also shields incumbents to a degree because of the heuristic it provides. Functionally, non-partisan judges decide salient cases in a fashion that is more consistent with their constituency's ideology (Canes-Wrone, Clark, and Kelly 2014). As such, we suspect that when judges craft their opinions in these courts, they will consider how the public will react to their opinion and will adjust accordingly in order to avoid potential public backlash, while weighing how likely that backlash is to occur. Some may wonder if this backlash could ever occur: we know judicial elections are low salience events, especially when compared to federal elections. Even if the backlash never materializes, the fact that justices fear its possibility is enough to affect their behavior (see Hall 1987). However, new research (Hughes 2019) has demonstrated that when the media do report on judicial elections, voter turnout is significantly and substantively influenced. This effect is magnified even further when the reporting focuses on "candidates' voting behavior, qualifications, mud-slinging, and the horse-race" (Hughes 2019; 30). Justices, like other elected representatives, should consider their audience, especially in light of the fact that when the media do pay attention, their constituency receives the message. Whether this message is positive or negative, is in the hands of the judges who write the opinions.

Contrarily, judges in the states can also be retained by elite reappointment; meaning either by the governor or legislature, depending on the state. While the primary audience of the opinion in these systems should still be the other judges on the court, the secondary audience is not the electorate. Since these judges need to be retained by an elite body to stay in office, their behavior should be modified to cater to a more elite audience. Langer (2002) finds that these judges were significantly less likely to engage in judicial review and overturn laws. Furthermore, we know that the political knowledge and level of sophistication of political elites is significantly higher than that of the public. In light of these systematic differences between the two audiences, we also assume that there should be some variation in what issues they consider to be salient. The elite audience is more knowledgeable than the public, prioritizes issues differently, and is likely to play closer attention without the mitigating role of the media. We expect that this combination of factors should strongly influence not only how judges write opinions, but also in what issue areas we should see the effect.

The last mechanism of retention used by states puts incumbents before the public in what amounts to an uncontested referendum on the judge's time in office. Generally, these elections are low salience, and experience a high degree of ballot roll-off (Klein and Baum 2001). However, in recent years, judges in retention elections systems have become targets of organized campaigns to unseat them, generally after they have been part of an unpopular opinion (Pariente and Robinson 2016). Thus, while the judges in retention election systems are retained by the public, the public seems to pay less attention to these contests than those in partisan and non-partisan systems. These judges do not need to consider elite institutions for their retention, and thus likely do not view the governor or legislature as their secondary audience. It remains to be seen, however, whether they will behave in a similar fashion to judges in the contested electoral systems. While the public is the retention audience specifically, we know that a large portion of this constituency is not "tuned in" to these state supreme court justices. As previous research has determined that retention election systems are the least accountable institution used by states (Curry and Hurwitz 2016), justices in this system may behave consistently with what Baum hypothesizes for judges on the federal bench. While retention election judges do not have life tenure, they are exceedingly insulated, and may be able to simply write for a secondary audience of their own individual choice.

Plan for the Book

Our primary goal in this text is to evaluate and examine how language and institutional context impact the opinions written by state court judges. Unlike previous studies that have focused primarily on aggregate data from the courts in order to understand how the institutions function, we rely on the words of the court specifically in order to understand how judges strategize when resolving legal disputes. In the chapters that follow, we attempt to show how language changes when judges are confronted with different legal and institutional circumstances, and how this language impacts the decisions made by the court at any particular time.

In Chapter 2, drawing on work from judicial behavior, political communications, and political theory, we articulate specifically how state court judges can be conceptualized as political representatives, even if their method of selection or retention does not reside in the hands of the electorate. Using historical context as a motivator, we discuss the development of both the modern judicial opinion and the various methods of retention and selection used to staff state supreme courts. From there, we examine the evolution and modern use of the judicial opinion and focus specifically on how judges prioritize language use in order to speak to the multiple audiences who may interact with a decision. Our primary theory is that judges will prioritize justifying their decisions over attempting to persuade others dependent on variations in institutional context, case context, and potential for negative audience response (based on retention audiences used to maintain the bench). The chapter concludes with our primary motivation for the empirical chapters that follow: a judge's external audience is dependent on the mechanism of judicial retention in the state, and judges will adjust their writing in order to appease these audiences.

Chapter 3 has two goals. First, we introduce the reader to the data that will be used through the rest of the book, which consists of 5,260 death penalty and 1,413 education decisions made by state supreme courts from 1995 to 2010. We provide some descriptive statistics on these decisions in order to assist the reader in better understanding our measures, and formulate some initial hypotheses concerning how language may be impacted by variations with state courts. Second, we start our empirical analysis by examining how judges frame their decision in salient (death penalty) and non-salient (education) cases. We start with an analysis of opinion frame as this will provide the first context in understanding how and why judges made a particular decision. We find that judges do have particular strategies when crafting opinions, and they appear to be cognizant of how their words will be interpreted by broader audiences once a decision is released.

Chapter 4 begins to focus more directly on the internal and external audiences of the court. In this chapter we assess two interrelated questions regarding dissenting opinions. First, we assess whether institutional variations and linguistic traits of the majority opinion affect the decision to dissent from any particular case. We argue that when judges prioritize justification, and specifically discount or leave un-discussed particular alternative arguments, others on the bench should be more likely to write separately, and specifically to write dissents that highlight these alternative arguments. Second, there is reason to believe that a published dissent will also have an effect on the language usage in the majority opinion. The decision to dissent usually is not taken in isolation, and we know that language bargaining occurs on collegial courts. Utilizing the findings from our first models, we consider the decision to dissent as the selection step and focus on how the choice to dissent has a direct impact on the clarity of the majority opinion as well as its argumentative complexity. We conclude that judges writing for the majority pay close attention to the arguments made by dissenters, and that the decision to dissent has a marked impact on the resulting precedent established by the court.

Chapter 5 examines an understudied aspect of judicial opinions, the per curiam. We focus on the per curiam specifically as it provides a unique opportunity for the court to avoid direct confrontation with external audiences by removing identifiers from the opinion and leaving the author ambiguous. We believe that per curiam opinions therefore present the court with a unique opportunity to engage with disputes and craft law while avoiding potential backlash from audiences who may disagree with the outcome of a case. We start by highlighting the development of per curiam opinions in the United States, focusing on the creation, growth, and strategy of the opinion at both the federal and state level. We then proceed by outlining basic data about their use, before modeling under what conditions per curiam opinions are more likely to be employed, and how judicial language changes the likelihood the court will decide anonymously rather than through the use of a signed opinion.

Chapter 6 changes the focus of our observations from trying to understand variations in judicial opinions, to using those variations to predict the likelihood of a non-unanimous decision. Because the other judges on collegial courts are the primary audience for judicial opinions, different qualities of the majority opinion should affect the likelihood that a judge chooses to sign on to any opinion. Ties to the electorate, however, may mute the effectiveness of the opinion author in successfully persuading their colleagues to agree with their assessment in a case. We choose to focus specifically on the probability of coalition breakdown and how the language of the opinion along with other institutional factors mitigate or exacerbate the likelihood that judges will come to full agreement on a case. We find that it is here where judges are presented with a unique "Goldilocks dilemma" in which the majority opinion author must work to strike a clear balance between justifying their decision and persuading various audiences to its validity.

Our conclusion in Chapter 7 summarizes and unifies our theoretical contributions and empirical findings. We then discuss what our arguments concerning language and judicial strategy tell us about the broader judiciary more generally, and state courts specifically. Finally, we provide some suggestions for future research on state courts and the judiciary, and outline some key takeaways in order to guide future work on how judges craft law through judicial opinions.

Notes

1 According to the Tennessee Penal Code, the death penalty can be sought for a variety of circumstances; however, it can be requested only if the crime has particular aggravating circumstances, such as first-degree murder, homicide in connection with arson, rape, or involving law enforcement; as well as crimes considered, "heinous, atrocious, or cruel." For more information, see Tennessee Penal Code 39-13-201, et seq.; 37-1-102; 40-23-114.
2 Information comes from the Tennessee Department of Corrections website on Capital Punishment in the state: www.tn.gov/correction/article/tdoc-death-penalty-in-tennessee. More information at: www.deathpenaltyinfo.org/tennessee-1

References

Aldisert, R. J., Rasch, M., & Bartlett, M. P. (2009). Opinion Writing and Opinion Readers. *Cardozo Law Review*, 31(1), 1–44.

Baum, L. (2006). *Judges and Their Audiences: A Perspective on Judicial Behavior*. Princeton: Princeton University Press.

Bivens, J. S. (2015). *State of Tennessee v. Rickey Alvis Bell, Jr*. No. W2012-02017-SC-DDT-DD. Majority.

Black, R. C., Owens, R. J., Wedeking, J., & Wohlfarth, P. C. (2016) *U.S. Supreme Court Opinions and their Audiences*. Cambridge: Cambridge University Press.

Box-Steffensmeier, J. M., Christenson, D. P., & Hitt, M. P. (2013). Quality Over Quantity: Amici Influence and Judicial Decision Making. *American Political Science Review*, 107(3), 446–460.

Broockman, D. E. & Butler, D. M. (2017) The Causal Effects of Elite Position-Taking on Voter Attitudes: Field Experiments with Elite Communication. *American Journal of Political Science*, 61(1), 208–221.

Bullock, J. G. (2011) Elite Influence on Public Opinion in an Informed Electorate. *American Political Science Review*, 105 (3), 496–515.

Canes-Wrone, B., Clark, T. S. & Kelly, J. P. (2014). Judicial Selection and Death Penalty Decisions. *American Political Science Review*. 108(1), 23–39.

Choi, S. J., Gulati, G. M., & Posner, E. A. (2010). Professionals or Politicians: The Uncertain Empirical Case for an Elected Rather than Appointed Judiciary. *Journal of Law, Economics, and Organization*, 26(2), 290–336.

Clark, T. S., & Carrubba, C. J. (2012). A Theory of Opinion Writing in a Political Hierarchy. *Journal of Politics*, 74(3), 584–603.

Collins, P. M., Corley, P. C., & Hamner, J. (2015). The Influence of Amicus Briefs on U.S. Supreme Court Opinion Content. *Law & Society Review*, 49(4), 917–944.

Collins, P. M., Ringhand, L. A. (2017). *Supreme Court Confirmation Hearings and Constitutional Change*. Cambridge: Cambridge University Press.

Corley, P. C. (2008). The Supreme Court and Opinion Content: The Influence of Parties' Briefs. *Political Research Quarterly* 61(3), 468–478.

Corley, P. C., & Wedeking, J. (2014). The (Dis)Advantage of Certainty: The Importance of Certainty in Language. *Law & Society Review*, 48(1), 35–62.

Corley, P. C., Collins, P. M., Calvin, B. (2011). Lower Court Influence on U. S. Supreme Court Opinion Content. *Journal of Politics*, 73(1), 31–44.

Curry, T. A. and Hurwitz, M. S. (2016). Strategic Retirement of Elected and Appointed Justices: A Hazard Model Approach. *Journal of Politics*, 78(4), 1061–1075.

Curry, T. A. and Romano, M. K. (2018). Ideological Congruity on State Supreme Courts. *Justice System Journal*, 39(2), 139–154.

Dahl, R. A. (1956). *A Preface to Democratic Theory*. Chicago; University of Chicago Press.

de Vreese, C. H. & Neijens, P. (2016). Measuring Media Exposure in a Changing Communications Environment. *Communication Methods and Measures*, 10(2–3), 69–80

Dillard, S. L. (2017). #Engage: It's Time for Judges to Tweet, Like, & Share. *Judicature*, 101(1), 11–13.

Fix, M. P., Kingsland, J. T., & Montgomery, M.D. (2017) The Complexities of State Court Compliance with US Supreme Court Precedent. *Justice System Journal*. 38(2), 149–163.

Garner, B. A. (2002). *The Elements of Legal Style*, 2nd ed. New York: Oxford University Press.

George, J. J. (2006). *The Judicial Opinion Writing Handbook*. 5th ed. New York: William S. Hein.

Goelzhauser, G. & Cann, D. M. (2014) Judicial Independence and Opinion Clarity on State Supreme Courts. *State Politics and Policy Quarterly*, 14(2), 123–141.

Hall, M. G. (1987). Constituent Influence in State Supreme Courts: Conceptual Notes and Cast Study. *Journal of Politics*, 49(4), 1117–1124.

Hall, M. G. (1995). Justices as Representatives: Elections and Judicial Politics in the American States. *American Politics Quarterly*. 23(4), 485–503.

Hall, M. G. (2015). *Attacking Judges: How Campaign Advertising Influences State Supreme Court Elections*. Stanford: Stanford University Press.

Hinkle, R. K. 2015. Into the Words: Using Statutory Text to Explore the Impact of Federal Courts on State Policy Diffusion. *American Journal of Political Science*, 59(4), 1002–1021.

Hinkle, R. K. 2017. Panel Effects and Opinion Crafting in the U.S. Court of Appeals. *Journal of Law and Courts*, 5(2), 313–336.

Hinkle, R. K., Martin, A. D., Shaub, J. D., & Tiller, E. H. (2012). A Positive Theory and Empirical Analysis of Strategic Word Choice in District Court Opinions. *The Journal of Legal Analysis*, 4(2), 407–444.

Hughes, D. A. (2019). Does Local Journalism Stimulate Voter Participation in State Supreme Courts? Forthcoming in the *Journal of Law and Courts*.

Klein, D. & Baum, L. (2001). Ballot Information and Voting Decisions in Judicial Elections. *Political Research Quarterly*, 54(4), 709–728.

Krupnikov, Y. & Searles, K. (2018). New Approaches to Method and Measurement in the Study of Political Communication Effects. *Political Communications*, 00, 1–5.

Langer, L. (2002). *Judicial Review in State Supreme Courts: A Comparative Study*. New York: SUNY Press.

Leonard, Meghan E., and Joseph V. Ross. 2016. Understanding the Length of State Supreme Court Opinions. *American Politics Research*, 44(4), 710–733.

Maltzman, Forrest, James F. Spriggs, & Paul L. Wahlbeck. 2000. *Crafting Law on the Supreme Court: The Collegial Game*. Cambridge: Cambridge University Press.

Marbury v. Madison (1803), 5 U.S. 137.

McCleary v. State (2012), 269 P.3d 227.

Murphy, W. F. 1973. *Elements of Judicial Strategy*. Chicago: University of Chicago Press.

Nelson, M. J. & Hinkle, R. K. (2018). Crafting the Law: How Opinion Content Influences Legal Development. *Justice System Journal*, 39(2), 97–122.

Owens, R. J. & Wedeking, J. (2012). Predicting Drift on Political Insulated Institutions: A Study of Ideological Drift on the United States Supreme Court. *Journal of Politics*, 74(2), 487–500.

Pariente, B. J, & Robinson, F. J. (2016). A New Era for Judicial Retention Elections: The Rise of and Defense Against Unfair Political Attacks. *Florida Law Review*, 68(6), 1529–1567.

Peretti, T. J. (1999). *In Defense of a Political Court*. Princeton: Princeton University Press

Pitkin, H. F. (1967). *The Concept of Representation*. Berkeley: University of California Press.

Pritchett, C. H. 1948. *The Roosevelt Court*. New York: Macmillan.

Rehfeld, A. (2006). Toward a General Theory of Political Representation. *Journal of Politics*, 68(1), 1–21.

Rehfeld, A. (2009). Representation Rethought: On Trustees, Delegates, and Gyroscopes in the Study of Political Representation and Democracy. *American Political Science Review*, 103(2), 214–30.

Saward, M. (2010). *The Representative Claim*. New York: Oxford University Press.

Schubert, G. R. (1965). *The Judicial Mind: Attitudes and Ideologies of Supreme Court Justices, 1946–1965*. Evanston: Northwestern University Press.

Segal, J. A. & Spaeth, H. J. (2003). *The Supreme Court and the Attitudinal Model Revisited*. Cambridge: Cambridge University Press.

Sellers, P. (2010). *Cycles of Spin: Strategic Communication in the U.S. Congress*. Cambridge: Cambridge University Press.

Tennessee Penal Code 39-13-201, et seq. 37-1-10240-23-114.

Valenzuela, S., Correa, T. & De Zúñiga, H. G. (2018). Ties, Likes, and Tweets: Using Strong and Weak Ties to Explain Differences in Protest Participation Across Facebook and Twitter Use. *Political Communication*, 35(1), 117–134.

2

JUDICIAL REPRESENTATION, WRITTEN OPINIONS, AND AUDIENCES

The federal judiciary really is not a democratic institution. Federal judges exist within an environment where life tenure and constitutionally-based decisions shield the judges from nearly all types of accountability. The defining character-istic of a democratic institution is a requirement to revitalize the representative connection with the authorization constituency in order to maintain legitimacy. While some federal judges – particularly those not on the US Supreme Court – may cater to a constituency in order to achieve their own personal goals or ambitions, the US Supreme Court is easily the most unaccountable court in the United States. State courts of last resort are exceedingly different.

All state courts of last resort, minus three, have terms instead of life tenure.[1] Judges on these courts are dependent upon an authorizing constituency tasked with deciding whether judges are properly upholding their oath of office. In order to maintain their position on the court, these judges must prove that they are making decisions in a way that is in line with the community values of the state (Lebovitz and Hidalgo 2009; Mullins 2016; Wald 1995). That is, judges must be responsive, and persuasive, to a constituency. While this authorization constituency can come in the form of the electorate or an elite institution such as the governor or legislature, judges should engage in strategic behavior with this constituency in mind. These judges, unlike the justices of the US Supreme Court, reside in democratic institutions.

Revitalization of the authorization link between judges and their constituen-cies is just one step in order to maintain judicial legitimacy, however. For repre-sentatives to maintain their power, they must provide some justification for their policy choices (Pitkin 1967; Montanaro 2012; Saward 2010). This justification is especially important for judges, as their role is the least understood among the branches of government. Uncertainty over the role and purpose of the judiciary in government historically can be traced to debates and dialogues over the power of judicial voice. In the United States, judicial power (at both the state and federal levels) is said to be derived from two primary sources: either from the people themselves (who are often called upon to legitimize judicial choices through their acceptance of the "rule of law") (see especially Blackstone 1765 [2016]; Tiller and Cross 1999; Keith 2002; Keith, Tate and Poe 2009; Hamilton 1788 [1999]; Montesquieu 1748 [1994]; O'Donnell 2004), or more technically through the various articles of incorporation that craft the scope and power of the judicial branches constitutionally (for example, the US Supreme Court's "Article III" power). Thus, to strike a balance between accountability and independence, the judicial branch adopted the tactic of publishing written, public opinions as part of the communicative process of justifying and codifying their decisions. Judge Wald (1995, 1372) makes the point succinctly, "Tradition aside, modern judges write opinions . . . to reinforce our oft-challenged and arguably shaky authority to tell others – including our duly elected political leaders what to do." This claim changes when the judges have a constituency, like the vast majority of judges at the state level. The written opinion evolves from an attempt to build upon a judge's shaky authority into a campaign promise and/or a claim of credit. Our argument, in this chapter and throughout this book, is that the judiciary will use these public opinions as a strategic tool in order to placate or persuade the constituency responsible for their retention, be it the governor, legislature, or the electorate.

In order to examine the relationship between the judicial opinion and a judge's audience, we assume that one role of judicial opinion writing is message communication. At its base level, the communicative relationship between elites and the public is an expectation concerning the proper functioning of a representative government. Practically, the relationship has a fundamental connection with the ability of an audience to make an informed choice in the retention context (Canes-Wrone, Brady, and Cogan 2002; Carey 2008; Grimmer, Westwood and Messing 2012; 2014; Snyder and Strömberg 2010). It is not unreasonable to state, therefore, that the ability to address others in order to help explain and define problems and solutions through the mechanism of the spoken or written word is fundamental to modern democratic societies. Communication is central to political knowledge and participation as it is the primary means through which individuals, representatives, and other political actors persuade one another toward some action.

Legal writing, however, is often maligned as being abstruse and indecipherable. Despite the significant value attached to the opinion, the common critique is that judicial writing is arcane: "glazing the eyes and numbing the minds of readers" (Wydick 1998, 3). Notwithstanding this complaint, substantial time and energy has been devoted to improving the clarity and accessibility of judicial prose (for an excellent literature review on this subject see Vance 2011). Judges themselves are conscious of this problem, and often are the most critical of abstruse legal writing (Aldisert 2009; Aldisert Rasch and Bartlett 2009; Kravitz 2009; Posner 1995; Federal Judicial Center 1991; Wald 1995). We argue that while some judges may wish to improve the quality of the writing contained within judicial opinions, there may be strategic reasons for some judges, under certain conditions, to write in a less than clear fashion. In this chapter, we devote our time to explaining why judges may write in clear, or unclear, ways. We believe that judges will write differently when the issue being considered is salient to the audience which is responsible for their retention in office. These salient issues, however, will vary along with the retention constituency dependent upon the institution which is responsible for maintaining membership in the judiciary.

Judges as Political Representatives

Across institutional structures, a vital component to a functioning democratic society is the perception that the system is working for the benefit of citizens. Inevitably, examinations that hinge on this belief must focus their attention on the ability of political actors to serve as representatives of the peoples' interests, both ideologically and in making substantive policy decisions (Dahl 1956; Pitkin 1967). Nowhere is this representational link more strongly debated than in the scholarship on the judicial branch. The federal judiciary was constitutionally designed to keep judges "out of politics" by insulating them from popular pressure. The image of a judge conforms most often to a legal model wherein judges make choices based on fact and law, without regard for whether they should "stand for" a particular group or belief. This conception of judging is most often espoused by judges when seeking judicial appointments, such as Chief Justice John Roberts' belief that his job was to act as an "umpire" who calls balls and strikes, rather than actively playing the game. Even in the empirical literature on judicial politics, where scholars openly accept that judicial decisions can be based on ideology and strategy, the view that judges act as political representatives is not openly accepted. Collins and Ringhand (2013) come closest to accepting judges as representatives, noting that nominees for the U.S. Supreme Court are confirmed only if they represent the majority's ideas of appropriate jurisprudence.

The argument that judges are not representatives becomes unsatisfactory once we consider variations in the method of selection that are utilized to populate courts in the United States. Whereas the method of selection for institutions such as the legislature and executive have changed very little since the nation's founding, the ways in which most members of the judicial branch in the United States are selected and retained has undergone several, sometimes drastic, revisions with the goal of increasing the amount of accountability or independence that is requisite in the judicial office. Interesting for the examination here, these changes often occurred in conjunction with the institution of rules surrounding the written opinion.

Based upon the method by which judges are retained, we should see these institutions incentivize certain behavior. Much like any political actor, judges have goals. Minus crafting their legacy, these goals are attainable only while maintaining power in office. If judges are retained by political elites, either the governor or legislature, it is likely the judges will consider their audience when making decisions and writing opinions, especially when the issue involves governmental policies (Langer 2002). Similarly, if judges are retained through contested elections, the judges will consider the public when the issue is salient (Brace and Boyea 2008, Canes-Wrone, Clark, and Kelly 2014).

Two factors are particularly relevant for understanding the role of judges as representatives: the audience of the representative, and the justifications used by judicial representatives in order to make "claims" to representation. Manin (1997) first designs the concept of "audience democracy" to distinguish between changes in representative systems that have occurred throughout history. Succinctly, audience democracy emphasizes the role of individual actors and personalities over formal/informal institutional structures such as parties, and authenticity over perceived competence in governing. That is to say, democratic representation is a communicative process in which actors *perform* and try to convince constituents of their ability to govern through the use of ritual and symbols (Edelman 1967; Manin 1997). Audience is important as it helps us to conceptualize the constituencies a representative is attempting to stand for in the political arena and this concept has become more significant in modern representative systems owing to the reliance on electoral selection mechanisms that give citizens greater power to choose representatives.[2] Conceptualizing representation in this way does not mean that representation ends with electoral institutions, as representation is only a *claim* until the audience recognizes and accepts it (Rehfeld 2006; Saward 2010). This opens up actors to become representatives despite their not being directly elected (Montanaro 2012). Once a claim is accepted as legitimate, representatives are better able to provide voice to affected constituencies, thus increasing the potential for the affected to have an impact on policy choices (Goodin 2007). In this way, "Representatives are thus no longer spokesmen; the personalization of electoral choice has, to some extent, made them trustees. But they are also *actors* seeking out and exposing cleavages" (Manin 1997: pg. 226).

The method used to populate the court is a vital first step to understanding judicial representation by identifying the appropriate selection agent and decision rules that structure the institution (Rehfeld 2009). Identifying the method of selection and retention, however, only informs us of one facet of representation. Our argument here expands beyond the simple claim that judges act as representatives due to the forging of an accountability link through elections or retention through elite actors. We argue particularly that *because they are representatives*, judges routinely engage in the act of justifying their choices in order to appease their constituent audiences. That is to say, judges exist in a constant state of *claim-based representation*.

A new, and growing, body of literature has begun examining how agents make claims to representation, and how such claims aid the production of a representative link with constituents (see Saward 2010). According to Pitkin's (1967) initial formulation of political representation, a representative must not only stand for another group when making substantive decisions, but also must *justify* their actions to constituents. This justification step is generally waved off as part of the reelection process. However, *how* actors justify has a substantial impact on opinion formation in both elite and mass audiences (Broockman and Butler 2017). Opinion formation is largely dependent upon outside sources, such as the media, interest groups, and policy elites. Importantly, the constituents often base their beliefs on how political elites develop arguments in view of the public. Elite communication, when wielded in this way, is strategic (Disch 2011; Druckman 2014; Mutz, Sniderman and Brody 1996) and is often part of an ongoing competitive marketplace where messages interact in order to gain public attention. Justification is a key component in the transformation of a political actor from passive representative of an audience into an active representative of their wants and desires in the public sphere.

In order for judges to be fully accepted as representatives there must not only be an authorization to act on behalf of others and the opportunity for those affected to influence the decision – referred to by Goodin (2007) as the "affected interests standard" of representation – but they also must provide some form of *justification* for their actions. The justification step, the majority opinion in the judicial context, allows representation to occur by providing a formal outlet for judges to explain and defend their decisions to the audiences they are seeking to speak for or influence. The methods used in the states to select and retain judges provide variations in the opportunities for judges to provide such steps. Elite level appointments constrain judges from acting specifically as representatives of the public, however through the use of the published judicial opinion, judges are able to provide discursive representation (Dryzek and Niemeyer 2008) by acting as a voice for the public when working with other branches of government. Methods of selection that offer greater accountability to the public – such as partisan and non-partisan elections – provide such opportunities through the campaigning process, as well as through the issuance of public statements concerning recent decisions. Furthermore, as all judges must write opinions to justify their decision-making, these written opinions also serve another purpose: they represent the justification for their action to their constituency. According to Justice Breyer (2010, 43), while significant for several other reasons, the opinion is a vital tool for judges seeking to persuade readers and should make "a lasting impression on the minds of those who read it." In this sense, the claim of representation is actually *stronger* for judges than most other representatives in the American context. Not only do judges have to meet the same requirements as other representatives, they must publicly defend not some, but all of their decisions in writing. Few other representatives we know of would meet this standard.

Our focus on the crafting of judicial opinions substantively relates to this process of justification by providing judges with an outlet to speak with their various audiences. We believe that judges are selected as representatives, but methods of retention modify the representative connection over time (see Curry and Romano 2018), and thus will change the way a judge thinks and, central to our inquiry, speaks. While the average citizen likely feels judges should remain outside of the political system to produce fair decisions, the simple reality is that it is impossible to subtract judges from the enterprise of representative government in the United States (*Republican Party of Minnesota v. White* 2002). The method of selection and retention used to populate courts – specifically state courts of last resort – will have an effect on how judges communicate with their authorizing constituency. Systematically, variations in the method of retention change whom the judges speak to and attempt to represent. We argue that the systems of retention used by the states create an accountability check on judges, giving them authority by crafting a legitimization link between judges and their constituent publics or elites. This link provides judges an opportunity to make "claims" to representation in a variety of ways, the most important of which is the requirement of a written, public opinion on which a judge may be judged by their audience.

Changing Audiences and Changing Standards in State Judiciaries

Following the American Revolution, the various states began developing plans for how to design their newly established governments. While most states had some governing structures in place by the end of the Revolutionary War, the cementing of formal institutions had not yet completed, leaving states with a wide degree of variation in how to proceed. One such area of multifariousness included what to do with the judiciary. Procedurally, pre-revolutionary judges had been considered tools of the King, leaving colonists suspicious of common law and its interpreters (Popkin 2007). Institutional designers within the states had to take great care to balance the needs of having a formal check on government in an unbiased judiciary with the perceived mistrust of judges by the new sovereign public. Some states, such as New Jersey, New York, and Pennsylvania, were implicitly dismissive of judging and judicial power in crafting their new governments, while others (such as Massachusetts) explicitly tethered such power to the public. Inevitably, the experimentations of institutional designers focused on two key features of the judicial system in an attempt to strike balance: the method of selection and retention, and the role of the judicial opinion, both of which follow a unique, often parallel path in American institutional development.

One key point of contention over the judiciary was the question of how to ensure the right judges were placed in office. Largely, institutional designers in the states settled on utilizing a method of elite appointment to ensure that judges would not be beholden to popular pressure in the same way that other representatives of government were. In *Federalist 78*, Hamilton provides the reasoning for selecting judges in this fashion, arguing that the judiciary in its current state was not a powerful institution on its own, though it was necessary to place such an institution "outside of government" in order to protect minorities from government encroachment. The judiciary was unable to enforce decisions, depending instead on the other two branches of government to lend their strength in order for judgments to be carried out. However, Hamilton (1788 [1999], 468) notes that the independence of judges from popular pressure allowed them to act as a voice of reason against the "ill humors" that "have a tendency in the meantime to occasion dangerous innovations in the government, and serious oppressions of the minor party in the community." Since the judiciary was viewed as the weakest branch of the newly formed governments, it was assumed that judges would not handle important political decisions since they would have no means through which to enforce their conclusions. The executive and the legislature instead would handle these decisions, as they were provided with formal mechanisms to legitimize their decisions. As such, the need for oversight from the public or the other branches in the form of term limits was assumed unnecessary and possibly dangerous (Streb 2007).

While the need to keep judges separate from "politics" was viewed with utmost importance by institutional designers in the states, this was coupled with the desire to ensure that their decisions would be seen as legitimate law by the public as well. In order to project institutional authority, judges had to develop a method through which they could convey their decisions to the newly enfranchised "people," in whom the power of government resided. The tradition of English common law, which consisted of a mixture of spoken law and codified written decisions, was largely obscure to those who did not have access to time and legal training (Kempin 1959; Healy 2001). Much of the reporting of decisions was unofficial, and in the United States the judiciary's power to declare decisions without the requirement of justification was considered obsolete and (to some) tyrannical, since this was the method often used by the previous royal government to maintain power over colonists (Popkin 2007). Following the lead of the Marshall Court, states began to adopt practices of printing opinions, a practice that culminated in a rich, codified set of judicial laws that could be referenced by future litigants.[3] Early legislation attempted to buttress and entrench this requirement by institutionalizing the role of court reporters and tying compensation of the early reporters to requirements of quality and timeliness (Popkin 2007). These institutional practices became so engrained in the early understanding of judicial voice and authority that by the time Kentucky entered the union in 1792, its newly developed constitution included some of the strictest requirements for the publication of judicial opinions of any state in the union, including strict guidelines on compensation tied explicitly to the timeliness of delivery of a written, public opinion.

Starting in the early to mid-1800s, changes in American political culture and politics began to challenge the notions of early institutional designers with regard to the judicial branch. These challenges climaxed in the development of two new institutional variations for judges. In the area of judicial selection/ retention, the wave of populist politics during this period led to the use of elections as a system for selecting judges. Most notably, Mississippi's constitutional requirement in 1832 that all judges be popularly elected is often pointed to by scholars as one of the first "turning points" in the historical debate over methods of selection. As the populist movement began to grow in the United States, states quickly began to adopt elections – primarily partisan elections – as a means of selecting judges.[4] This push for the partisan election of judges can be linked to numerous contributing factors. First, following the publication of *Marbury v. Madison* (1803) and the establishment of judicial review as the power of the judiciary, a worry emerged that unaccountable judges would begin to overturn law in the states. These judges were not directly accountable to the public, or to other elected officials. By making judges responsible to the same constituency as legislators, this concern could be mitigated. Second, following on the heels of the Jacksonian Democrat revolution, it was generally believed that elite appointments to the judiciary amounted to little more than another example of the spoils system that was rampant in politics (Dubois 1980). Under the system of appointment, the judges were thought to be beholden to those that selected them, namely the governor or legislature. By removing their means of selection and retention out of the other two branches of government, judges were thought to be more independent of those branches. Third, moving retention into the hands of the electorate allowed a means by which to remove inept judges from the bench that did not involve impeachment (Streb 2007). Partisan elections ultimately provided a means to keep judges accountable to the public in a fashion that did not exist under appointment systems that still used life tenure.

This increase in partisan elections did not eliminate all issues concerning judicial selection in the states. The dominant political machines largely chose judicial candidates at the time, and the increased strength of the party system in this era brought with it an increased belief that the spoils of (electoral) battle went to the victors. Judgeships were not immune to this conviction. The move to elections, which was thought to increase independence from the other branches of government, had created a system where the judges were perceived as dependent on the political machines. In the late 1800s, many nascent state bars decried a partisan elected bench as contaminating the neutral application of the law with politics (Dubois 1980). During the Progressive Era, in an attempt to curtail control by the political machinery of the time, non-partisan elections were floated as a means to maintain public accountability, while insulating judges from the perceived vulgarity of partisan politics and thus diminishing cronyism. Non-partisan elections were perceived to help remove power from the political machinery at the time, allowing the public to choose directly who would be judges without the exacerbating role of the party.

The shift from appointment-based selection to electoral mechanisms was not the only means by which judges were forced to become more accountable, however. The developing conflict over the best method by which to fill the judiciary leaked over into new debates over the role, practice, and requirement of judicial opinions as well. Particularly, the argument over the requirement for judges to write seriatim and new state requirements dictating that judges provide a written opinion in *every* case likewise were tied to attempts to ensure judges remained accountable to various audiences. The argument over the seriatim opinion has its roots, particularly, in the animosity between the Jefferson administration and the Marshall Court. Starting with his tenure on the Court, Marshall began a practice of writing decisions per curiam; that is, "for the Court."[5] Jefferson and his allies in the states campaigned for changes to judicial statutes which would require judges write separate opinions in all cases, in order to "expose judging to political scrutiny" (Popkin 2007, 92). State laws requiring seriatim opinions were instituted in some states only to be repealed, most notably due to noncompliance by judges (Berring and Edinger 1999; Casto 1995; Popkin 2007; Sanders 1963).[6] Unlike the early federal court, however, judges recognized the need to maintain some accountability with the public, particularly as their positions became dependent upon votes. Marshall's practice of per curiam did not find a foothold in the states as a result, with judges largely complying with a practice of signing their names to opinions, as well as the development of a system of signed concurrences and dissents being included after the issuance of majority opinions. Likewise, the continued practice of publishing opinions in this way may have ensured substantial accountability for judges (Berring and Edinger 1999), and "might also have secured the legal profession and judicial law from too much interference by appearing to accede to democratic pressure" (Popkin 2007, 92). While the institutional requirement for the written opinion was not necessarily new by the time elections became en vogue (Connecticut was one of the first to require the written opinion in some cases in 1784), as Popkin (2007) and Radin (1930) note, the proliferation of the requirement especially building up to and after the Civil War had a markedly populist tinge. And most notably, the *fight* over such requirements took a stark turn during this timeframe, with judges frequently deriding commentators' distrust and openly balking at legislatively imposed requirements (Popkin 2007; Radin 1930).

By the end of the nineteenth century, the debate over whether state judges ought to be accountable to, and thus justify their decisions with, the public had reached boiling point. Various audiences in the states, including the legal community, government officials, the public, and judges themselves, wanted a court that was at once independent of all outside pressure, but still conformed to the belief that at its heart, America was ruled by the people. Normatively, the argument was that judges need not be "political" in order to be accountable, and that states should institute systems that would ensure accountability and independence while mitigating the "nastiness," that was electoral politics. Beginning in the early 1900s, the American Judicature Society and the American Bar Association (ABA) began pushing for an alternative method for selecting judges in order to balance these normative goals. Initially termed "merit selection," the ABA pushed for the inclusion of non-partisan/bipartisan commissions to evaluate individuals seeking judgeship in the states. The commission would submit a list of names to the chief executive, who would then choose one from the list. After a short period of time, a judge would then stand in a retention election, which is a referendum on their judgeship (Dubois 1980). In 1940, the state of Missouri became the first state to adopt the system, leading scholars and commentators to dub the new system as the "Missouri Plan." The ABA argued that this method of selection would shield candidates from politics because a list of candidates would arise from a non-partisan/bi-partisan commission from which the governor would select a judge. These judges would remain accountable to the public because of the judicial "confidence" vote, which was built into the system.

Since the spread of the Missouri Plan, it has become clear that this selection and retention method is also not immune from critique. While the nomination commissions are functionally non-partisan, they ultimately are tools of the state's lawyers and bar associations (Dann and Hansen 2001). Instead of removing politics from judicial selection, therefore, they shield it to a large extent from public view. The retention portion is also not immune. Retention in the Missouri Plan takes the form of an uncontested confidence vote. Because of the lack of a challenger, and generally low levels of campaigning, retention elections generally experience a significant amount of ballot roll-off (Klein and Baum 2001), meaning that from the top of the ballot to where judges are retained, as many as 60% of voters don't vote for judges. This combination makes the Missouri Plan a poor institution to keep judges accountable (Bonneau and Hall 2009; Curry and Hurwitz 2016), and also a poor institution to leash the ideology of judges to the electorate (Curry and Romano 2018).

Following along with the continued discussion of ethics and the normative implications of selecting and retaining judges through public vote, judicial norms of structuring and writing public opinions began to solidify in order to ensure that the opinion was viewed as the legitimate voice of law, regardless of the method by which a judge reached the bench. For judges, the question concerning judicial voice and power focused strongly on whether or not judges should write separately, or should confine their decisions to a single, majority opinion. Early attempts at cultivating this standard, such as the 1924 *Canons of Judicial Ethics* by the American Bar Association, explicitly promulgated the importance of restraint (in writing separately), and solidary between members of the bench. These early advocates were primarily concerned with the loss of respect that might arise from a judiciary that appeared too discordant, however their arguments also display some desire to ensure that the public voice of the court remained as apolitical as possible in order to stave off criticisms that the court was biased. Particularly, non-unanimity rates in state courts have been targeted as being one tell-tale sign of increased polarization by critics who link such acts directly with the methods of retention and selection used in a state (Popkin 2007). According to Popkin (2007, 129), "if it is true that judges view a united front as one way to head off public dissatisfaction with judicial performance . . . an ethic of discouraging separate opinions might be internalized as a norm of judicial behavior."

Opinions, however, are a unique tool in a judges' arsenal; they exist to serve numerous purposes to a variety of audiences. Judicial opinions as they have evolved from their historic form are shaped not only by the author and other judges on the court, but also the retention audience for the court at the state level. If we accept that judges act as representatives, the next obvious question becomes just *what purpose* the opinion has beyond the simple conveyance of a decision.

The Role of the Modern Judicial Opinion

Judicial opinions do not exist merely to communicate the winner and loser of any given case. The language, and the way the decision is communicated, serves a multitude of purposes. Foremost, these opinions establish the rationale for why judges choose a particular outcome. They represent the public reasoning for a private decision and become part of the opinion author's track record. It is something that the authors can be evaluated on. Therefore, as it is the public representation of a judge's private thoughts, judges should consider other factors external to the court when choosing how to say what they say.

The opinion also serves as the primary means by which judges communicate with non-judges; that is, with their constituency. As judges have significant control over the content, judicial opinions offer judges the ability to frame both the law *and* how it is perceived by various audiences. It is not difficult to surmise, therefore, that to achieve their goals judges write to specific audiences they wish to impress or show support toward. This is especially true at the state court level, where an individual judge's desire to stay in office takes priority over their policy-based goals (Brace and Hall 1997; Baum 2006; Hall 1987; 1992; 1995; Hall and Bonneau 2006; Hall and Brace 1992; Langer 2002). As such, to please disparate groups, judges must find a way to present themselves in a manner that audiences will find acceptable. The written opinion is therefore tied to a judge's self-presentation and self-preservation, an attempt by the authors to craft a positive self-image with a document's intended audience. More than just the simple conveyance of a decision, the opinion can best be understood as a judge's attempt to "win popularity and respect" (Baum 2006, 28) to make a favorable impression.

Of the multiple types of opinion, the most important to our argument is the majority opinion of the court. This opinion, joined by a majority of the judges, articulates which party the court ruled for and why. Indeed, the opinion of a court has been called its "most powerful weapon," (Maltzman, Spriggs, and Wahlbeck 2000: 6) as, foremost, it establishes precedent, and thus law, and sets the standards for decision-making in lower courts as well. Shapiro (1968, 39) notes that opinions are crucial to understanding the political behavior of the appellate courts, "since it is the opinion which provides the constraining direction to the public and private decision makers who determine the 99 percent of conduct that never reaches the courts." Simply put, focusing on the decision of the court may tell us that gay marriage is legal, for example, but not that it is legal because marriage is a 14th Amendment substantive due process right.

There are two other types of opinion that exist for the judges to explain themselves and speak directly to their audience. The concurring opinion, written by a judge in the majority, agrees with the outcome of the case, but usually would have reached the decision differently, perhaps emphasizing different points of law. A dissenting opinion, written by a judge who did not vote in the majority, explains why they feel the decision reached is wrong, and explains how they would have ruled had they been in the majority. Functionally, the last two types of opinion serve no legal purpose in that they do not change the decision of the court. According to Baum (2006), these decisions are written for the benefit of some audience that the judge is trying to please: an action only necessary if the judge is attempting to court favor or approval as a representative

For judges, the act of writing accomplishes three general purposes (Alito 2009; Mullins 2016), each of which reveals and caters to particular judicial audiences. The first three of these audiences are displayed in Figure 2.1 At the most basic level, the judicial opinion needs to garner a majority of the votes on the bench. To that end, the first and most important audience to the opinion author should be her fellow judges (Hettinger, Lindquist, and Martinek 2007; Maltzman, Spriggs & Wahlbeck 2000). State supreme courts, like most appellate courts, make decisions based on majority rule. Without the backing of other judges, the power of a decision wanes substantially. To provide a unified front, the opinion must strategically account for the viewpoints of all judges on the panel. As Kastellec (2011) notes with regard to the federal courts, collegiality on the court is vital to decision making, especially when the panel is made up of opposing ideological views. When judges choose to write separately, this also has an impact on audience perception going forward. To maintain strong judicial voice, therefore, the first priority of a judge is to ensure their colleagues do not oppose them. As we will discuss in Chapter 4, this may be more difficult for some judges, in some institutions, to achieve.

At the next level, judges must respond directly to those in conflict. The opinion author acts as an adjudicator of the law by resolving the exact dispute between the parties of the case. This role is most consistent with the concept of judging, and also with the need for a judiciary in a democratic society (Blackstone 1765 [2016]; Hamilton 1788 [1999]; Locke 1660 [1988]). This immediate

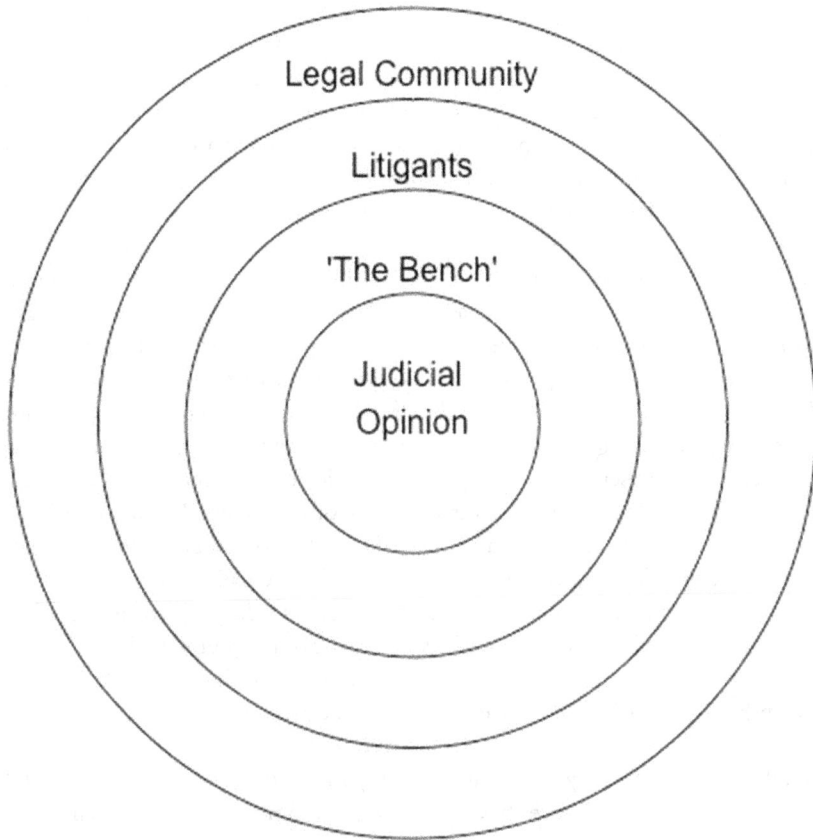

FIGURE 2.1 Initial Range of Judicial Audience Dispersion
Figure Created by Authors

audience consists specifically of the litigants and their lawyers; the idea being that these players are the primary stakeholders in any conflict and in need of the most attention from judges. Judges must therefore tailor their writing as to justify their interpretation of the law given the particular context that the parties present. In the strictest sense, this amounts to pure application of the law, wherein "the judicial opinion informs these readers of the disposition and the reasons for it" (Mullins 2016, 327).

Dispute resolution is one of the most simplistic purposes for a judicial opinion, however. Its purpose is to choose the side which is most correct given the current legal landscape. If the opinion only served this purpose, they could be reasonably direct and relatively short as judges would be simply required to state plainly "what the law is," and which party should receive relief. Judicial opinions are rarely (if ever) so succinct and to the point. Inevitably, judges expand the scope of their audiences beyond the primary litigants when crafting opinions and do so for two other complementary purposes.

Aside from dispute resolution, opinions need to provide consistency in the law. Consistency is an important function of the opinion, as it helps to connect the current decision to past precedent, as well as acting as a bridge between the narrowness of dispute resolution and broader societal impacts that judges may affect by issuing an opinion. In doing so, judges utilize the opinion as a means of *justification* to their audience, the intent being to show how the disposition of a case fits in line with past precedent. In the sense, judges must demonstrate consistency in application of the law given the case context so that the *broader legal community* can evaluate the decision based on past benchmarks. By using past precedent in deciding present cases, judges provide this consistency, and the opinion is meant to highlight this fact by providing the progeny of cases which helped the court reach their decision. Beyond this, judges must display consistency by presenting not only to the parties but to other judges, lawyers, and legal actors how their choice fits with previous decisions. The opinion serves as a benchmark for the law in many respects and serves to guide future courts. Within the broader legal community, we must also recognize the role that lower court judges have in disseminating the high court's ruling. These intermediate appellate judges are one of the groups that the majority opinion author wishes to reach, as these intermediate appellate courts implement the decisions. As Judge Kozinski (2001, 1176–77) indicates, "Writing an opinion is not simply a matter of laying out the facts and announcing a rule of decision. *Precedential opinions are meant to govern, not merely the case for which they were written, but future cases as well.*"

There are other audiences beyond the legal community, however, and these secondary audiences also play a role in the content and crafting of a judicial opinion. As the opinion is the central creation of a court, it serves the purpose of acting as a paper trail so that judges may maintain accountability with the various audiences responsible for their retention. Figures 2.2 and 2.3 provide us with some examples of how these broader communities might be located and structured dependent on the method used by the state to select and retain a judge. Since all state courts engage in the production of opinions, either due to explicit requirements through statute or implicitly because of judicial norms, judges engage constantly in the process of representative claims-making by affirming and explaining how they are upholding community values within the state (Saward 2010). Since the judiciary is considered to be a passive institution, it makes sense that one role of the opinion would be to attempt to frame the decision in a way that is responsive to the community a judge lives within. Despite evidence that elite communications (such as the opinion) often structure public perception rather than vice versa, the classic conception of representative democracy portrays political actors as heavily constrained by constituent publics. Public officials are expected to shy away from policy positions that do not receive some backing from constituents (Canes-Wrone, Brady, and Cogan 2002;

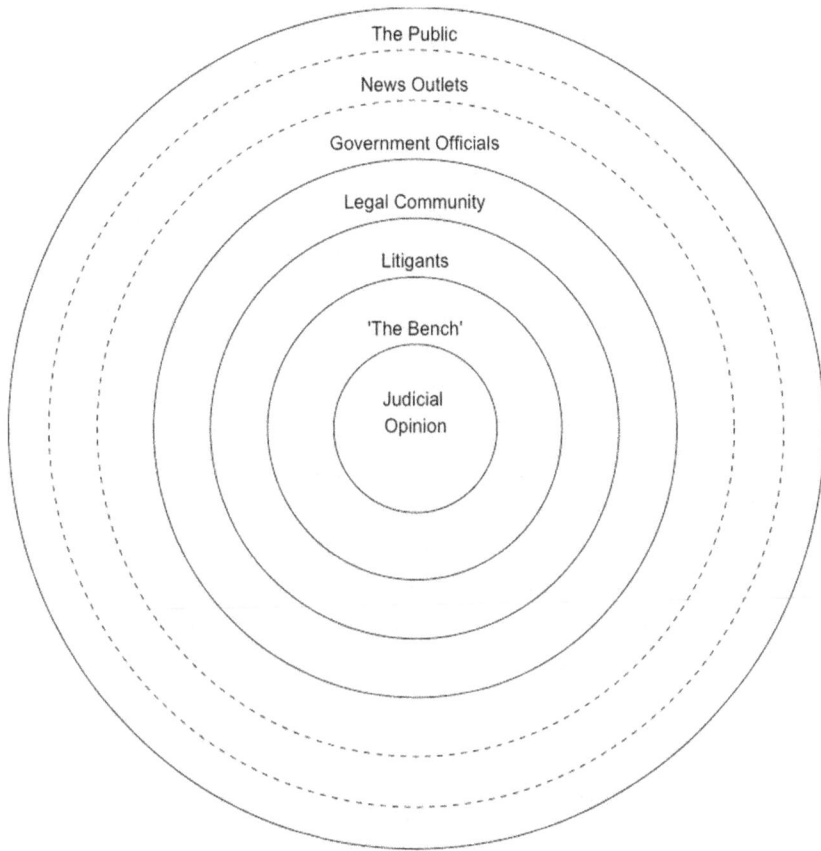

FIGURE 2.2   Judicial Audience Dispersion in States Where Government Officials Play a Role in Judicial Selection and Retention

Figure Created by Authors

Carey 2008; Druckman 2014; Grimmer Westwood and Messing 2012; 2014; Snyder and Strömberg 2010), lest they risk backlash from constituents when they go up for retention.

The requirement for a written opinion was first institutionalized as a way to ensure that judges shy away from decisions that did not uphold community values, so that judicial decisions are, "met with communal acceptance" (Alito 2009, 51). As methods of selection and retention have evolved, different audiences began to take priority as the audience for the opinion. These broader audiences exist in a more amorphous condition, wherein information and perceptions may "bleed through," from one audience to another through the process of dialogue and communication. Initially, and in those states where government officials (legislatures, executives, or bi-partisan committees) play

Government Officials

The Public

News Media

Legal Community

Litigants

'The Bench'

Judicial
Opinion

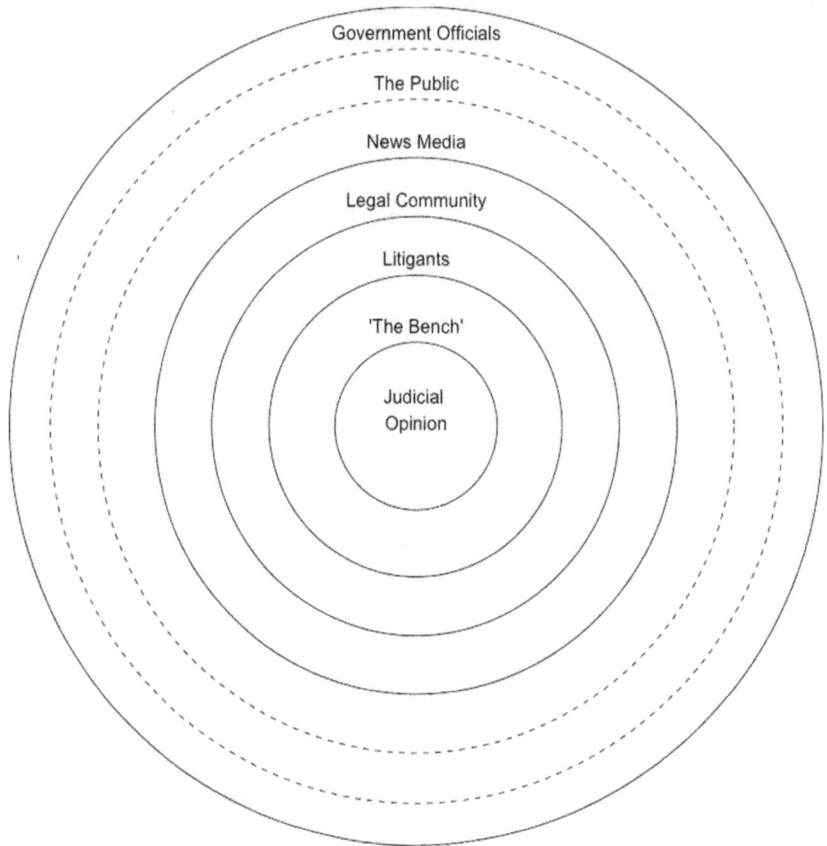

FIGURE 2.3 Judicial Audience Dispersion in States Where the Public Plays a Role in Judicial Selection and Retention

Figure Created by Authors

some role in either the selection or retention of a judge, the opinion will take a form that speaks directly to these more elite audiences, as we see in Figure 2.2. Elites may then release statements concerning a particular opinion to the news media, who will report on these findings accordingly, thus informing the public. Since the mass public has only a tacit connection with these judges in these elite appointment systems, their opinions and views on judges and decisions will be heavily influenced by external sources and will likely suffer from substantial information asymmetries.

Elected judges do have to be mindful of the public (Hall 2014), but the connection between a judge and the mass public is generally not a linear path. It is most common for the public to learn about a judge's justification for a decision through some form of media exposure. While most citizens do not actively engage with a judicial opinion, they do become informed of a judge's rhetoric – particularly on salient issues (Collins and Cooper 2012; Zilis 2015). Black et al. (2016) have shown there is an indirect relationship between public mood and court rhetoric, and this finding may exist even when the case itself is not considered salient (Casillas, Enns, and Wohlfarth 2011). As Figure 2.3 shows, therefore, once the opinion spreads past the legal community, the news media are the first (or most likely) to digest the opinion. Dependent on the newsworthiness of the opinion, journalists then transmit information about the opinion (including the judge's justification) to the mass public. In cases such as this, the frame used by a judge may substantially impact the understanding of the public, something we investigate further in Chapter 3.

The fact that the opinion may reach further than the legal community, coupled with the various institutional modifications present in state courts, is an indicator that the opinion may have serve a third general purpose. As judges may consider audiences beyond the legal community, it theoretically follows that if a specific audience is also the judge's constituency, they may write with them in mind. Occasionally, the law may constrain the judge to an unpopular decision, or the judge makes a decision she knows will be unpopular but is normatively right. In these cases, convincing their constituency it is the right decision may be the only strategy left for them to use.

Communicative Strategy and the Persuasive Power of Judicial Opinions

If the judiciary is to act as an effective branch of government, wield the force of law, and achieve policy goals, then strong, well-crafted opinions must be produced and publicly disseminated (Aldisert, Rasch, and Bartlett 2009; Garner 2002; George 2006; Federal Judicial Center 1991). The general consensus amongst political and legal authorities is that in order for an opinion to convey authority to a variety of audiences, judges must write in a way that is clear, concise, and easily digestible.[7] In the legal literature, opinion clarity is regularly linked to evaluations of judicial performance; with examinations generally emphasizing that good legal writing ought to be written "in plain English" (Garner 2002, 1). As Aldisert, Rasch, and Bartlett (2009) assert, the precedential value of an opinion is diminished substantially when a judge's writing is vague or unclear since the audience will find it difficult to draw conclusions from awkwardly expressed opinions. "Detective mysteries and narratives with O. Henry surprise endings have their place – in fiction. Apply these techniques to the writing of opinions and you risk losing your audience" (Aldisert, Rasch, and Bartlett 2009, 3). Clarity has also been shown to link strongly with opinion quality in empirical literature as well (Clark and Carrubba 2012; Lax and Cameron 2007; Choi, Gulati, and Posner 2010), however most recent studies have shown that opinion quality and clarity may be more strongly based on prevailing norms of professionalism, and less on audience considerations or case salience (Goelzhauser and Cann 2014; Owen and Wedeking 2011).

But while conflict resolution and consistency matter greatly to the function of the judiciary, the fact that the judicial opinion evolved into a public, written account rationalizing the decision of the court indicates a desire to go beyond simply justifying a choice in order to attempt audience persuasion. While there is some disagreement over whether judges should prioritize writing in this way (see especially Cappalli 2000; Hopkins 1969; Leflar 1983), the simple fact is that judges recognize they *must* emphasize persuasion in order to offset their often-questioned ability to engage in the policy-making process through their interpretive power (see Wald 1995). Persuasion likewise transforms the judicial opinion from the simple resolution of a dispute into something greater; a political statement by a court. "Persuasion is ubiquitous in the political process," (Mutz, Sniderman and Brody 1996, 1), and as a tool of the court the opinion serves as the means by which judges may best influence the various audience-spheres' behaviors and beliefs.

The primary issue in unpacking how to translate and discover the communicative power of the judicial opinion lies in the amorphous differences between "justification" on the one hand, and "persuasion" on the other. Justification is based within the judge's ability to provide consistency with the law in an opinion and is arguably a tool used for democratic responsiveness in order to avoid audience backlash. As Mullins (2016) notes, general understanding of the term 'justification' assumes that there is an inherently positive value to the subject (or in this case, choice), and that the author merely presents evidence to back up this intrinsic positive value. For justification to appear valid, the author must contend that there is only one true choice and display why the choice being made is the correct one. Judges who focus on justifying a choice will thus display traits of clear, rules-based thinking; their general argument being that in their opinion there is no option other than the choice made. In this way, justification tends to require the assumption that the audience a judge is speaking to is relatively well versed in legal understanding or logic and can follow a judge's line of argument without question. It assumes a general sort of information symmetry, wherein both judge and audience come to the table with similar understandings and can make reasonable arguments based on a shared context. As such, justification is not an ideal strategy when a judge's secondary audience is the electorate.

Persuasion, to the contrary, has its basis within elite communication strategy. The general assumption behind persuasion begins with supposition that there are at least two alternatives and that the audience must be shown which is most valid given the context of a decision. Persuasion therefore focuses on how an author presents information in order to move an audience in their favor. In order to influence an audience, speakers strive to structure arguments in ways that are easily comprehensible to their intended audience in hopes that the argument will be internalized and accepted as truth. The inevitable problem, however, is that the level of information between individual audience members, the audience as a body, and the speaker, is asymmetrical. Thus, the resulting interpretation by the audience is entirely exogenous to the speaker. This results in a sort of persuasion game wherein audience response is tied to two considerations: (a) the information possessed by the speaker at the time of the communication; and (b) how she chooses to divulge this information to the audience. According to Glazer and Rubinstein (2006), among the multiple considerations that may restrict a speaker, chief among them are the audience's ability to process information, and the speaker's ability to show a common "shared interest" between themselves and the audience such as "the common good," or "democratic values" (see also Grice 1989).

For a judge to be persuasive then, they must not only know how to apply the law consistently, but *what* law to apply consistently. Judges therefore selectively single out information in order to maximize the success of their opinion, based on what they perceive will be most useful to the various audiences of the opinion. Persuasion and justification are not mutually exclusive, however, and can be difficult to fully distinguish from each other in empirical analyses. It is our argument that while judges may wish to perform both functions simultaneously in an opinion, the various institutions of the judiciary as well as the constraints set upon judges when making decisions will lead to the prioritization of one feature or the other. When judges seek to persuade, they do so through engaging in a communicative strategy which highlights the complexity of an argument, engaging multiple threads and showing how they will eventually lead to a chosen, "correct" decision. This complexity is necessary, since judges must speak to a variety of audiences, all of whom may have some stake in their continued retention. In this way, we can begin to break apart the two meanings and begin to apply judicial voice to judicial practice. We contend ultimately that judges prioritize persuasion to influence specific audiences; in particular, the other justices on the court. This prioritization of persuasion deteriorates as justices coalesce around a decision, ultimately translating into a justification tactic in order to appear responsive to a more general audience; that is, the mass public.

Inherently, prioritizing persuasion or justification should lead to a trade-off between readability (or "comprehension") on the one hand, and rhetorical complexity on the other. Comprehension, as a concept, is based on the ability of an individual to read and understand the arguments of a particular text (Aijina, Laouiti, and Msolli 2016; Benoit, Munger and Spirling 2017; Coleman and Liau 1975; Dale and Chall 1949; Flesch1948; Gunning 1952; Sawyer, Laran, and Xu 2008; Terblanche and Burgess 2010). Originally developed in the education literature, "readability" statistics have been a central tool for analyzing the comprehensibility of complex speech in several fields, including political science (see Reilly and Richey 2011; Owens and Wedeking 2012; Owens, Wedeking and Wolfarth 2013; Black, Owens, Wedeking, Wohlfarth 2016; Nelson and Hinkle 2018) and business (Aijina, Laouiti, and Msolli 2016; Terblanche and Burgess 2010).[8] Readability is used here as a proxy for justification for one simple reason: it takes the subject matter under discussion as inherently positive (that is, correct), and simply focuses on how well a judge conveys this in the opinion. As stated previously, the root difference between justification and persuasion, based on their definitions, lies in whether the outcome is viewed as inherently correct, or a matter of debate. When a judge justifies a decision, the clarity of their writing should be based on how simple, or "common sense," their choice actually was. Reilly (2009) finds that in order to reach a general audience of American citizens, authors must write to approximately an 8th grade reading level. Even if we start with the assumption that the opinion is merely post hoc, acting as a capricious justification for a judge's desired policy outcome, the opinion must still be written in a way that conveys this choice in a manner that appears within the letter of the law, and thus must show clear justification for a judge's interpretation. Judges who struggle with clear legal writing may be showing signs that their argument is not as clear-cut as they wish it to be. Thus, a higher reading difficulty should be a sign that a judge may be forgoing reading clarity and justification for a strategy of persuasion.

We recognize that a single measure likely does not account for all the ways in which an author may attempt to justify their arguments. As we are specifically interested in analyzing the trade-off that occurs between persuasion and justification, we need a way to examine the variety of ways that judges attempt to justify their decisions. As justification is primarily focused on emphasizing the common-sense reasoning behind a decision, we believe that the level of analytic language present in an opinion is indicative of justifying behavior. Analytic thinking, according to our measures, focuses on the level of formal, logical reasoning in a document compared to more personal, "here and now" narrative style that we argue would be inherent in persuasion (see Pennebaker et al. 2015). Nearly all opinions display a high degree of analytic language; however, we contend that the higher the proportion of analytic to non-analytic language present in the opinion is indicative that the author has taken the outcome as factually correct and is simply outlining how they came to the chosen decision. This line of argumentation is not only in line with our theory as it pertains to justification, it also follows from what Popkin (2007) refers to as the "authoritative" tone, which stressed as more magisterial, impersonal, and technical reasoning for a decision.

Contrary to justification, persuasion accepts as a default that people will come to different conclusions when presented with similar circumstances. Decisions are not made purely on mechanical logic, and individuals may be susceptible to changing their minds if the argument is effective. As such, persuasion requires advocacy from the writer, the ultimate goal to be the swaying of an audience to your side. As Zaller (1992) points out, however, elites must ensure that arguments are clear if they are going to be successful at convincing outside audiences. "When elites uphold a clear picture of what should be done, the public tends to see events from that point of view (Zaller 1992, 8)." To be convincing, therefore, elites must show that their choice was not the only best choice, it was the *only choice*. In doing so, texts that are convincing will likely display a higher degree of cognitive complexity, or cognitive clarity, in their writing. Measures of cognitive clarity have been utilized previously by Owens and Wedeking (2012) to predict ideological drift on the U.S. Supreme Court and are popular when analyzing textual data in political science in order to investigate the behavioral components of political speech (see Tetlock, Bernzweig, and Gallant 1985; Gruenfeld and Presten 2000; Gruenfeld 1995; Tetlock 1986; Gibbons 1990; Romano 2018). As developed in psychology and cognitive science, measures of cognitive clarity are used to measure a speaker's ability to evaluate complicated situations and arrive at a decision. Generally, empirical examinations of cognition have measured cognitive complexity by first determining the levels of differentiation and integration used in a speaker's language, and then collapsing these into a single score to measure the extent of a speaker's evaluative and decision-making power. Differentiation focuses on the capacity of an individual to relate to and adopt a variety of perspectives when introduced to a particular event or issue. In their case study of press conferences held by Rudy Giuliani between 1993 and 2001, Pennebaker and Lay (2002) show, for example, that Giuliani began to convey a greater sense of differentiation when considering multiple perspectives and compromise as a result of his personal battle with cancer and the terrorist attacks on September 11. Put plainly then, differentiation examines whether individuals see the world in "black and white" or "shades of gray." The second dimension, integration, takes a step past differentiation and indicates that an individual has the capacity to recognize connections between divergent perspectives. Complex thinkers tend to consider an extensive range of issues as they attempt to reconcile different, sometimes contradictory strains of thought, whereas less complex thinking generally adheres to attitudinal decision-making and dogma (Winters 1996).

To round out our measures of persuasion, we also include a measure of authenticity in the language of a judicial opinion. Authenticity, the "genuineness and sincerity" of an author (Baker and Martinson 2001). Measures of authenticity focus particular attention on the level of personal and disclosing discourse in text compared to impersonal, guarded language; providing a clear but mutually exclusive counter to our measure of analytic language discussed previously. This translates particularly well to a personal tone (Popkin 2007), which is argued to be more useful for judges attempting to craft strong, persuasive arguments. Personal voice, according to Popkin (2007, 3), "locates the source of law in the nonprofessional community, with the judge speaking as a fellow member of that community." This style of writing is incredibly useful for judges attempting to mollify or sway an audience, and should be better suited at presenting them as responsive to various arguments and voices.

Our primary argument throughout this book is that variations in the institutional framework of the state judiciary will have a substantial impact on how judges utilize persuasion and justification throughout a judicial opinion. Particularly, we believe that variations in the methods of retention used to sustain the bench will lead judges to write strategically in order to placate and influence the audiences responsible for their retention. Currently, the landscape of judicial retention in the various states exhibits a wide range of variation, but the patterns that remain are, to a degree, holdovers from the previously discussed political movements that have instigated changes in the judiciary since the 1800s.

Partisan electoral systems and non-partisan electoral systems make the claim of judicial representation the clearest. These judges are elected by the public and retained by the public, and the public is their audience. This provides the public with the explicit authority to make a choice between whom they wish to represent them. Considering that these judges need to justify their decisions not only during their elections, but also in writing following every decision, it may be argued that elected judges more easily meet the qualifications for representatives than other elected officials in the U.S. context. We should expect that judges in these states will start from a perspective that they need to be heavily persuasive in their arguments in order to protect themselves from backlash. This strategy is likely to be altered dependent on the unique contexts of each case, however, which we will explore more fully in the chapters that follow.

While removing the explicit connection to the electorate, appointment systems simply shift the accountability mechanism for judges to either the legislature or governor of the state. In doing so, these systems simply make an elite body or individual the audience for judicial decisions and opinions, shifting the audience but not diminishing the representative nature of the judiciary. While the public may play a role in retention through a tacit form of representation, they are not the direct body responsible for retention. As the primary judicial audience consists of government officials, with the public watching from the wings, judges should be more likely to prioritize justification in these states, dependent on case context and other institutional factors such as term length.

Courts that use the Missouri Plan share a similar audience with those states which use contested elections, but with a significant modification. While retention in all these systems is dependent upon the electorate, salience and participation is significantly lower in Missouri Plan systems. Recall, retention elections in the Missouri Plan are plagued by ballot roll-off and next to no campaigning. This leaves the electorate less energized and active. To this end, justices may not need to consider their retention audience nearly as consistently as those judges in contested electoral systems.

Summary

Establishing the foundations of judicial authority and legitimacy has always been a difficult task for the institution. For scholars of judicial behavior, the puzzle is equally perplexing, with researchers often being split over how judges overcome constraints in order to exercise power. The fundamental issue from this perspective tends to be focused on how a seemingly undemocratic institution exercises its authority over a democratic populace. The common foundation of judicial legitimacy stems from the belief that the bench requires a judge to stand for and protect minority rights from majority tyranny; however in the states often-times we find that judges are beholden to the majority in order to maintain their power. Only a minority of judges in the United States have the benefit of life tenure, and many more judges must face the public as an electorate in some form of retention. Given this, we should expect that judges act as representatives of the public trust, and we should expect that they will behave in a manner consistent with the values of representation.

Once we accept that judges fit the definition of representatives, the primary question of concern should be how the public can enforce or police institutions such as the judiciary when they use their power illegitimately (Peretti 1999). As the self-promoted bastions of the rule of law, judges are important to the modern foundation of democratic society. If judges are allowed to make political decisions free from the confines of representation, what stops judges from becoming simply "partisans in robes"? In order to investigate judicial representation and the use and scope of judicial power, we argue that a focus on the judicial opinion is vital. The public opinion is a cornerstone of the contemporary legal system in the United States, and is also a quintessential piece of the representative process; a process that judges are often constitutionally required to take part in. In the opinion, judges must consider various audiences at the elite, legal, and public levels, and must also find a way to balance the views of these audiences in order to satisfy their constituent audiences while still acting within the guidelines of judicial ethics. While the judicial opinion is often considered to be primarily a source of justification, we argue that the opinion acts more as a tool for persuasion in order for judges to protect their authority *and achieve their own policy goals*. To find balance, judges often must emphasize justification or persuasion when crafting opinions and writing law, and as we will show, a judge's ability to prioritize one over the other is often linked to whether they are "shielded" from popular backlash during retention.

In the next chapter, we begin our investigation of how judges craft opinions in order to justify and persuade. Specifically, we begin our investigation by examining thoroughly how judges craft frames within opinions, paying special attention to whether and how judges balance these two competing forms of rhetoric and to their impact on the accessibility of an opinion in salient and non-salient cases.

Notes

1 Rhode Island is the only state to truly have life tenure, but the states of Massachusetts and New Hampshire allow judges to serve without terms until the age of 70.
2 To be perceived as representative agents by a population, potential representatives must be recognized and validated through two sets of rules. The first set of rules recognized by Rehfeld (2006) is designed via the governing institutions to designate the way in which representatives are officially selected (a method of selection). Specifically, these rules "specify a *Selection Agent* who uses a *Decision Rule* to select a representative from

a *Qualified Set*" (Rehfeld, 2006: pg. 5). The selection agent may take any number of variations depending on the decision rules used to provide accountability. For example, in electoral systems the selection agents are citizens, the decision rule is based on the method chosen to populate the institution itself (such as "majority rule" or "plurality" voting), and the qualified set are those citizens eligible to vote in an election.

3 It is noteworthy to point out that while states did begin making moves toward codifying law through the written opinion, the practice was not uniform in its adoption, nor was the adoption an instant tread at the state level. Many states did not begin adopting reporting practices similar to those instituted by the Marshall Court until the 1840s and 1850s (see Kempin 1959; Healy 2001 for a more thorough discussion of the expansion of precedent through the written opinion at the state and federal level).

4 According to Evan Haynes (1944, 100), "In the year 1850 alone, seven states changed to popular election of judges." Following the conclusion of the Civil War, a majority of the states in the union, twenty-four of thirty-four, used elections as the way to staff their judiciary.

5 As we will develop further in Chapter 5, this early form of per curiam opinion is a far cry from the system used today. Marshall's opinions were "signed," however, these opinions were written explicitly to state what the court's decision was, and the Justices often shied away from writing separately, particularly in salient cases.

6 Notably, Connecticut's requirement starting in 1784 was largely ignored by members of the judiciary after being enacted, with judges largely continuing a practice of writing a majority opinion with dissents. Louisiana's requirement of seriatim in 1821 was repealed one year after it was instituted. As noted by Sanders (1963, 677) the practice was largely disbanded after judges would submit the statement, "I concur in the opinion for the reasons adduced," attached to the majority opinion in a case.

7 We will revisit this aspect of the opinion more in Chapter 3.

8 While there may be no uniquely "best" measure of readability for every research question (Benoit, Munger, and Spirling 2017; Cann, Goelzhauser, and Johnson 2014), the base measure still provides us with a distinct way of evaluating a judge's ability to justify themselves.

References

Ajina, A., Laouiti, M., & Msolli, B. (2016). Guiding Through the Fog: Does Annual Report Readability Reveal Earnings Management? *Research in International Business and Finance*, 38, 509–516.

Aldisert, R. J. (2009). Judicial Declarations of Public Policy. *The Journal of Appellate Practice and Process*, 10(2), 229–245.

Aldisert, R. J., Rasch, M., & Bartlett, M. P. (2009). Opinion Writing and Opinion Readers. *Cardozo Law Review*, 31(1), 1–44.

Alito, S. A. (2009). The Second Conversation with Justice Samuel A. Alito, Jr.: Lawyering and the Craft of Judicial Opinion Writing. *Pepperdine Law Review*, 37(5), 33–62.

Baker, S. & Martinson, D. L. (2001). The TARES Test: Five Principles for Ethical Persuasion. *Journal of Mass Media Ethics*, 16(2&3), 148–175.

Baum, L. (2006). *Judges and Their Audiences: A Perspective on Judicial Behavior*. Princeton: Princeton University Press.

Benoit, K., Munger, K., & Spirling, A. (2017). Measuring and Explaining Political Sophistication Through Textual Complexity https://ssrn.com/abstract=3062061 (accessed on May 16, 2019).

Berring, R. C., & Edinger, E. A. (1999). *Finding the Law: An Abridged Edition of How to Find the Law*. 11th ed. Bethesda: West Group.

Black, R. C., Owens, R. J., Wedeking, J., & Wohlfarth, P. C. (2016) *U. S. Supreme Court Opinions and their Audiences.* Cambridge: Cambridge University Press.

Blackstone, W. (1765). *Commentaries on the Laws of England.* Edited by Paley, R. (2016). Oxford: Oxford University Press.

Bonneau, C. W., & Hall, M. G. (2009). *In Defense of Judicial Elections.* New York: Routledge.

Brace, P. & Boyea, B. D. (2008). State Public Opinion, the Death Penalty, and the Practice of Electing Judges. *American Journal of Political Science*, 52(2), 360–372.

Brace, P. & Hall, M. G. (1997). The Interplay of Preferences, Case Facts, Context, and Rules in the Politics of Judicial Choice. *Journal of Politics*, 59(4), 1206–1231.

Breyer, S. (2010). *Making Our Democracy Work: A Judge's View.* New York: Vintage.

Broockman, D. E. & Butler, D. M. (2017) The Causal Effects of Elite Position-Taking on Voter Attitudes: Field Experiments with Elite Communication. *American Journal of Political Science*, 61(1), 208–221.

Canes-Wrone, B., Brady, D. W., & Cogan, J. F. (2002). Out of Step, Out of Office: Electoral Accountability and House Members' Voting. *American Political Science Review*, 96(1), 127–140.

Canes-Wrone, B., Clark, T. S. & Kelly, J. P. (2014). Judicial Selection and Death Penalty Decisions. *American Political Science Review*, 108(1), 23–39.

Cann, D. M., Goelzhauser, G., & Johnson, K. (2014). Analyzing Textual Complexity in Political Science Research. *PS: Political Science and Politics*, 47(3), 663–666.

Cappalli, R. B. (2000). Improving Appellate Opinions. *Judicature*, 83(6), 286–287.

Carey, J. M. (2008) *Legislative Voting and Accountability.* Cambridge: Cambridge University Press.

Casillas, C. J., Enns, P. K, & Wohlfarth, P. C. (2011). How Public Opinion Constrains the U.S. Supreme Court. *The American Journal of Political Science*, 55(1), 74–88.

Casto, W. R. (1995). *The Supreme Court in the Early Republic: The Chief Justiceship of John Jay and Oliver Ellsworth.* Columbia: University of South Carolina Press.

Choi, S. J., Gulati, G. M., & Posner, E. A. (2010). Professionals or Politicians: The Uncertain Empirical Case for an Elected Rather than Appointed Judiciary. *Journal of Law, Economics, and Organization*, 26(2), 290–336.

Clark, T. S., & Carrubba, C. J. (2012). A Theory of Opinion Writing in a Political Hierarchy. *Journal of Politics*, 74(3), 584–603.

Coleman, M. & Liau, T. L. (1975). A Computer Readability Formula Designed for Machine Scoring. *Journal of Applied Psychology*, 60(2), 283–284.

Collins, T. A. & Cooper, C. A. (2012). Case Salience and Media Coverage of Supreme Court Decisions: Towards a New Measure. *Political Research Quarterly*, 65(2), 396–407.

Collins, P. M., Ringhand, L. A. (2017). *Supreme Court Confirmation Hearings and Constitutional Change.* Cambridge: Cambridge University Press.

Curry, T. A. and Hurwitz, M. S. (2016). Strategic Retirement of Elected and Appointed Justices: A Hazard Model Approach. *Journal of Politics*, 78(4), 1061–1075.

Curry, T. A. and Romano, M. K. (2018). Ideological Congruity on State Supreme Courts. *Justice System Journal*, 39(2), 139–154.

Dahl, R. A. (1956). *A Preface to Democratic Theory.* Chicago; University of Chicago Press.

Dale, E. & Chall, J. S. (1949). The Concept of Readability. *Elementary English*, 26(1), 19–26.

Dann, B. M. & Hansen, R. M. (2001). Judicial Retention Elections. *Loyola of Los Angeles Law Review*, 34, 1429–1446.

Disch, L. (2011). Toward a Mobilization Concept of Democratic Representation. *American Political Science Review*, 105(1), 100–114.

Druckman, J. N. (2014). Pathologies of Studying Public Opinion, Political Communication, and Democratic Responsiveness. *Political Communication*, 31(3), 467–492.

Dryzek, J. S., & Niemeyer, S. (2008). Discursive Representation. *American Political Science Review,* 102(4), 481–493.

Dubois, P. L. (1980). Public Participation in Trial Court Elections: Possibilities for Accentuating the Positive and Eliminating the Negative. *Law and Policy*, 2(2), 133–160.

Edelman, M. (1967). *The Symbolic Use of Politics.* Champaign: University of Illinois Press.

Federal Judicial Center. (1991). *Judicial Writing Manual.* Washington, D.C.: Federal Judicial Center.

Flesch, R. (1948). A New Readability Yardstick. *Journal of Applied Psychology*, 32(3), 221–233

Garner, B. A. (2002). *The Elements of Legal Style.* 2nd ed. New York: Oxford University Press.

Garner, B. A. (2009). *Legal Writing in Plain English.* Chicago, University of Chicago Press.

George, J. J. (2006). *The Judicial Opinion Writing Handbook.* 5th ed. New York: William S. Hein.

Gibbons, F. X. (1990). Self-attention and Behavior: A Review and Theoretical Update. *Advances in Experimental Social Psychology*, 23(2), 249–303.

Glazer, J. & Rubinstein, A. (2006). A Study in the Pragmatics of Persuasion: A Game Theoretical Approach. *Theoretical Economics*, 1, 395–410.

Goelzhauser, G. & Cann, D. M. (2014) Judicial Independence and Opinion Clarity on State Supreme Courts. *State Politics and Policy Quarterly*, 14(2), 123–141.

Goodin, R. E. (2007). Enfranchising All Affected Interests, and Its Alternatives. *Philosophy and Public Affairs*, 35(1), 40–68.

Grice, H. P. (1989). *Studies in the Way of Words.* Cambridge: Harvard University Press.

Grimmer, J., Westwood, S. J., & Messing, S. (2012). How Words and Money Cultivate a Personal Vote: The Effect of Legislator Credit Claiming on Constituent Credit Allocation. *American Political Science Review*, 106(4), 703–719.

Grimmer, J., Westwood, S. J., & Messing, S. (2014). *The Impression of Influence: Legislator Communication, Representation, and Democratic Accountability.* Princeton: Princeton University Press.

Gruenfeld, D H. (1995). Status, Ideology, and Integrative Complexity on the U.S. Supreme Court: Rethinking the Politics of Political Decision Making. *Journal of Personality and Social Psychology*, 68(1), 5–20.

Gruenfeld, D. H. & Preston, J. (2000). Upending the Status Quo: Cognitive Complexity in the U.S. Supreme Court Justices Who Overturn Legal Precedent. *Personality and Social Psychology Bulletin*, 26(4), 1013–1022.

Gunning, R. (1952). *The Technique of Clear Writing.* New York: McGraw-Hill

Hall, M. G. (1987). Constituent Influence in State Supreme Courts: Conceptual Notes and Cast Study. *Journal of Politics*, 49(4), 1117–1124.

Hall, M. G. (1992). Electoral Politics and Strategic Voting in State Supreme Courts." *Journal of Politics*, 54(2), 427–446.

Hall, M. G. (1995). Justices as Representatives: Elections and Judicial Politics in the American States. *American Politics Quarterly*, 23(4), 485–503.

Hall, M. G. (2015). *Attacking Judges: How Campaign Advertising Influences State Supreme Court Elections.* Stanford: Stanford University Press.

Hall, M. G., & Bonneau, C. W. (2006). Does Quality Matter? Challengers in State Supreme Court Elections. *American Journal of Political Science*, 50(1), 20–33.

Hall, M. G. & Brace, P. (1992). Toward an Integrated Model of Judicial Voting Behavior. *American Politics Quarterly*, 20(2), 147–168.

Hamilton, A. (1788). Federalst No. 78. in Rossiter, C. (1999). *The Federalist Papers*. New York: Signet Classic.

Haynes, E. (1944). *The Selection and Tenure of Judges*. Clark: The Lawbook Exchange.

Healy, T. (2001). Stare Decisis as a Constitutional Requirement. *West Virginia Law Review* 104: 43–121.

Hettinger, V. A., Lindquist, S. A., and Martinek, W. L. (2006). *Judging on a Collegial Court: Influences on Federal Appellate Decision Making*. Charlottesville: University of Virginia Press.

Hopkins, J. D. (1969). Notes on Style in Judicial Opinions. *Trial Judges Journal*, 8, 49–70.

Kastellec, J. P. (2011). Hierarchical and Collegial Politics on the U.S. Courts of Appeals. *Journal of Politics*, 73(2), 345–61.

Keith, L. C., Tate, C. N., & Poe, S. C. (2009). Is the Law a Mere Parchment Barrier to Human Rights Abuse? *Journal of Politics*, 71(2), 644–660.

Keith, L. C. (2002). Constitutional Provisions for Individual Human Rights (1977–1996): Are They More than Mere "Window Dressing?" *Political Research Quarterly*, 55(1), 111–143.

Kempin, F. G. (1959). Precedent and stare decisis: The critical years, 1800 to 1850. *The American Journal of Legal History*, 3(1), 28–54.

Klein, D. & Baum, L. (2001). Ballot Information and Voting Decisions in Judicial Elections. *Political Research Quarterly*, 54(4), 709–728.

Kozinsk, A. (2001). *Hart v. Massanari*. 266 F.3d 1155 (9th Cir.).

Kravitz, M. R. (2009). Written and Oral Persuasion in the United States Courts: A District Judge's Perspective on Their History, Function, and Future. *The Journal of Appellate Practice and Process*, 10(2), 247–272.

Langer, L. (2002). *Judicial Review in State Supreme Courts: A Comparative Study*. New York: SUNY Press.

Lax, J. R. & Cameron, C. M. (2007). Bargaining and Opinion Assignment on the US Supreme Court. *Journal of Law, Economics, and Organization*, 23(2), 276–302.

Lebovits, G. & Hidalgo, R. (2009). Advice to Law Clerks: How to Draft Your First Judicial Opinion. *Westchester Bar Journal*, 36(1), 29–37.

Leflar, R. A. (1983). Quality in Judicial Opinions. *Pace Law Review*, 3(3), 579–592.

Locke, J. (1660). *Two Treatise of Government*. Edited by Laslett, P. (1988). Cambridge: Cambridge University Press.

Maltzman, Forrest, James F. Spriggs, & Paul L. Wahlbeck. (2000). *Crafting Law on the Supreme Court: The Collegial Game*. Cambridge: Cambridge University Press.

Manin, B. (1997). *The Principles of Representative Government*. Cambridge: Cambridge University Press.

Marbury v. Madison (1803), 5 U.S. 137.

Montanaro, L. (2012). The Democratic Legitimacy of Self- Appointed Representatives. *Journal of Politics*, 74(4), 1094–1107.

Montesquieu, C. (1748). *The Spirit of the Laws*. Edited by Cohler, A. M., Miller, B. C., & Stone, H. S. (1994). Cambridge: Cambridge University Press.

Mullins, A. E. (2016). Jedi or Judge: How the Human Mind Redefines Judicial Opinions. *Wyoming Law Review*, 16(2), 325–342.

Mutz, D. C., Sniderman, P. M., & Brody, R. A. (1996). *Political Persuasion and Attitude Change*. Ann Arbor: University of Michigan Press.

Nelson, M. J. & Hinkle, R. K. (2018). Crafting the Law: How Opinion Content Influences Legal Development. *Justice System Journal*, 39(2), 97–122.

O'Donnell, G. (2004). Why the Rule of Law Matters. *Journal of Democracy*, 15(4), 32–46

Owens, R. J. & Wedeking, J. (2012). Predicting Drift on Political Insulated Institutions: A Study of Ideological Drift on the United States Supreme Court. *Journal of Politics*, 74(2), 487–500.

Owens, R. J., Wedeking, J., & Wohlfarth, P. C. (2013). How the Supreme Court Alters Opinion Language to Evade Congressional Review. *Journal of Law and Courts*, 1(1), 35–59.

Pennebaker, J. W. & Lay, T. (2002). Linguistic Styles: Language Use and Personality during Crises: Analyses of Mayor Rudolph Giuliani's Press Conferences. *Journal of Research in Personality*, 36(1), 271–282

Pennebaker, J. W., Booth, R. J., Boyd, R. L., & Francis, M. E. (2015). *Linguistic Inquiry and Word Count: LIWC2015*. Austin, TX: Pennebaker Conglomerates (www.LIWC. net).

Peretti, T. J. (1999). *In Defense of a Political Court*. Princeton: Princeton University Press.

Pitkin, H. F. (1967). *The Concept of Representation*. Berkeley: University of California Press.

Popkin, W. D. (2007). *Evolution of the Judicial Opinion: Institutional and Individual Styles*. New York: New York University Press.

Posner, R. A. (1995). Judges' Writing Styles (And Do They Matter?). *The University of Chicago Law Review*, 62(4), 1421–1449.

Radin, M. (1930). The Requirement of Written Opinions. *California Law Review*, 18(5), 486–496.

Rehfeld, A. (2006). Toward a General Theory of Political Representation. *Journal of Politics*, 68(1), 1–21.

Rehfeld, A. (2009). Representation Rethought: On Trustees, Delegates, and Gyroscopes in the Study of Political Representation and Democracy. *American Political Science Review*, 103(2), 214–30.

Reilly, S., & Richey, S. (2011). Ballot Question Readability and Roll-Off: The Impact of Language Complexity. *Political Research Quarterly*, 64(1), 59–67.

Republican Party of Minnesota v. White (2002), 536 U.S. 765.

Romano, M. K. (2018). Legislators Off Their Leash: Cognitive Shirking and Impending Retirement in the U.S. House. *Social Science Quarterly*, 99(3), 993–1005.

Sanders, J. W. (1963). The Role of Dissenting Opinions in Louisiana. *Louisiana Law Review*, 23(4), 673–679.

Saward, M. (2010). *The Representative Claim*. New York: Oxford University Press.

Sawyer, A. G., Laran, J., & Xu, J. (2008). The Readability of Marketing Journals: Are Award Winning Articles Better Written? *Journal of Marketing*, 72(1), 108–117.

Shapiro, M. (1968). *The Supreme Court and Administrative Agencies*. New York: Free Press.

Snyder, J. J., & Strömberg, D. (2010). Press Coverage and Political Accountability. *Journal of Political Economy*, 118(2), 355–408.

Streb, M. J. (2007). *Running for Judge: The Rising Political, Financial, and Legal Stakes of Judicial Elections*. New York: New York University Press.

Terblanche, M., & Burgess, L. (2010). Examining the Readability of Patient-Informed Consent Forms. *Open Access Journal of Clinical Trials*, 2, 157–162.

Tetlock, P. E. (1986). A Value Pluralism Model of Ideological Reasoning. *Journal of Personality and Social Psychology*, 50(4), 819–827.

Tetlock, P. E., Bernzweig, J., & Gallant, J. L. (1985). Supreme Court Decision Making: Cognitive Style as a Predictor of Ideological Consistency in Voting. *Journal of Personality and Social Psychology,* 48(4), 1227–1239.

Tiller, E. H., & Cross, F. B. (1999). A Modest Proposal for Improving American Justice. *Columbia Law Review,* 99(1), 215–234.

Vance, R. C. (2011). Judicial Opinion Writing: An Annotated Bibliography. *The Journal of the Legal Writing Institute,* 17, 197–231.

Wald, P. M. (1995). The Rhetoric of Results and the Results of Rhetoric: Judicial Writing. *University of Chicago Law Review,* 62, 1371–1419.

Winter, D. G. (1996). *Personality: Analysis and Interpretation of Lives.* New York: McGraw-Hill.

Wydick, R. C. (1998). Plain English for Lawyers. *California Law Review,* 66(4), 727–765.

Zaller, J. R. (1992). *The Nature and Origins of Mass Opinion.* Cambridge: Cambridge University Press.

Zilis, M. A. (2015). *The Limits of Legitimacy: Dissenting Opinions, Media Coverage, and Public Responses to Supreme Court Decisions.* Ann Arbor: University of Michigan Press.

3

WRITING FOR AN AUDIENCE

Framing and Opinion Content

As part of the opinion, judges make conscious choices about what topics and arguments they will pay attention to, and what arguments they will ignore or deemphasize. In the opening vignettes from Tennessee and Washington in Chapter 1, Justice Bivens and Stephens craft strategic statements not only about the court's role in government, but also how the court and future judges ought to examine cases. By the time a case reaches a state's highest court, the information resources provided to it by plaintiffs, defendants, outside parties, other judges, and the states leave judges with a vast number of resources to draw from as they write the decision. The choice of what to focus on (and not focus on) is important, as it can be used as a signal to a judge's respective audience. Whether it be to guide future litigants attempting to draw parallels between their cases and past precedent or an appeal to retention audiences that a judge is acting justly on their behalf, the language and discursive structure of a judicial opinion carries substantial weight when measured against a judge's goals. Our question is this chapter is what information becomes prevalent or ignored in the opinion, and why might judges choose to highlight certain arguments over others?

One way to evaluate how judges emphasize or deemphasize information within an opinion is by examining how judges frame their arguments. Framing, or the presentation of information through a specific reference point, is important for understanding the intentions of an author when addressing and persuading an audience. We believe that judges select the frame of their opinions differently depending upon the level of insulation they have from the voting public and based upon their decision in the case. Previous findings by Canes-Wrone, Clark, and Kelly (2014) have shown that judicial selection mechanisms have significant influence over the decision in death penalty cases. We build upon these findings and demonstrate that judges also carefully decide how they will explain themselves when making a variety of decisions. The choice of how to frame an opinion is conditioned by the belief that it may be an important factor in their retention.

As the opinion is the quintessential "product," of the judiciary, it is reasonable to assume that the internal structure and arguments made in the opinion will have some substantial impact on a judge's ability to appeal to various retention audiences. As Bonneau and Cann (2015, 72) correctly point out, "a judge cannot send free mailings to his or her constituents trumpeting recent decisions the judge made, nor can a judge call a press conference to call attention to a pressing issue and inform his or her constituents how the judge plans to deal with the issue." What a judge *can do*, however, is provide a clear rationale for their decision after the fact, which can be used by audiences when evaluating a judge's performance later. Judges should therefore take great care when crafting the frames of their argument in order to satisfy various goals while on the bench.

In this chapter, we begin our investigation into how judges consider their audiences by examining the extent to which judges frame their arguments differently in both salient (death penalty) and non-salient (education) issues. Our primary purpose in this chapter is twofold. First, the chapter provides us with an opportunity to present our data descriptively and discuss some of the unique features of the dataset that will provide us with avenues for investigation in the following chapters. Second, this chapter acts as our first attempt to understand the discursive nature of the judicial opinion writing. In order to draw some conclusions concerning how judges selectively frame their choices, we analyze 5,206 death penalty opinions and 1,413 education opinions written by members of a state's court of last resort from 1995–2010. Utilizing a topic modeling approach, we calculate the topic prevalence of various judicial frames, and examine how language choice affects the framing of judicial decisions – specifically focusing on the trade-off between language of justification and persuasion as discussed in Chapter 2. Briefly, we find that judges do select frames based on their decision to justify their choices, and only apply persuasive language carefully to avoid backlash from the public. We likewise find that framing and frame consistency is largely dependent on method of retention used to maintain the bench.

Framing Choices and Judicial Opinions

Studying framing, as a general practice, involves the examination of how actors structure the political process and substantively, "narrow the available political alternatives" (Tuchman 1978, 156). Particularly, actors attempt to, "promote perceptions and interpretations that benefit one side while hindering the other" (Entman 2003, 417), and when effective, limit the public's consideration to specific issues. Within this process, authors organize symbols and other signifying elements that advocate certain ideas and encourage audiences to adopt and internalize these elements in their own thinking as well (see Iyengar and Simon 1993;

Kim, Scheufele and Shanahan 2002; Pan and Kosicki 1993). Fully developed frames perform several functions beneficial to the speaker and audience. At a basic level, frames define problems, specifically by "organizing everyday reality" (Tuchman 1978, 193, Shah et al. 2002) and limiting the grounds for discussion and debate to specific questions and concerns. Secondarily, frames provide causal analysis linking problems to potential alternatives and solutions, which then leads to the development of a moral judgement as to why certain solutions exist or are viable alternatives. For our purposes, this function is significant as it relates to the ability of judges to justify their decision. For political framing specifically, the final function of a well-developed frame is some kind of remedy promotion, which acts as a guidepost for the audience moving forward (Entman 1993; 2004; 2007) and solidifies the speaker's argument as the best alternative, or most often, the *only choice* that will properly remedy the situation. By raising an audience's awareness and focusing their thoughts on specific aspects of information, frames function as a fundamental core of the communication process (Entman and Usher 2018), providing them with a strategic persuasive element as well.

Recalling our model of judicial target audience dispersion from Chapter 2, an analysis of framing is important as it helps us explain how language permeates outward from an opinion and disseminates to different audiences. Entman's "cascade model," (1993; 2004) is useful here to understand how framing assists in this information flow. From an author's perspective, the process of framing helps in dictating the rules that govern discussion of policy problems or decision (Gamson and Modigliani 1987). By institutionalizing specific arguments over others, judges can make strategic choices which will inevitably shape policy discussions in each ripple as the opinion is dispersed. According to the cascade model, communication flows trickle outward as elites refine statements and distribute them out to various audiences such as the news media or the general public (see also Scheufele 1999; Sellers 2010). While each layer may have some power to shape and remold information to satisfy their own goals, the initial crafting of a message is important, as it effectively limits the debate (Entman 2004). For high court judges, the choice in argument definition may also have an impact on discussions of judicial quality later, however. Thus, judges should be expected to frame arguments carefully to both protect themselves from backlash as well as achieve their policy goals.

Framing, however, is not a simple process. Particularly for members of the court, communication strategies such as those inherent in judicial opinions require us to take more holistic approach to understanding what occurs when judges craft law. For a political actor such as a judge to win popularity and gain respect, they must frame issues and arguments in ways that will mobilize audiences in their favor, be those audiences their constituency or fellow judges and attorneys. To do so, they must determine first what they want to say and how they want to say it. Politicians frequently adopt communication frames used by other elites, such as the media and other politicians, but they also have been found to be influenced by citizen discussions (Riker 1996; Edwards and Wood 1999;

Druckman, Jacobs, and Ostermeier 2004). Frames are linked most prominently to the ability of one institution to influence others when making policy. In the courts, persuasion and speech have been linked to the ability of lower courts to influence higher courts (Corley, Collins and Calvin 2011; Curry, Romano, and Romero, n.d.), as well as the influence of party briefs (Corley 2008) and amicus briefs (Box-Steffensmeier, Christenson, and Hitt 2013) on court decision making. Most notably, Brace and Boyea (2008) and Hall (1987) both show that public support for the death penalty has its most powerful effect on judicial institutions that utilize election mechanisms; an indication that public sentiment does influence judicial decisions.

Frames can also vary significantly, even over the same issues (Chong and Druckman 2007). This can lead to a wide differentiation in how individuals discuss issues, giving some agency to groups in other audience spheres. The opinion writing process itself introduces multiple opportunities for other institutions, actors, and interests to influence the composition of a court's opinion; including legal precedent (Caldeira 1985; Kassow, Songer, and Fix 2012, Hansford and Spriggs 2006), interest group signals and participation (Box-Steffensmeier, Christenson, and Hitt 2013; Collins 2008) as well as strategic motivations such as institutional legitimacy, compliance, and institutional legitimacy (Owens, Wedeking, and Wolfarth 2013; Spriggs 1996). The initial selection of a frame of reference by a judge, however, has a long-lasting impact on the overall interpretation of an issue (Chong and Druckman 2007).

To understand how frames may go beyond their basic structural function and grant judges the ability to justify and, more importantly, persuade audiences using an opinion, we must take into consideration how individuals process information and evaluate a speaker's arguments. As discussed briefly in Chapter 2, the literature on elite opinion dissemination and persuasion emphasizes the role played by officials and other elite actors in structuring political discourse by strategically manipulating public sentiment toward individual and party goals (see particularly Chong 1993; Chong and Druckman 2007; Gabel and Scheve 2007; Lenz 2009; 2012; McCombs and Shaw 1972; McCombs 2005; Schuman and Presser 1981; Tewksbury and Scheufele 2009; Zaller 1992). Even when there is no overt manipulation of the public, attitudes often tend to shift sometimes arbitrarily, exhibiting a substantial amount of instability when measured by surveys (Converse 1964; Converse 2000; Delli Carpini and Keeter 1996; Kinder and Kalmoe 2017; Zaller 1992). According to Chong (1996) a key factor in rectifying this shortcoming is the provision of a "common frame of reference" or popularized account that can be easily adopted when discussing political issues. Chong (1996, 196–97) particularly emphasizes the role of "norm" references as a basis for opinion formulation, and how norms and principles provide individuals an outlet through which they can, "set aside arguments that may recommend decisions that are inconsistent with their principle [or norm] – even though they may agree with these arguments in isolation."

Our question, as we develop our theories in this chapter and beyond, is how these norms develop and entrench themselves within various audiences. We argue that judges hold the ability to solidify norms and principles in the mass public through the use of a well-crafted and strategically framed opinion. Furthermore, we claim that through the use of framing, judges can deemphasize the importance of opinions that would be unpopular with the public. Just as the choice of a particular frame can amplify attention within the public, another frame could as easily mute the attention a specific decision receives. In this sense, the choice of the frame should be affected not only by the cases itself and the individual writing the opinion, but also by how the public perceives the issue.

Analyzing Frames in Judicial Opinions

Frames help us to understand communication by identifying how authors agenda-set and prime individuals to adopt specific views when engaging in discussion. Previous research on judicial opinions has focused considerable attention to how language is transmitted or adopted between party briefs, other sources of information, and the final opinion (Corley 2008; Corley Collins and Calvin 2011; Box-Steffensmeier Christenson and Hitt 2013); however, to our knowledge few studies have paid considerable attention to how judges *utilize* language itself to narratively explain their decisions through frame adoption. While investigations of language transference are of considerable worth and value to understanding how judges craft law, also vital to a strong opinion is the way in which the ideas and messages are conveyed to an audience. The clarity of an opinion is important to ensure that these audiences do *read* the opinion, but judges must also consider what message they are conveying. One way that judges may safeguard themselves and ensure audience approval is through the selective use of frames when crafting the written opinion. Fundamentally, the framing of an opinion helps determines its contents, as well as the aspects of law that will be the basis for future precedent through the establishment of discourse. Discourse theory and analysis attempt to understand how meaning is generated through the selective use of language. As part of framing, discourses help provide boundaries on the meaning of objects and subjects by endowing them with particular identities (Dunn and Neumann 2016). According to Dunn and Neumann (2016, 2), "Analyzing discourses reveals how we come to take a certain phenomenon or an entire social reality for granted, and what kind of effects it has to naturalize that reality rather than another."

Discourses are also heavily linked to the concept of power and the development of social truths (Derrida 1974; Foucault 1970; 1973), attempting to centralize our understanding and craft our beliefs by signifying a fixed understanding and meaning. Relating this to judicial opinions, we argue that judges attempt to utilize opinions to center reality on specific concepts that serve to justify their decision-making as socially "correct." Thus, while judges are engaged in the creation of social reality, we believe they are constrained by what the public wishes to see done. Judges engage in a form of communicative action by attempting to coordinate their actions (the decision) with the shared goals of the audiences in question. It is a strategic action, according to Habermas (1996), as the judge (as principle actor) is not interested primarily in mutual understanding of the decision but aligning the decision with audience and individual goals.

Framing analysis is thus a quintessential first step for understanding the power and impact of judicial opinions, as they show us just how judges attempt to justify their choices and persuade an audience. Before moving forward, we must recognize that frames can be defined "only in relation to specific issues, events or political actors" (Chong and Druckman 2007, 106). Frames provide us with a common vocabulary which we can use to understand political issues, and different contextual frames will be applied to different issues or events (see also Entman 2004). As such, the choice in what context we use is important, as it will serve to limit or generalize our understanding of the world and how judges structure their thoughts in order to resolve legal disputes. Most often, studies of judicial behavior and opinions have paid special attention to the question of salience or non-salience to provide some contextual clarity toward their analyses (Epstein and Segal 2000; Fix 2014; Unah and Hancock 2006). We believe that this focus is conducive to our analyses, as judges should be likely to frame salient events differently in order to speak directly to audiences that are vital to their retention and maintaining institutional legitimacy.

For this reason, we choose to focus on legal opinions on death penalty decisions and education decisions in the states, which we believe to be representative of salient and non-salient cases respectively.[1] While support for the death penalty has been declining regularly from its all-time high of 80% in 1994, a solid base of support still exists for capital punishment for murder convictions (61% approval as of 2016) (Gallup 2016). The death penalty is thought of as an "easy issue" (Carmines and Stimson 1980) or "morality policy" (Mooney and Lee 2000), that is an issue which elicits a "gut response" from individuals. Such cases are also likely to garner substantial coverage from the media, as they are easily framed and often include scenarios and information that is easy to sensationalize. Education cases, on the other hand, are often more mundane in their discussions, and most often do not elicit the same kinds of affective reactions from audiences. Most frequently, such cases involve issues involving testing standards, union disputes (in some states), or education funding for the fiscal year. While such decisions may be deemed important by some, they are more difficult to frame in exciting ways that might elicit attention, leading to decreased awareness from audiences.

A single document may include several different frames and elements that help to structure the argument, and as a result we must also find a way to consider how particular frames may dominate an opinion over others (Chong and Druckman (2007). As Gamson and Modigliani (1987, 144) suggest, elites have a set of "culturally available frames," which they can use to develop their argument. Identification of these frames, and measurement of how strictly judges adhere to one frame over others help us understand how judges control debate around a policy issue. We can separate our examination here into two distinct parts. First, what types of frame are most common in death penalty and education opinions, and what language is most common in particular frames vs. others? Secondly, how might institutional context and audience considerations impact the selection and dominance of one frame over others in a given opinion?

To begin our investigation, we collect data on 5,206 death penalty opinions and 1,413 education opinions written by members of a state's court of last resort from 1995–2010. The full dataset is comprised of opinions from over 400 judges in all 50 states for cases involving education, and all 37 states that currently utilize the death penalty. Data for education cases was collected using the Westlaw Legal Library,[2] and death penalty cases were collected through the Lexis Legal Archive. For each subset, we collect opinions from the high court when the decision includes a formal, published opinion,[3] since these cases are instances in which judges attempt to directly influence the interpretation of law through codified, written precedent as discussed in Chapter 2.

Word Usage and Language Selection in State Judicial Opinions

Before discussing how judges select frames when crafting legal arguments, it is useful to examine directly language choice and how words develop a particular narrative in a case. The common conception that judicial decisions are at least partially dependent upon the context and facts of a case assumes that context is highly conditional; that is, each case is different and thus a judicial opinion will be heavily weighted by the specifics of a particular dispute. By analyzing the choice of words used, we can begin to see that judges view cases not based on such differences but based upon similar conditions that exist across cases and contexts. Functionally, judges do not view cases as unique, but a reiteration of previously established trends. To examine how word frequency may impact or be impacted by context, Figures 3.1 and 3.2 below graphically present the most frequent one hundred words found in either death penalty (3.1) or education (3.2) cases. Far from providing some support for precedent adherence, what we show here is that *context* tends to boil down to keywords that judges may use to identify common trends, which can be useful in quickly dispensing with judgment and justifying the use of some precedent over others. For example, in death penalty decisions, the primary contextual focus appears to be on appellate complaints. This makes sense, as appellants are likely to be individuals convicted of a capital crime and will be most likely to bring their appeal to the state supreme court to seek relief. As such, many of the terms most frequently used in opinions focus on factors that such appellants find important to the case, including general terms such as "mitigate," "circumstance," as well as more specific terms like "mental," and "ineffective." By comparison, an examination of word frequencies in education cases tells us how judges' order such cases into separate policy domains to structure an argument. Terms such as "school" and "board" indicate some need to focus on education leadership, whereas "teacher," "employ," and "contract," indicate the need to focus on education hiring. Most interesting, the frequency of terms such as "year," "fund," and "legislature," indicate that the courts frequently must answer questions of paying for public education, which identify the need for judicial oversight in the education process more generally; something we do not find with frequency in death penalty cases.

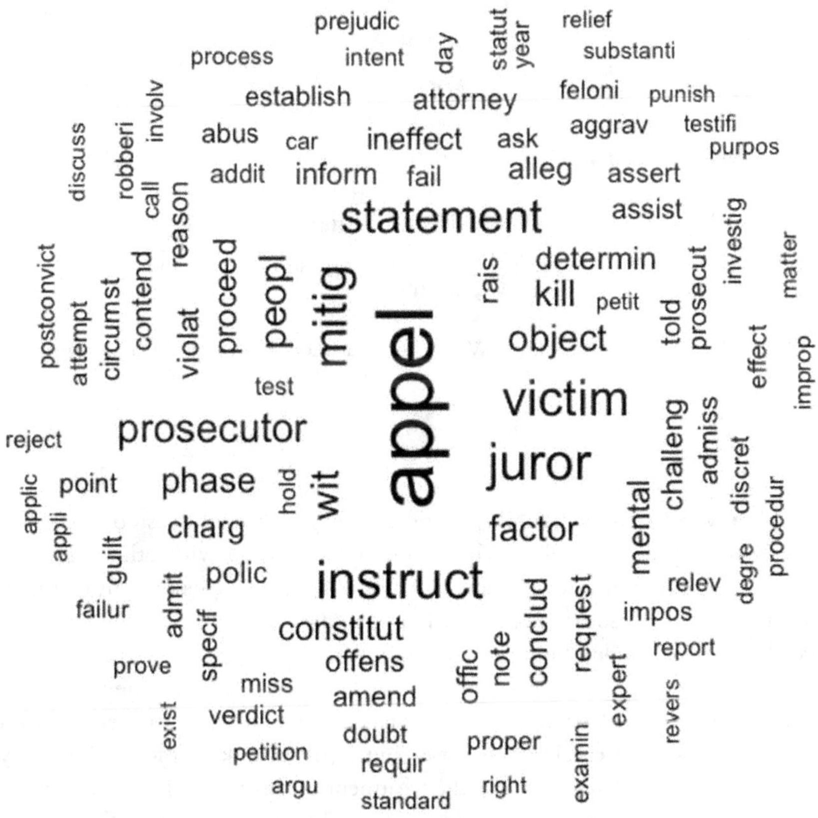

FIGURE 3.1   100 Most Frequent Words in Death Penalty Decisions in State Supreme Courts

Figure Created by Authors

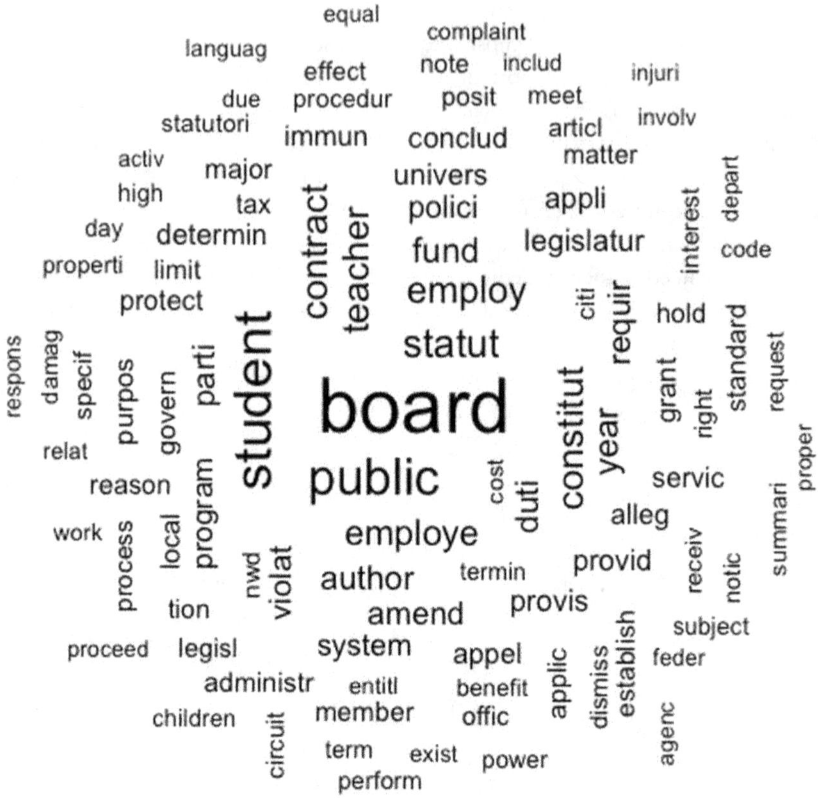

FIGURE 3.2 100 Most Frequent Words in Education Decisions in State Supreme Courts

Figure Created by Authors

While word frequencies tell part of the story of how judges contextualize decisions, they cannot tell us what words are associated with others directly. Framing requires not just that particular words appear frequently, but that they occur *together* with some frequency. For example, in Figure 3.3 we graph the word association index between two words of interest from the word clouds above. For death penalty decisions it may be of interest to map the associative link for the word "mental," to determine how judges treat the term within their decisions. As mental assessment is contingent in seeking the death penalty in the majority of states sampled, the treatment of this particular word may be of particular benefit in understanding how judges use context to frame their decisions. As Figure 3.3 shows, the term has the strongest association with discussions of condition, specifically the terms "retardation," "health," and "illness" all appear to be strongly correlated. If we examine more closely, we

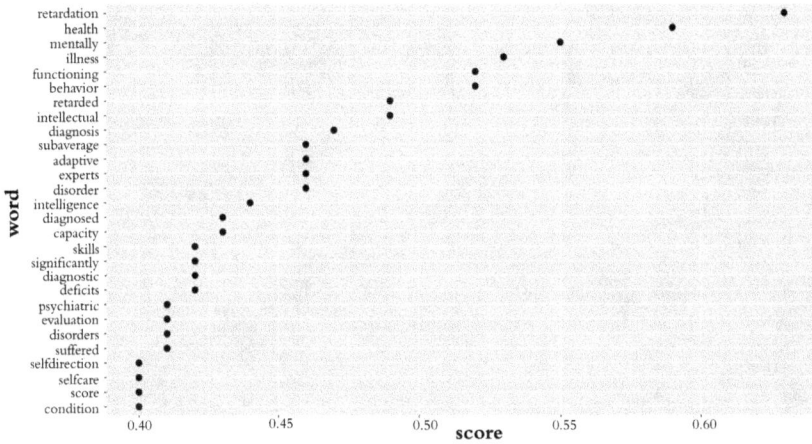

FIGURE 3.3 Word Associations with "Mental" in Death Penalty Decisions

Figure Created by Authors

can start to see distinctive patterns emerging in term associations, particularly focused on the use of testing and diagnostics, the role of expertise in determining mental condition, and finally a specific focus on intelligence testing as the primary means through which judges determine mental capacity when evaluating death penalty decisions.

Similarly, we may be interested in understanding just what terms and potential disputes are involved with usage of the term "student" in education cases. As education seems most likely to be salient when disputes involve students directly, examining the word associations with the term may key us in to understanding why education cases tend to be considered less interesting to the public. In Figure 3.4, we graph the common correlative associations with the term, similar to our examination of "mental" with death penalty cases in Figure 3.3. As Figure 3.4 indicates, the primary focus of student issues in the judiciary appears to involve testing and scores. This makes sense, given that student standardized tests are linked with graduation in many states. Terms such as "test," and "grade," stand out as key to understanding the correlations within these associations. Likewise, we can see how judges tend to focus on student testing and student issues by framing these questions with terms associated with positive sentiment, such as "important," "achieve" (and "achievement"), and "significant."

As we have seen thus far, words do appear to matter in providing us with context across different cases in our chosen policy areas. While the analysis thus far has given us an interesting start and helped in developing a few key insights, to fully understand the versatility of opinion frames and how judges may use strategy when selecting particular framing cues over others, we move from an

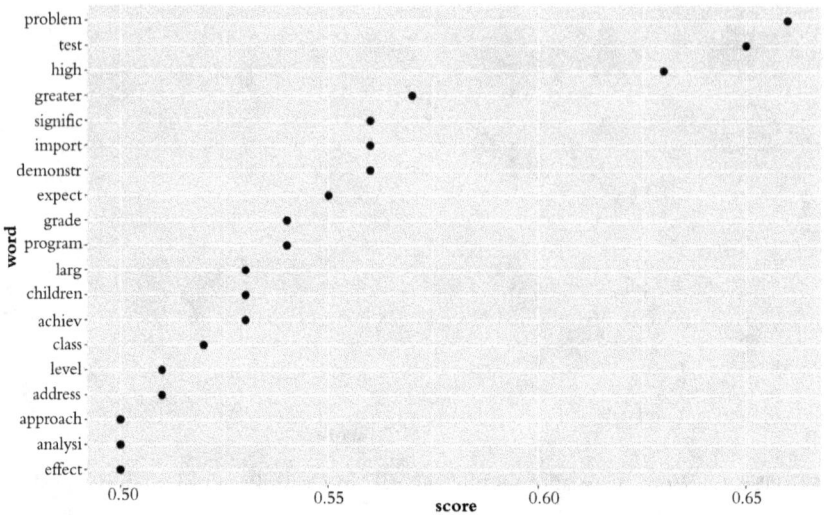

FIGURE 3.4 Word Associations with "Student" in Education Cases

Figure Created by Authors

analysis of word frequency into the development and discussion of topic modeling and the link between various words and particular decision outcomes.

From Words to Frames: Topic Selection and Frame Adherence in Opinions

While examining word groupings is an important step, word correlates may or may not be identifiable frames. The choice of what word to use is generally dependent upon the other words that appear around it. Word choice is not independent. Specific and focused word choice is framing, or the writing of content in a specific way to emphasize (or deemphasize) a particular topic.

To categorize the frames of judicial opinions, we implement an organization structure utilizing a Latent Dirichlet Allocation (LDA) as prescribed by Blei (2012). The intuition behind the use of LDA here is that we seek a way to intuitively organize the structure of a document, while recognizing that each document may contain a number of framing conventions, or "topics." LDAs try to capture this intuition by assuming a generative process by which words gain meaning through random association with other words within a corpus (Blei, 2012). In probabilistic topic modeling, LDAs treat data "as arising from a generative process which includes hidden variables. This generative process defines a joint probability distribution over both the observed and hidden random variables" (Blei 2012, 79). Topic models assume that all documents begin as a "bag of words," and meaning is derived for a document based upon the organization and structure those words produce. In this way, utilizing a topic modeling approach allows us to dig deeper into the hidden thematic structure of a text and uncover the frames important to an author's argument.[4]

The resulting topic model provides us with a baseline understanding of how judges categorize their decisions in death penalty and education cases, as well as how significant each frame is to a judge's considerations when crafting an opinion. In death penalty cases, we find that judges rely on a greater variety of frames compared to education cases, however we cannot say for certain whether this is due to the prevalence of death penalty cases in state courts compared to their counterpart (we find 5,206 death penalty cases between 1995–2010 vs. 1,413 education cases). Table 3.1 lists the top ten terms in each expressed opinion frame for death penalty cases. Examining the language used in each topic, we can develop distinctive frames for each topic by investigating the interpretive correlation between words. For example, terms such as "attorney," and "prosecutor," occur frequently in opinions concerning the death penalty. While at first glance such terms may not hold much interpretive value (lawyers are an obligatory part of criminal proceedings), the resulting topic models provide us with more clarity concerning when judges may frame decisions around the legal profession. Particularly, we find that judges frame death penalty decisions in three distinct ways when discussing the role of lawyers in the process, as shown in Table 3.1. While judges may focus attention on general legal matters and the role of either the defense or prosecution procedurally (as indicated by the category labeled "Attorney – General"), we also find that judges have distinctive frames for legal failures on the part of either the prosecution or defense. Prosecutorial errors occur and are generally framed when the state's attorney improperly handles evidence or witnesses during the trial phase (as indicted by the frequency of the term "improper" appearing within the category). With regard to the defense, judges in state courts primarily concern themselves with evaluating the ability of counsel to effectively represent their clients (with negative terms such as "fail," and "ineffect" occurring frequently in the category).

Contrary to death penalty decisions, education cases tend to borrow from fewer frames comparatively. We believe that this may be a product of case salience, as judges find there is less need to draw from several different argumentative strands to make their decision. Salience here matters, as judges are not struggling to ensure that they are appeasing multiple audiences, something we will investigate in greater detail in the next section. As we show in Table 3.2, the frames produced by our topic models neatly encompass the various issues surrounding education policy in the various states. Student performance, as discussed previously, does appear to be a distinctive category of interest to judges when discussing education policy and resolving disputes in such cases. Interestingly, state courts appear to devote a substantial amount of time focused on the administration of the education system at

TABLE 3.1 Top 10 Terms Found in Each Death Penalty Opinion Frame

Legal Factors	Trial – General	Case Facts	Jury Instructions	Precedent	Jury Challenges	Procedural Issues	Witnesses
statut	instruct	car	peopl	miss	juror	appel	statement
constitut	charg	shot	prosecutor	instruct	challeng	point	witness
amend	offens	gun	instruct	circuit	prospect	mitig	admiss
applic	intent	robberi	factor	revers	voirdir	fail	testifi
suprem	degre	kill	prosecut	object	peremptori	overrul	inform
punish	kill	told	phase	remand	reason	offens	admit
appli	feloni	shoot	contend	bar	excus	specif	crossexamin
process	verdict	back	object	merit	strike	articl	hearsay
determin	count	polic	special	code	imparti	object	call
violat	element	hous	constitut	cite	select	kill	prosecut

Questioning	Mental Illness	Ineffective Counsel	Sentencing Phase	Prosecutorial Error	Physical Evidence	Attorney – General
statement	mental	ineffect	mitig	prosecutor	victim	proceed
offic	expert	postconvict	factor	instruct	blood	attorney
polic	compet	petition	aggrav	object	bodi	plea
confess	retard	assist	victim	victim	test	request
detect	mitig	relief	circumst	improp	dna	repres
right	evalu	rais	feloni	comment	rape	appoint
suppress	report	fail	weight	proposit	sexual	file
arrest	test	alleg	statutori	contend	home	day
search	disord	petit	phase	statement	child	waiv
interview	medic	evidentiari	proport	close	apart	notic

Source: Table Created by Authors

TABLE 3.2 Top 10 Terms Found in Each Education Opinion Frame

Administration	Complaint	Funding	Employee Relations	Injury	Constitutional Requirements	Student Performance
board	univers	fund	employ	duti	public	student
appel	parti	system	contract	immun	statut	program
superintend	process	tax	teacher	injuri	amend	high
circuit	alleg	constitut	employe	damag	author	test
applic	procedur	local	year	neglig	govern	children
author	complaint	cost	servic	liabil	legislatur	parent
offic	dismiss	year	posit	nwd	provis	polic
petit	due	articl	termin	alleg	purpos	standard
member	attorney	legislatur	work	tort	constitut	particip
meet	request	equal	benefit	summari	violat	class

Source: Table Created by Authors

the local and state level and discuss the constitutional prerogative of education to a substantial degree as well. According to the Education Commission of the States (Parker 2016), all 50 states enshrine public education in their constitutions, with some variation. We find distinctive categories for education funding specifically, as well as other issues stemming from the constitutional requirement for education enshrined in most state constitutions (for example only nine states – Arizona, Delaware, Indiana, Michigan, Mississippi, Nebraska, Ohio, Oklahoma, and West Virginia – include protections for disabled students within the state constitution). Education frames also appear to be highly contextual in nature compared to death penalty cases.[5]

We believe that frames become more prevalent, and thus more likely to become their own particular "topics" when modeling language, when judges are interested in signaling to an audience their view on a specific issue. That is, judges may utilize specific frames to make it clear to audiences why a decision was reached ultimately avoiding either confusion or backlash, and to indicate to potential audiences how a judge should rule in the future. To understand how this may lead to a trade-off between the use of justification and persuasion in judicial opinions, we focus the remainder of this chapter on an analysis of how judges apply a singular frame to an opinion, measured by evaluating the frame consistency from the output of our topic models. As noted by Chong and Druckman (2007) frames can vary substantially even in discussions of the same issue. While some of these frames may be contextually based and thus unique to the opinion itself, we believe that the extent to which a judge relies on one of the predominant frames identified during the topic analysis is indicative of an attempt to draw audiences into a dialogue in order to either justify or persuade them and establish consistent rules governing policy within the states. Frame consistency is therefore useful as a first test, as our measures for justification and persuasion should have clear, marked effects controlling for other factors we believe should affect judicial communications.[6]

The Role of Language in Framing Judicial Opinions

Invariably, our theory posits that the amount of attention judges will place on opinion frames is based upon their desire for audience approval. Frame adherence, or domination, is important to recognize, as judges may be limited to particular reference points when writing an opinion, which will inevitably limit their ability to impact the interpretation of law. Thus, in this chapter we specifically analyze the dominance of a particular opinion frame, using the values generated in the previous topic models. For each topic discovered, we start by determining the most frequently emphasized frame. We then calculate the percentage of the document that uses the dominant frame's language, binding the variable between 0 and 1 to create our final measure of opinion frame consistency.

For a judge to provide a sound justification, the opinion must be written a way that is not only legally sound but also accessible. To determine the extent to which judges are successful, we use two measures of the opinion language which we believe are indicative of a "justification tone" in an opinion, as well as the interaction between these two. To measure the soundness of a judge's argument, we calculate the use of analytic tone in an opinion measured by collecting data on the use of terms correlated with formal, logical, and hierarchical thinking.[7] We argue that as analytic language use increases, judges are likely to be presenting their arguments in an attempt to provide firm justification, rather than attempt at persuasion. More formally:

- Hypothesis 1: As use of analytic language in a judicial opinion increases, the consistency of the opinion frame should increase.

We believe that the analytic style of argumentation will lead to greater frame consistency overall, as judges will tend to focus specifically on outlining the reasoning for their primary argument, and only discuss alternative frames in order to distinguish that they have no bearing on a particular case. By writing in this way, judges focus on properly justifying why the decision made was the correct choice. All opinions will (and based on a preliminary examination of the data do) display a substantial degree of analytic language, as the work of the opinion is to provide a sound argument to back up a decision. Death penalty and education cases are decidedly similar in the average level of analytic language, with death penalty cases averaging scores of 0.932, and education cases averaging 0.964. This makes sense, at first glance, as all opinions are required to justify to some degree in order to provide an answer to legal disputes. We believe, however, that this should result in an increase in the frame consistency when judges are particularly focused on justification for their decision, rather than attempting to write persuasively, as judges will focus primarily on a singular frame to emphasize why it is not only the correct choice, but the *only* choice that could be made.

Analysis alone does not necessarily mean justification, however, and to fully examine the role of justification in judicial language, we also examine the clarity of the arguments made to further examine justification's role. To determine accessibility of a frame, we focus on the reading clarity of the language being used in an opinion with a unique measure of readability based upon factor analysis of several measures collected for each opinion.[8] We suspect that opinions that prioritize justification will be highly accessible (and thus, more "readable") and should utilize "black-and-white" logic. This should result in a more consistent frame overall, as judges can draw from simpler language and develop an argument that is easier to follow without attempting to include multiple strands of logic. More formally:

- Hypothesis 2: As judicial opinions become more readable, the consistency of an opinion frame should increase.

As Figure 3.5 suggests, preliminary examinations of topic readability in death penalty cases indicate that topic frames have a readability score of 4.456 on average, which approximates to a college-level comprehension score for most standard measures. Topic categories range from 6.243 for opinions framed

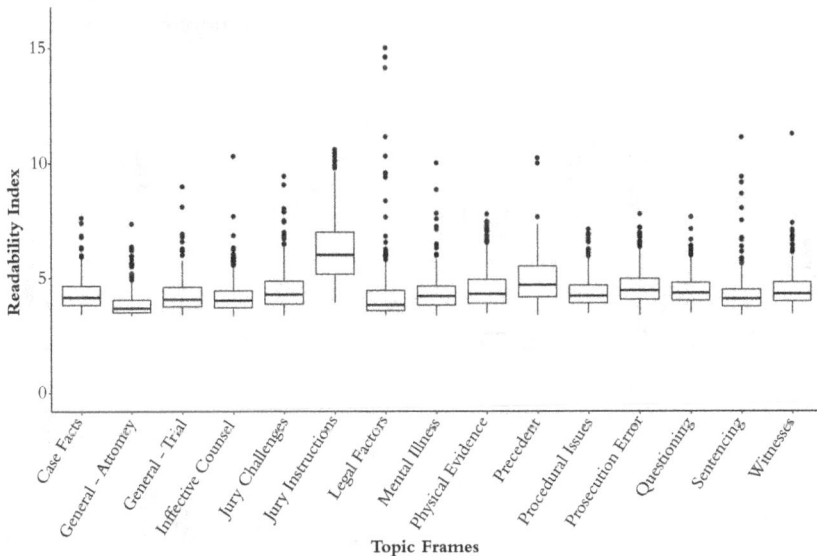

FIGURE 3.5 Readability of Topic Frames in Death Penalty Cases

Figure Created by Authors

around jury instructions (which would indicate approximately a high-school reading level), to 3.893 for opinions primarily focused on questions of general legal counsel and legal requests for post-conviction relief. Thus, we find preliminary evidence that frames which may impact the public directly (frames focused on the role and procedures of juries) are much more likely to use consistent messages and frames in order to ensure greater clarity with the mass public. Education cases, contrarily and as shown in Figure 3.6, are written to a substantially different level of accessibility. While the average readability falls within similar parameters as death penalty cases (4.443 on average), topic readability maintains a relatively standard level of accessibility compared to the wide degree of variation found in death penalty cases. Topic categories range from 4.795 for opinions focused on tort-based injury cases, to 4.236 for school funding questions and disputes.

The difference in readability between death penalty cases and education cases is notable and we believe it is a function of the underlying differences between the case types rather than a conscious choice on behalf of the opinion authors. First, most death penalty cases are heard via mandatory appeals. That is, even in states that have discretionary jurisdiction for their courts of last resort, they must hear at least one appeal in death penalty cases. As such many of the cases are "easy," requiring very little in the way of exposition to justify their decisions. Second, death penalty jurisprudence is a highly litigated area of law. This makes the review of the cases formulaic in nature, perhaps the area where jurisprudence gets its closest to mechanical. Third, education cases cover a wider range of issues and are generally a less settled area of law. This will cause the judicial opinions to become longer, and more complex. In this

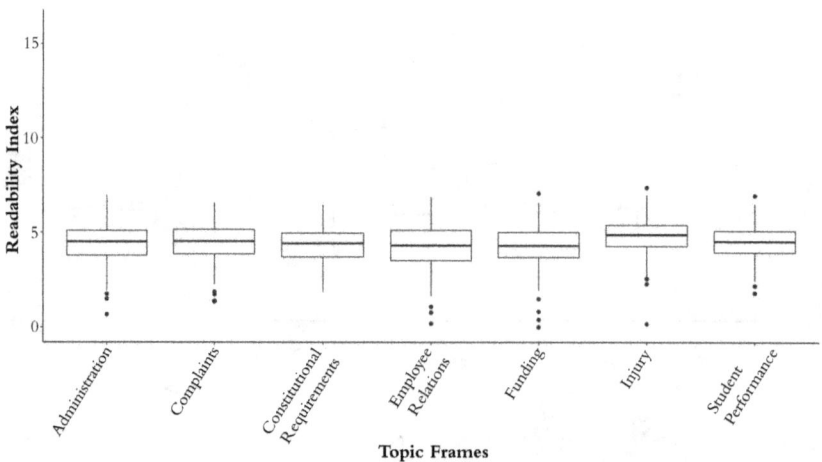

FIGURE 3.6   Readability of Topic Frames in Education Cases

Figure Created by Authors

book however, death penalty and education cases will only be compared to each other indirectly, never appearing in the same statistical model.

Taken together, we suspect that opinions that highlight justification should be more analytic and more readable when controlling for other factors. We argue that these two factors are constituent parts of justification, and we suspect that the interaction between the two measures should have a significant and substantive effect. This interaction should highlight the complexity of the justification-tone in judicial opinions. While taken individually, analytic language and readability should increase frame consistency (thus arguably indicating that judges are attempting justification), when interacted together, we suspect that these two features of judicial opinions should have the opposite effect; which is also in line with our expectations concerning justification. Recall from our discussion in Chapter 2, we believe that judges, when justifying their decisions, must show not only that they made the right choice, but that this choice was the *only* option. To do this, and to make the argument valid, judges must divide their focus in an opinion and discuss alternative choices, so that they may ultimately reject the arguments not chosen. This should increase analysis, as well as reading clarity, but have the overarching effect of decreasing the frame consistency when taken together. By writing in this fashion, judges can craft a strong argument rejecting alternative options, ostensibly "proving their point," that there was no other, logical alternative to the choice made in the decision.

- Hypothesis 3: As the overall tone of justification in an opinion increases, the consistency of a frame will decrease.

Justification is just one half of the strategy available in writing a legal opinion. The second set of variables of interest to us focus on how *persuasive* judges are when crafting a frame in the process of writing an opinion. As discussed in Chapter 2, persuasion in a judicial opinion may be understood by focusing on the cognitive complexity of a decision, as expressed by a judge's choice of language. For an opinion to be persuasive, we argue that judges must find a way to tie multiple, sometimes divergent arguments together into a cohesive statement. Opinions that attempt this necessarily trade off clarity and justification for greater persuasive power, as judges work through several arguments to determine which one reaches the best decisions, not just the "only" decision. While a singular frame may firmly cement the boundaries of a discussion, this may lead audiences to question the logic of an opinion, since a judge appears not even to consider alternatives when reaching their conclusion. By making the opinion more complex, judges show more forethought to various audiences in hopes that the opinion can act as a guide for others. The addition of a secondary, or tertiary frame muddles the reality a judge is trying to create, however, introducing caveats and clarifications into an opinion. While this should lead to a reduction in the justification power of an opinion, the inclusion of alternative frames in an opinion can serve to send signals to judicial audiences that a judge is paying attention to their desires. And depending on the level of insulation or accountability a judge is required to have, utilizing a variety of alternative frames can also serve to protect judges from potential backlash either from other governing institutions or from the public itself.

In political psychology, analyses of language focus largely on the complexity of statements by specifically examining how various viewpoints and arguments are (or are not) assimilated into an author's speech (Gruenfeld 1995; Gruenfeld and Presten 2000; Owens and Wedeking 2012; Tetlock Bernzwig and Gallant 1985; Winters 1996). Per Gruenfeld (1995, 134), "complexity measures are generally used to assess the conceptual organization of decision-relevant information and are derived from individuals' verbal rationales for their preferences." When complexity is low, individuals tend to rely on strict, inflexible rules based on only a few salient pieces of information when making decisions. This would be indicative of a more justification-based style and would explain the greater use of analytic writing as well as greater writing clarity. When complexity is high, individuals will rely on multiple perspectives, taking a more multidimensional view when deciding (Winters 1996). To develop our measure of complexity, we collect data on factors which are generally presumed to indicate greater cognitive considerations in writing (Gruenfeld 1995; Gruenfeld and Presten 2000; Owens and Wedeking 2012; Tetlock Bernzwig and Gallant 1985; Winters 1996).[9] Judges' cognitive complexity tends to be rather low in both death penalty and education cases on average, indicating an overall reluctance to engage in overt persuasive behavior. As we show in Figure 3.7, death penalty cases overall resist substantial complexity, averaging a score of -0.197 overall, with decisions focused on precedent (-0.060) and jury challenges (-0.064) being the most "complex"

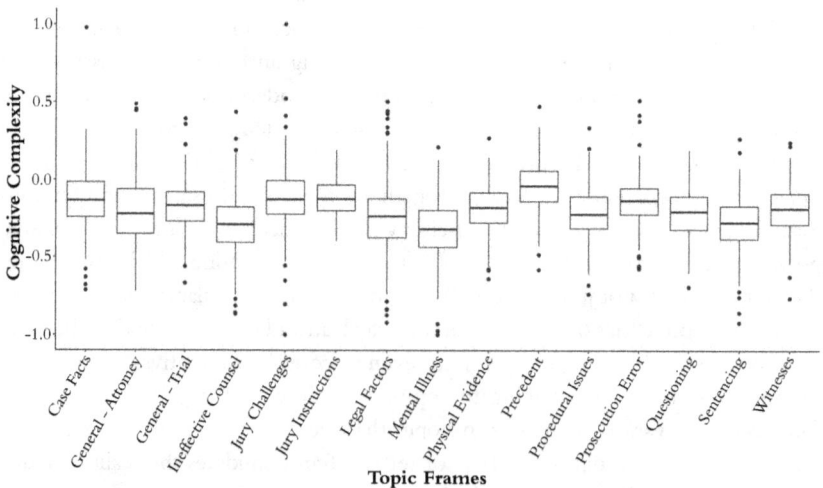

FIGURE 3.7 Cognitive Complexity of Death Penalty Opinions by Topic Frame
Figure Created by Authors

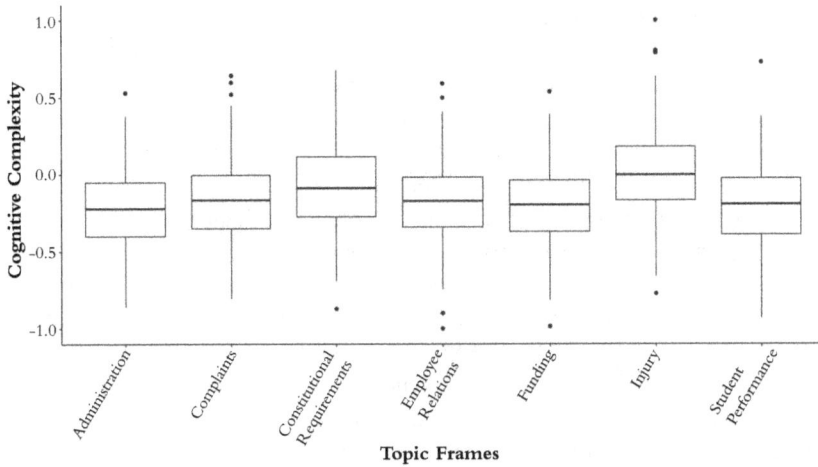

FIGURE 3.8 Cognitive Complexity of Education Opinions by Topic Frame
Figure Created by Authors

kinds of decision on average. Similarly, in Figure 3.8, we find that education cases display an average complexity of -0.150. Interestingly, the greatest degree of complexity occurs in injury cases (0.008), which we would suspect is due to the personal, individual nature of such cases and the potential for these cases to gain some public attention.

What is important to recognize here is that higher complexity is indicative of stronger lexical style, which has been found to be more persuasive in the communications literature (Bradac, Desmond, and Murdock 1977; Hosman 2002). Likewise, Williams and his colleagues (Goss and Williams 1973; Williams 1980; Williams and Goss 1975) find that the vagueness of a message tends to make the audience more receptive, and generally leads to greater recall by the audience later. As Hosman (2002, 377) notes, "receivers [can] easily reject clear, attitudinally incongruent messages, but [receivers] could not easily reject vague, attitudinally incongruent messages." As cognitive complexity requires the author to craft an argument using a multitude of positions and contrasting arguments, these opinions ought to be vaguer by comparison, thus decreasing the readability of the argument, but also increasing its cognitive complexity. As a result, audiences should be more receptive to these arguments since the various strands of thought provide the audience with ample opportunities to internalize the judge's argument; however, the consistency of the frame should also decrease in such case. Therefore, we believe as follows that:

- Hypothesis 4: As judicial opinions become more cognitively complex, the consistency of an opinion frame should decrease.

While persuasion as measured by cognitive consideration and complexity may act to decrease the consistency of a frame on its own, we suspect that this effect may be mitigated to some degree by the extent to which a judge personally believes in their decision. To account for this, we include one final measure of persuasive language use we believe will provide a clearer indication that a judge is choosing persuasion over justification: authenticity. As discussed in Chapter 2, authenticity in language is primarily based upon the willingness and comfort that an author has in engaging a discourse (Baker and Martinson 2001; Langan 1992; Taylor 1991). Such authenticity brings with it an air of sincerity and confidence, according to Baker and Martinson (2001, 162), who argue that authors/persuaders "believe in the product, service, or cause they are advancing . . . should sincerely believe that the product will benefit persuadees, and that the persuasion campaign is truthful, respectful, fair, equitable, and responsible." Authors who feel more confident in their arguments tend to have an easier time providing evidence and discussing why their chosen decision is the correct course of action, compared to inauthentic authors who generally display less comfort and engagement in their writing. We believe that authenticity is, therefore, a systemic attribute of persuasion necessary for a judge to convince an audience to their opinion. Put more formally:

- Hypothesis 5: As authenticity in judicial language increases, the frame consistency will also increase.

As with justification, we believe that our two measures of persuasion may also work in tandem to present an overall measure for persuasive tone. Unlike justification, however, we believe that the interactive effect of complexity and authenticity should increase the frame consistency of an opinion. We believe this is due to the relationship between being able to differentiate and integrate arguments together (complexity) with the wiliness to fully commit to and believe in the choice and an opinions reasoning. Authentic, complex, and persuasive authors should display an increase in frame consistency, as they will feel comfortable with the subject frame they have chosen to rely on, thus increasing the overall dominance of a particular frame over others. Judges who are less confident will display lower authenticity as they try to break down several arguments to convince the audience their choice was right. This act of trying to convince is, we believe, integral to the justification process, as judges try to lay out counter-arguments, so audiences can understand why they were rejected, rather than focusing on one particular frame and expounding upon the accuracy of their choice. Thus, our final linguistic hypothesis is framed as follows:

- Hypothesis 6: As the overall persuasiveness in an opinion increases, the consistency of a frame will likewise increase.

Retention Audience and Frame Consistency

One final area of interest to us in this and forthcoming chapters is just *who* the audience for judicial opinions is, and how this may impact variables such as frame consistency. The literature on judicial behavior tends to treat audience as synonymous with the groups responsible for selecting and retaining judges, and this argument is generally backed up by the more recent literature on audience and representation generally (see particularly Rehfeld 2006). Specifically, we should expect that judges that go through some form of public retention will write opinions more strategically to appease the public and protect themselves from backlash. We hypothesize, therefore, that variations in the method of election will emphasize this strategic consideration. Judges retained via partisan election should be most attuned to writing to an audience, and therefore act as a baseline for our expectations with regard to strategic writing styles. Particularly, electoral systems that insulate judges from partisanship should have a negative impact on frame consistency, as judges should be more likely to couch their decisions using multiple perspectives and arguments.[10] In direct contrast, judges who are insulated from the public completely through elite appointments should be more consistent in their frame use, as they can speak and write to more focused policy suggestions to engage an elite audience in institutional dialogue. Thus, for each method of retention, we expect the following:

• Hypothesis 7: Judges retained by non-partisan elections and retention elections will write with lower frame consistency.
• Hypothesis 8: Judges retained via elite appointment will write with a higher frame consistency.

Results

We are primarily interested in determining what factors influence the consistency of a judicial opinion frame. Since our data consist of several layers of variability, we opt to utilize a multilevel modeling strategy to account for the fact that we are observing the individual writing styles of judges, who exist in states with varying institutional contexts and shifting social and political environments dependent on the year in which their opinion is issued. Since our dependent variable – frame consistency – is structured continuously, a standard linear hierarchical model is most appropriate to account for changes in the expected value of the dependent variable (Gelman and Hill 2007). To account for the fact that judges are selecting specific frames over others, we also include a fixed effect for the frame chosen in an opinion to account for variations that existed across topics found in our previous analysis. Here, the analysis includes indicators for each of the 403 judges included in our time frame, as well as indicators for the year a decision was made. We also include a categorical indicator for the state to account for random in-state variations that may affect judicial decisions. The multilevel model allows us to specify random intercepts for individual judges and year and allows the slope to vary by the state in which the decision was made. This allows us to consider by-judge and by-year variability in the model, recognizing that these two variables co-occur within each state in the data as well.

We begin our analysis by focusing first on death penalty cases, as we suspect that these cases will display the greatest variation in justification and persuasive tones due to the salience of the issue. We find that judges do tend to display some degree of trade-off when writing opinions, and particularly judges rely more heavily on writing justifications for their decisions rather than attempt at persuasion. This trade-off has a direct and significant effect over the consistency with which judges apply frames in these cases. As we show in Figure 3.9, the use of analytic tone in death penalty cases has a strong and significant effect on frame consistency, and follows our expectations as laid out in Hypothesis 1. We find that as analytic tone increases in salient decisions, the consistency of the applied frame increases by 0.442 points, indicating a substantial focus on a singular frame in an attempt to firmly reject other potential alternatives in a decision. Likewise, following our expectations in Hypothesis 2, frame consistency also allows judges to write in simpler, "plain English," which we argue is indicative of an attempt at justification. Increased readability based upon our measure results in a subsequent increase in the frame consistency of an opinion by 0.178 points.

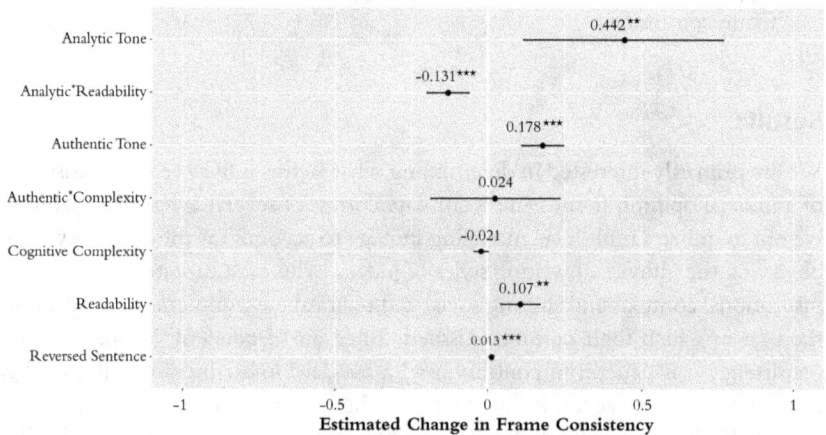

FIGURE 3.9 Expected Effects of Justification and Persuasive Tone and Decision Reversal on Frame Consistency in Death Penalty Cases

Figure Created by Authors

Contrary to our findings concerning justification and frame consistency, we find less clear evidence of the impact of persuasive language choice on judicial writing. Specifically, the complexity of legal arguments, which we measure using the cognitive complexity of the language of the opinion, does not have a statistically significant effect in our models. We believe that this may be indicative of judges attempting to avoid potential backlash from a decision by couching their language in more definitive, "black-and-white" terminology, which inevitably leads to greater emphasis on confirming and explaining decisions, which is indicative of justification. We do find evidence, however, that greater authenticity does have a significant and positive effect on frame consistency (Hypothesis 5). We find that as authenticity in language increases, the frame consistency increases by 0.178 points. This suggests that persuasion is present and strategically considered as part of judicial writing, and that judges may attempt to signal to audiences their beliefs; however, in salient cases, specifically, judges appear to be more heavily influenced by justification when framing their decisions.

As one final check, we examine the interaction of the two sets of variables measuring justification and persuasion to determine their coordinated power on frame consistency. We find judges emphasizing justification do have significantly lower levels of frame consistency, providing evidence of Hypothesis 3. Persuasive language does not exhibit a significant effect on frame consistency. Thus, we can conclude that while there may be some trade-off between the two tones, justification does appear to dominate judicial frames. We find this interesting, as it indicates that judges may be "gun shy" when attempting to exercise persuasive power from the bench. The general expectation for judges is to remain unbiased, which is difficult to maintain when openly advocating for a particular decision; a necessity when attempting to persuade audiences. In salient cases such as the death penalty, such persuasion can be useful in ensuring the public agrees with a judge's actions; however, there is potential for backlash if the public disagrees with the court's rationale. We believe that this potential for backlash will keep judges from exercising persuasion to its fullest extent, and instead will focus their attention on justification so as to appear unbiased in their decisions.

Shifting our attention from salient to non-salient cases, we find interestingly that judges may emphasize persuasion to some degree when the public may not be paying attention. According to the results in Figure 3.10, across all of our measures for language and tone, only authenticity attains statistical significance. Following our initial hypothesis, as authenticity increases in education, the frame consistency of a decision increases by 0.232 points. The positive direction and magnitude of this finding indicate that, following our argument, judges who confidently convey their decision are more likely to rely on a single, dominant frame.

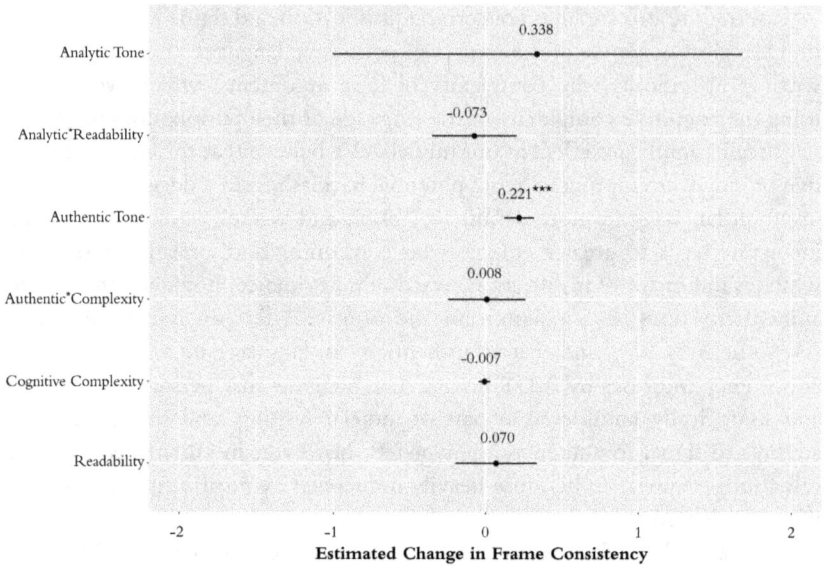

FIGURE 3.10   Expected Effects of Justification and Persuasive Tone in Education Cases

Figure Created by Authors

Along with our linguistic measures, we are also interested in seeing whether frame consistency varies by methods of retention. Variation in retention methods will force judges to consider different audiences when making decisions and crafting law. As a result, judges who are insulated from the public should be more likely to frame their arguments differently, specifically less consistently. As we show in Figure 3.11, we find evidence to indicate that this is the case, particularly in salient cases where judges are retained by election. Compared to other mechanisms, non–partisan and retention systems specifically write their opinions less consistently. In non-partisan systems, this reduction leads to a reduction of approximately 1.6 percent compared to other retention systems. For retention elections, we find a reduction in frame consistency of approximately 1.26 points. We feel this is because non-partisan and retention systems insulate judges from the public by removing competition (in the case of retention election systems) and by removing significant information heuristics (in the case of non-partisan and retention elections). Interestingly, we do not find a significant difference between appointment and partisan systems.

Partisan election systems and elite appointment systems share a common characteristic, despite the quite different ways the courts are staffed. Judges in each of these systems know their audiences and expect their audiences to know them. The constituents of partisan elections have a significant amount of information given to them through the ballot, and those in charge of retention in appointment

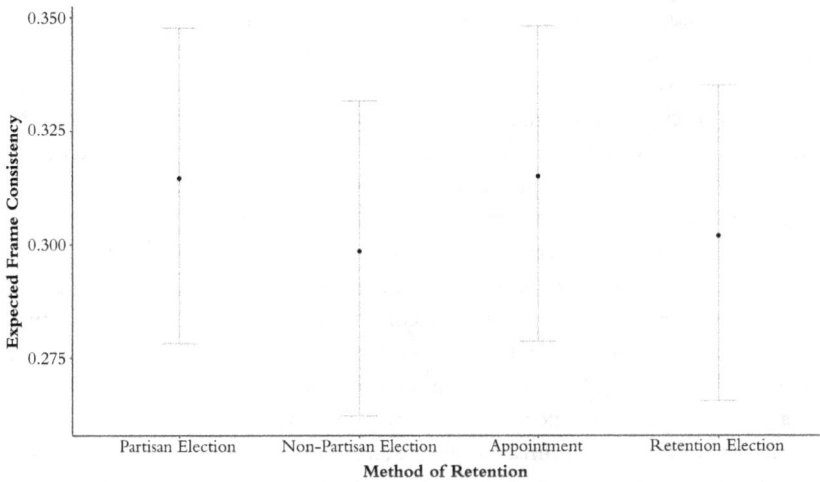

FIGURE 3.11   Expected Change in Frame Consistency by Methods of Retention in Death Penalty Cases

Figure Created by Authors

systems are even more familiar with the judges under consideration. We believe that, because of this, these judges do not need to cater to their audience nearly as much. They can choose to be very consistent in their frame choice, without having to use alternative explanations. Judges who are retained by non-partisan or retention elections need to use every advantage to appeal to or appease their audience as these are low salience, low information elections. As such, they should be less consistent in their use of frames, as they will want to explain, in more depth, to their less attentive audience.

Conclusions

Judges have audiences and will attempt to court – or appease – those audiences to gain approval. As Baum (2006, 158) notes, "judges' efforts to appeal to their audiences exert an impact even when those efforts are not fully conscious, as is often – indeed usually – the case." We argue, and our model demonstrates, that Baum's intuition concerning audience effects applies to state court judges and their choice of judicial frames. To appeal to audience concerns, judges select their language carefully so as to ensure that they are expressing their decisions in the most optimal way. This is particularly true for judges during salient cases, as judges protect themselves by using rationality and logic, markers of the language of justification. This is true for all judges and is part of the key norms of professionalization that proponents of an unbiased, accessible court contend ought to be a defining feature of the American judicial system.

Our findings in this chapter provide a first look at understanding the intricacies of legal decision-making and the crafting of judicial opinions. Utilizing the language of the opinion itself, we have analyzed the ability of judges on the state's high court to craft meaningful, accessible, and persuasive opinions in both salient and non-salient cases. Judges do have a legal language that they use when crafting opinions, and this language is useful in understanding just how opinions are crafted and how judges prioritize topic frames in legal analysis. Along with this, judges make clear decisions regarding the use of persuasion and justification within decisions, and these choices have significant impact on the framing of decisions.

We have demonstrated that judges consider their secondary audience, their retention constituency, when they choose how to frame majority opinions. This finding follows a long line of research on state courts which argues judges consider their retention audience when deciding cases. Much rarer in the literature is a demonstration that the primary audience affects the majority opinion at the state level. Our findings in this chapter set up our empirical argument for the chapters that follow: that judges write strategically in order to satisfy (or at the very least, not anger) the various audiences whom may come in contact with an opinion. In the next chapter, we examine whether and how dissention on the court causes majority opinion authors to augment or accommodate, in their opinion.

Notes

1 Unlike Epstein and Segal (2000) we cannot construct a direct measure of issue salience across 50 states and 52 state supreme courts. We feel that decisions concerning the death penalty follow the "easy issue" format for most constituents. Education cases range from union contracts, to tenure decisions, to academic eligibility to play sports. While important, the issues dealt with in education are more complex, and less likely to resonate with the public.

2 We would like to thank Meghan Leonard and Joseph Ross for their assistance and for providing us with data on education cases specifically.

3 We recognize that there are likely differences between published and unpublished decisions (see Ringquist and Emmert 1999), but our interest is in how the constituency of the judges shapes the content of the opinion. This influence is only likely to occur in opinions which, by their nature, are public.

4 One problem for unsupervised textual analyses such as LDAs is the determination of the number of topics that may exist in a corpus *a priori*, especially in cases where the number of documents in the corpus is significantly large. According to Arun et al. (2010, 391), "while estimating the right number of topics for a small image or text corpus might seem easy, it becomes unreasonable to guess the same when the corpus size is huge." Research on determination of topic numbers has recently attempted to develop measures that would "naturally" determine the number of topics that exist in a corpus through a variety of methods, including matrix factorization (Arun et al. 2010), nonparametric density-based analysis (Cao et al. 2008), Latent Concept Modeling (Deveaud, Sanjuan and Bellot 2014), and Markov Chain Monte Carlo estimation (Griffiths and Steyvers 2004). We utilize the formulations from these four different calculations to determine the appropriate number of frames in death penalty and education cases separately. According to an analysis of these separate tuning models, we find that the optimal number of topics in death penalty cases is 15, and seven for education cases.

5 A common concern with topic modeling approaches is the requirement that interpretation of the models occurs post hoc, which can sometimes lead to arbitrary assertions of the existence of patterns in the data. As we discuss in the text and in footnote 4, we ran our data through several iterations of topic modeling strategies in order to optimize the k-number of topics that occur within death penalty and education cases. Based on an analysis of the most frequent terms in each category, as displayed in the text, we believe that our classification for topics is facially valid.

6 To conserve space, we include a more detailed discussion of the variables utilized in this and other chapters to the appendix.

7 Our scores are calculated utilizing the most recent (2015) scores for analytic and authentic language from the Linguistic Inquiry and Word Count (LIWC) dictionaries (Pennebaker et al. 2015). The variables range from 0, indicating absolutely no analytic/authentic language content, to 1, which indicates a very high degree of analysis/authentic language.

8 In the appendix, we discuss the usefulness of readability scores when studying political phenomena and compare the various measures for reading clarity with our own created using PCA. Briefly, we find that there are substantial levels of collinearity in these measures, and while there is some argument to finding a specific "in-domain" measure of readability for political discourse (see Benoit, Munger, and Spurling 2018), currently such measures incur substantial costs unavailable to us for the purposes of our study. We argue that our measure of clarity is valid, as the scores used to generate our variable all correlate together, and load on a singular dimension which we determine is indicative of reading comprehension. Our measure is also beneficial to our analysis here, as it allows us to speak specifically to the direct relationship between readability and language use. As such, we can interpret our results simply as saying that "as readability increases, we expect X," rather than having to interpret the results as the inverse.

9 Much like our measure for readability, we analyze these indicators utilizing Principle Component Analysis and find that they load out two factors, which we deem to indicate greater differentiation or integration as discussed in Chapter 2. Following methods set down by Gruenfeld (1995), we subtract the scores for differentiation and integration in order to craft our initial score, and then bind the score between −1 and 1 for greater clarity in the analysis. A score of 0 on our measure, therefore, is indicative of an average level of complexity comparatively, and increases in the score indicate greater complexity in thinking, whereas lower scores indicate firmer "black-and-white" reasoning.

10 We are not alone in hypothesizing that non-partisan judges will behave differently, see Canes-Wrone, Clark, and Kelly 2014.

References

Arun R., Suresh V., Veni Madhavan C.E., & Narasimha Murthy M.N. (2010) On Finding the Natural Number of Topics with Latent Dirichlet Allocation: Some Observations. In: Zaki M.J., Yu J.X., Ravindran B., Pudi V. (eds) *Advances in Knowledge Discovery and Data Mining*. PAKDD 2010. Lecture Notes in Computer Science, vol. 6118. Berlin, Heidelberg: Springer.

Baker, S. & Martinson, D. L. (2001). The TARES Test: Five Principles for Ethical Persuasion. *Journal of Mass Media Ethics*, 16(2&3), 148–175.

Baum, L. (2006). *Judges and Their Audiences: A Perspective on Judicial Behavior*. Princeton: Princeton University Press.

Benoit, K., Munger, K., & Spurling, A. (2017). Measuring and Explaining Political Sophistication Through Textual Complexity. https://ssrn.com/abstract=3062061 (accessed on May 16, 2019).

Blei, D. M. (2012) Probabilistic Topic Models. *Communications of the ACM*, 55(4), 77–84.

Bonneau, C. W. & Cann, D. M. (2015). *Voters' Verdicts: Citizens, Campaigns, and Institutions in State Supreme Courts*. Charlottesville: University of Virginia Press.

Box-Steffensmeier, J. M., Christenson, D. P., & Hitt, M. P. (2013). Quality Over Quantity: Amici Influence and Judicial Decision Making. *American Political Science Review*, 107(3), 446–460.

Brace, P. & Boyea, B. D. (2008). State Public Opinion, the Death Penalty, and the Practice of Electing Judges. *American Journal of Political Science*, 52(2), 360–372.

Bradac, J. J., Davies, R. A., & Courtright, J. A. (1977). Richness of Vocabulary: An Attributional Analysis. *Psychological Reports*, 41(3), 1131–1134.

Caldeira, G. A. (1985). The Transmission of Legal Precedent: A Study of State Supreme Courts. *The American Political Science Review*, 79(1), 178–194.

Canes-Wrone, B., Clark, T.S. & Kelly, J.P. (2014). Judicial Selection and Death Penalty Decisions. *American Political Science Review*, 108(1), 23–39.

Cao, J., Xia, T., Li, J., Zhang, Y., Tang, S. (2009). A Density-Based Method for Adaptive LDA Model Selection. *Neurocomputing*, 72(7–9), 1775–1781.

Carmines, E. G. & Stimson, J. A. (1980). The Two Faces of Issue Voting. *American Political Science Review*, 74(1), 78–91.

Chong, D. (1993). Coordinating Demands for Social Change. *The Annals of the American Academy of Political and Social Sciences*, 528(1), 126–141.

Chong, D. (1996). Creating Common Frames of Reference on Political Issues. In Mutz, D. C., Sniderman, P. M., & Brody, R. A. (eds.). *Political Persuasion and Attitude Change*. Ann Arbor: University of Michigan Press, 195–224.

Chong, D. & Druckman, J. N. (2007). Framing Theory. *Annuals of Political Science*, 10, 103–126.

Collins, P. M. (2008). *Friends of the Supreme Court: Interest Groups and Judicial Decision Making*. Oxford: Oxford University Press.

Converse, P. E. (2000). Assessing the Capacity of Mass Electorates. *Annual Review of Political Science*, 3, 331–353.

Converse, P. E. (1964). The Nature of Belief Systems in the Mass Public. *Critical Review*, 18(1–3), 1–74.

Corley, P. C. (2008). The Supreme Court and Opinion Content: The Influence of Parties' Briefs. *Political Research Quarterly*, 61(3), 468–478.

Corley, P. C., Collins, P. M., Calvin, B. (2011). Lower Court Influence on U.S. Supreme Court Opinion Content. *Journal of Politics*, 73(1), 31–44.

Curry, T. A., Romano, M. K, & Romero, R. A. (n.d.). Influence or Necessity: Language Borrowing on State High Courts. *Paper Presented at the Annual Meeting of Midwest Political Science Association*, Chicago, IL.

Delli Carpini, M. X., & Keeter, S. (1996). *What Americans Know about Politics and Why It Matters*. New Haven: Yale University Press.

Derrida, J. (1974). *Of Grammatology*. Baltimore: Johns Hopkins University Press.

Deveaud, R. Sanjuan, E., & Bellot, P. (2014). Accurate and Effective Latent Concept Modeling for Ad Hoc Information Retrieval. *Revue des Sciences et Technologies de l'Information - Série Document Numérique, Lavoisier*, 61–84.

Druckman, J. N, Jacobs, L. R., & Ostermeier, E. (2004). Candidate Strategies to Prime Issues and Image. *Journal of Politics*, 66(4), 1205–1227.

Dunn, K. C. & Neumann, I. B. (2016). *Undertaking Discourse Analysis for Social Research*. Ann Arbor: University of Michigan Press.

Edwards, G. C., & Wood, B. D. (1999). The President, Congress, and the Media. *American Political Science Review*, 93(3), 327–344.

Entman, R. M. (1993). Framing: Toward Clarification of a Fractured Paradigm. *Journal of Communications*, 43(4), 51–58.

Entman, R. M. (2003). Cascading Activation: Contesting the White House's Frame After 9/11. *Political Communication*, 20(4), 415–432.

Entman, R. M. (2004). *Projections of Power: Framing News, Public Opinion, and U.S. Foreign Policy*. Chicago: University of Chicago Press.

Entman, R. M. (2007). Framing Bias: Media in the Distribution of Power. *Journal of Communication*, 57(1), 163–173.

Entman, R. M., & Usher, N. (2018). Framing in a Fractured Democracy: Impacts of Digital Technology on Ideology, Power and Cascading Network Activation. *Journal of Communication*, 68, 298–308.

Epstein, L., & Segal, J. A. (2000). Measuring Issue Salience. *American Journal of Political Science*, 44(1), 66–83.

Fix, M. P. (2014). Does Deference Depend on Distinction? Issue Salience and Judicial Decision-Making in Administrative Law Cases. *Justice System Journal*, 35(2), 122–138.

Foucault, M. (1970). *The Order of Things*. New York: Pantheon Books.

Foucault, M. (1973). *The Archeology of Knowledge*. New York: Pantheon Books.

Gabel, M. & Sheve, K. (2007). Estimating the Effect of Elite Communications on Public Opinion Using Instrumental Variables. *American Journal of Political Science*, 51(4), 1013–1028.

Gallup. 2016. *Topics: Death Penalty*. www.gallup.com/poll/1606/death-penalty.aspx (accessed May 16, 2019).

Gamson, W.A., & Modigliani, A. (1987). The Changing Culture of Affirmative Action. In Braungart, R. D. (1987). *Research in Political Sociology*. Greenwich: JAI, 137–177.

Gelman, A. and Hill, J. (2007). *Data Analysis Using Regression and Multilevel/Hierarchical Models*. Cambridge: Cambridge University Press.

Goss, B., & Williams, M. L. (1973). The Effects of Equivocation on Perceived Source Credibility. *Central States Speech Journal*, 24, 162–167.

Griffiths, T. L., & Steyvers, M. (2004). Finding Scientific Topics. *Proceedings of the National Academy of Sciences*, vol. 101, suppl. 1, 5228–5235.

Gruenfeld, D H. (1995). Status, Ideology, and Integrative Complexity on the U.S. Supreme Court: Rethinking the Politics of Political Decision Making. *Journal of Personality and Social Psychology*, 68(1), 5–20.

Gruenfeld, D. H. & Preston, J. (2000). Upending the Status Quo: Cognitive Complexity in the U.S. Supreme Court Justices Who Overturn Legal Precedent. *Personality and Social Psychology Bulletin*, 26(4), 1013–1022.

Habermas, J. (1996). Some Further Clarification of the Concept of Communicative Rationality. In Cook, M. (1996). *On the Pragmatics of Communication*. Cambridge: Massachusetts Institute of Technology Press, 307–342.

Hall, M. G. (1987). Constituent Influence in State Supreme Courts: Conceptual Notes and Cast Study. *Journal of Politics*, 49(4), 1117–1124.

Hansford, T. G. & Spriggs, J. F. (2006). *The Politics of Precedent on the U.S. Supreme Court*. Princeton: Princeton University Press.

Hosman, L. A. (2002). Language and Persuasion. In Dillard, J. P. & Pfau, M. (eds.). *The Persuasion Handbook: Developments in Theory and Practice*. Thousand Oaks: Sage.

Iyengar, S. & Simon, A. (1993). News Coverage of the Gulf Crisis and Public Opinion: A Study of Agenda-Setting, Priming, and Framing. *Communication Research*, 20(3), 365–383.

Kassow, B., Songer, D. R., & Fix, M. P. (2012). The Influence of Precedent on State Supreme Courts. *Political Research Quarterly*, 65, 372–384.

Kim, S., Scheufele, D. A., & Shanahan, J. (2002). Think About it This Way: Attribute Agenda-Setting Function of the Press and the Public's Evaluation of a Local Issue. *Journalism and Mass Communication Quarterly*, 79, 7–25.

Kinder, D. R., & Kalmoe, N. P. (2017). *Neither Liberal nor Conservative: Ideological Innocence in the American Public*. Chicago: University of Chicago Press.

Langan, J. (1992). The Just-War Theory After the Gulf War. *Theological Studies*, 53(1), 95–112.

Lenz, G. S. (2009). Learning and Opinion Change, Not Priming: Reconsidering the Priming Hypothesis. *American Journal of Political Science*, 53(4), 821–837.

Lenz, G. S. (2012). *Follow the Leader? How Voters Respond to Politicians' Policies and Performance*. Chicago: University of Chicago Press.

McCombs, M. E. (2005). A Look at Agenda-Setting: Past, Present, and Future. *Journalism Studies*, 6(4), 543–557.

McCombs, M. E., & Shaw, D. L. (1972). The Agenda-Setting Function of the Mass Media. *Public Opinion Quarterly*, 36(2), 176–187.

Mooney, C. Z. & Lee, M. H. (2000). The Influence of Values on Consensus and Contentious Morality Policy: U.S. Death Penalty Reform, 1956–82. *The Journal of Politics*, 62(1), 223–239.

Owens, R. J. & Wedeking, J. (2012). Predicting Drift on Political Insulated Institutions: A Study of Ideological Drift on the United States Supreme Court. *Journal of Politics*, 74(2), 487–500.

Owens, R. J., Wedeking, J., & Wohlfarth, P. C. (2013). How the Supreme Court Alters Opinion Language to Evade Congressional Review. *Journal of Law and Courts*, 1(1), 35–59.

Pan, Z., & Kosicki, G. (1993). Framing Analysis: An Approach to News Discourse. *Political Communication*, 10(1), 55–75.

Parker, E. (2016). *Constitutional Obligations for Public Education*. Denver: Education Commission of the States.

Pennebaker, J. W., Booth, R. J., Boyd, R. L., & Francis, M. E. (2015). *Linguistic Inquiry and Word Count: LIWC2015*. Austin, TX: Pennebaker Conglomerates (www.LIWC.net).

Rehfeld, A. (2006). Toward a General Theory of Political Representation. *Journal of Politics*, 68(1), 1–21.

Riker, W. H. (1996). *The Strategy of Rhetoric: Campaigning for the American Constitution*. New Haven: Yale University Press.

Ringquist, E. J. & Emmert, C. E. 1999. Judicial Policymaking in Published and Unpublished Decisions: The Case of Environmental Civil Ligation. *Political Research Quarterly*, 52(1), 7–37.

Scheufele, D.A. (1999). Framing as a Theory of Media Effects. *Journal of Communications*, 49(1), 103–122.

Schuman, H., & Presser, J. L. (1981). Context Effects on Survey Responses to Questions about Abortion. *Public Opinion Quarterly*, 45(2), 216–223.

Sellers, P. (2010). *Cycles of Spin: Strategic Communication in the U.S. Congress*. Cambridge: Cambridge University Press.

Shah, D. V., Watts, M. D., Domke D., & Fan, D. P. (2002). News Framing and Cueing of Issue Regimes: Explaining Clinton's Public Approval in Spite of Scandal. *Public Opinion Quarterly*, 66(3), 339–70

Spriggs, J. F. (1996). The Supreme Court and Federal Administrative Agencies: A Resource- Based Theory and Analysis of Judicial Impact. *American Journal of Political Science*, 40(4), 1122–1151.

Taylor, C. (1991). *The Ethics of Authenticity*. Cambridge: Harvard University Press.

Tetlock, P. E., Bernzweig, J., & Gallant, J. L. (1985). Supreme Court Decision Making: Cognitive Style as a Predictor of Ideological Consistency in Voting. *Journal of Personality and Social Psychology*, 48(4), 1227–1239.

Tewksbury, D., & Scheufele, D. A. (2009). News Framing Theory and Research. In Bryant, J., & Oliver, M. B. (eds.) *Media Effects: Advances in Theory and Research*. Hillsdale: Erlbaum.

Tuchman, G. (1978). *Making News*. New York: Free.

Unah, I. & Hancock, A. M. (2006). US Supreme Court Decision Making, Case Salience, and the Attitudinal Model. *Law & Policy*, 28(3), 295–320.

Williams, M. L. (1980). The Effect of Deliberate Vagueness on Receiver Recall and Agreement. *Central States Speech Journal*, 31, 30–41.

Williams, M. L. & Goss, B. (1975). Equivocation: Character Insurance. *Human Communication Research*, 1, 265–270.

Winter, D. G. (1996). *Personality: Analysis and Interpretation of Lives*. New York: McGraw-Hill.

Zaller, J. R. (1992). *The Nature and Origins of Mass Opinion*. Cambridge: Cambridge University Press.

4

ACCOMMODATING FOR DISSENT

The Effect of Minority Voices on Majority Opinions

In order to achieve their policy goals while in office, judges attempt to have their decisions correspond as closely as possible to their own personal preferences. The problem for judges working on a collegial court, including state supreme courts, is that they must make decisions while in communion with other judges. The atmosphere of collective decision-making on a court is part of the "collegial game" in which opinions are crafted and laws are made not by a single judge but by a group of judges. This requires majority opinion writers to consider their colleagues, "with whom they ultimately must negotiate, bargain, and compromise" (Maltzman, Spriggs, and Wahlbeck 2000, 16) in order to achieve policy goals. This deliberative role of the majority opinion author, however, does not necessarily require that other judges be open to compromise. And when judges fundamentally disagree with the arguments made by the majority, they may vocalize their dissatisfaction by issuing a contrasting opinion: the dissent. The dissent is a powerful tool (Douglas 1948) for judges, with authors often being motivated to issue a dissent with the hope of changing the shape, tone, or precedent of the majority opinion. Our question here is, just how substantially does the dissent impact the language of the law?

This chapter focuses on how the majority opinion author's most immediate audience, the other justices on the court, can influence changes in the majority opinion by signaling their displeasure with a written dissent. This chapter examines whether dissents force judges to write more persuasively, and whether these separate opinions may impact the justification power of the majority decision. While one purpose of a dissent is to signal disagreement with the majority opinion to the relevant legal community (an external audience), a written dissent may be drafted for another more strategic purpose. Judges may write a dissenting opinion in hopes to persuade the majority opinion author to consider a point that is lacking in their current draft. This is to say that the dissent may exist to spurn change, not in future decisions, but in the current opinion.

One way judges attempt to respond to the constraints placed upon them by their colleagues is through a strategy of accommodation; the utilization of language, citations, and arguments that comport with a colleague's preference in a particular case in order to increase the likelihood they will sign off on the final opinion. While accommodation is a key feature of a collegial court, it is also notoriously difficult to measure and examine since much of the court's deliberation occurs in conferences and in the margins of opinion drafts not available to the public. Thus, we are left with an interesting question: how might judges signal their desire for accommodation in a more public setting, thus putting pressure on colleagues to respond in order to maintain collegiality and legitimacy? Specifically, how might the majority opinion affect the likelihood that a judge becomes dissatisfied and thus chooses to dissent? And once a dissent is present, does the majority respond in order to account for a colleague's dissatisfaction? Opinion writers should be more likely to engage in the use of strategic rhetorical cues in order to increase the majority coalition dependent on the existence of dissensus signals from the minority coalition. Dissents can be viewed as "dissatisfaction" with the court's decision on a particular case, and can lead to subtle decreases in collegiality, especially within contentious issue areas. Thus, the majority opinion writer, to avoid such conflict, may make attempts to change their language to decrease the likelihood that a dissent is circulated.

In this chapter, we test the extent to which a written dissent can change the language of an opinion, and the extent to which insulation from public audiences may affect these outcomes. Following our primary theory and findings from previous chapters, this chapter adds into the mix the "problematic" condition of collegiality required in order to convince other judges that the opinion is the correct course of action. To test the effect of dissents on opinion writing, we first examine the impact of the issuance of a non-majority opinion on the language adopted by the majority opinion. We believe that, combined with other institutional factors such as method of retention, court jurisdiction, and ideology, dissents trigger a particular type of response from the majority in order to not only to defend against detraction amongst the panel, but also to accommodate dissenting voices. This reaction by the majority opinion author is indicative of small-group decision-making. In general, dissents occur at the intersection of what we have called the persuasive and justification powers of the majority opinion. We find that dissents are more likely when the majority opinion prioritizes persuasion through authentic writing. In contrast, dissents are less likely to occur when the majority opinion focuses strictly on analysis, the language of justification. Digging deeper into these findings, we find that the contextual environment in which dissents occur will lead judges inevitably to try to find a balance between justification and persuasion, with an eye not only toward the other judges on the bench, but to external audiences as well.

The Whys and Whens of Dissent

As discussed in previous chapters, while the simple vote in any given case determines the winners and losers, the opinion provides the justification, the resolution of the legal dispute, and provides context and precedent for future cases. To be effective, the majority opinion must not only be persuasive, but must also enjoy strong support from the voting coalition.[1] While this opinion tries to provide certainty to the intended audience, the existence of a dissent often inserts a level of doubt into the opinion in the case and magnifies internal conflicts between judges (Douglas 1948; Johnson 1979; Posner 2008). There is little doubt that judges have goals while in office (Baum 2006; Gibson 1978; 1983), chief among them being the enactment of ideologically consistent outcomes. While it is true that some judges derive satisfaction specifically *from* writing separately (see Scalia 1994 for example), inevitably the choice to dissent is taken after attempts by one or more parties to accommodate one another via the written opinion in order to avoid this uncertainty (Hall and Brace 1999; Maltzman, Spriggs, and Wahlbeck 2000).

Thus, a particularly interesting question in the judicial literature has focused on the rationale for dissent and the benefits of writing separately. The traditional legal model would argue that judges dissent when they disagree with the majority; however, "such an answer depends on an inadequate understanding of judges' incentives" (Epstein, Landes, and Posner 2010, 23). Examinations of dissenting opinions tend to fall into one of two theoretical camps. First, judges may write separately because of strong ideological differences between the majority opinion author and the objecting judge (Hettinger, Lindquist, and Martinek 2004; 2006; Lindquist and Martinek 2009; Collins and Martinek 2011). The existence of a dissent "constitutes an important indicator of the political nature of judicial decision making" (Hettinger, Lindquist, and Martinek 2006, 16), by presenting us with a judge's unbound opinion concerning precedent and legal rules (see also Songer 1986).

Contrasting the sincere ideological theory of judicial dissent, others have argued that dissents potentially act as strategic tactics to gain an ideological advantage in the opinion. At the level of the U.S. Supreme Court, Maltzman, Spriggs, and Wahlbeck (2000) provide a set of circumstances and internal constraints that determine whether a justice writes a dissent. While Maltzman and his colleagues start from the assumption of ideological considerations, they ultimately note that the dissent is "a justice's most powerful sanction," (Maltzman, Spriggs, and Wahlbeck 2000, 69) against the majority when used to attempt to strategically change the legal outcome to better represent their ideological preferences. This sort of ideological strategy is rare, however.[2] Particularly, Epstein, Landes, and

Posner (2010) find signs of "dissent aversion" dependent on variations in the institutional environment in which judges decide at the federal level. These findings back up previous studies which argue that specific institutional features condition judges to write dissents at the state court level. A litany of studies from Hall and Brace (1989; 1992; 1999; also Brace and Hall 1990; 1993) find indicators of strategic behavior at the state court level, specifically the avoidance of written dissents depending on electoral concerns.

Finally, some have argued that dissent may act as a signal to others within the legal system, rather than specifically attempting to affect the voting coalition (Cross and Tiller 1998; Kim 2009; Van Winkle 1997). Signaling theory tells us that judges write dissents in order to call attention to the legal conflict in a case with hopes that they will come under review by a higher court. The inclusion of a dissent with a majority opinion positively increases the probability that the case will be reviewed (Caldeira and Wright 1988; Caldeira, Wright, and Zorn 1999; George 1999; Giles, Walker and Zorn 2006; Ginsburg and Falk 1991), providing the dissenting judge with the ability to influence and possibly implicitly change the legal ruling later via a reversal from higher up in the judicial hierarchy. According to Blackstone and Collins (2014, 272), if we imagine a unidimensional policy space for any legal decision, the choice to dissent is dependent on whether or not doing so would positively increase the probability that a reviewing court reconsiders the panel outcome and moves policy closer to its ideal point. If the probability is in the negative, the judge "would be made worse off by review," and thus they will be dissent-averse.

Communicative Patterns and a Strategy of Dissent

Without a doubt, the inclusion of a dissent causes a ripple within the judicial system. Previous research has shown that the presence of a dissent does significantly increase the length of opinions (Epstein, Landes, and Posner 2010; Leonard and Ross 2015); however to our knowledge few studies have delved into whether dissents change the actual language and rhetorical structure of the opinion (but see Gruenfeld 1995). We argue that, when choosing to dissent, judges act as catalysts that affects the cognitive considerations judges make when deciding and writing the majority opinion. Judges are interested in the development of coherent, legally defensible precedent (Baum 1994) and care about the consequences of their decisions (Klein 2002). The addition of a dissent, as we argue, casts an air of uncertainty around the decision that may complicate this interest.

At the heart of our analysis is an attempt to understand the foundational cognitive processes that culminate in the written opinion. To understand these processes, we must examine how judges use language in order to influence colleagues to agree with their policy stances. We posit that the inclusion of a dissent has a distinct impact on the power of an opinion to act as a rhetorical tool. In order to understand exactly what this does to the majority opinion, we take these developments in two parts, which emphasize both the dueling nature and also collaborative requirements inherent in justification and persuasion. While the audience of a judicial opinion is generally external to the court (Baum 2006), colleagues are the most immediate audience to the decision and have the most direct ability to influence its language. The other judges on the panel are exceedingly important to the majority opinion author since they are "a means to advance [a judge's] goals of achieving good legal policy" (Baum 2006, 22). Language is key to understanding how this interplay in translated into social policy by giving us insight into the individual thought processes of actors involved in its development (Owens and Wedeking 2012; Tausczik and Pennebaker 2010).

When to Dissent?

To start, we first focus on what factors lead to the issuance of a dissenting opinion. Analyzing the effects of linguistic choices on the presence of a dissent, we focus specifically on the trade-off between analytic language and authenticity. We believe that dissents are issued when the majority focuses primarily on persuasion over justification, which we believe is indicative that the decision is tenuous amongst members of the bench. The tactic of persuasion implicitly acknowledges that there exist a multitude of ways to resolve the conflict, whereas justification begins from the logical standpoint that the outcome is preordained by the facts surrounding the case and the applicable law.

In order to test this assumption, the first part of our analysis focuses on a multilevel logistic regression predicting the occurrence of a dissent. As we found in Chapter 3, judges rely prominently on the language of justification when writing in salient cases, but the presence of a contrasting opinion should make judges more cognizant of their language choices in such cases. Specifically, we argue that opinions which emphasize the language of analysis – and thus attempt to justify their decision – will be less likely to lead to a dissenting opinion. If this is the case, we would expect the majority opinion to be more deterministic, amplifying the role of justification but eschewing persuasive power. Justification we believe will be a signal that there is very little disagreement on the bench, and even if this disagreement is present, the majority believes its decision is correct and thus does not feel the need for further debate.

- Hypothesis 1: As the analytic language of the majority opinion increases, the likelihood of a dissent should decrease.

Judges who rely predominantly on justification in their language when crafting a judicial opinion are sending a message to other judges: the decision is right, and the law is clear. When judges write in this way, we should expect that they will find the need to persuade their colleagues will be minimized; but what about when judges are unsure their audience will be convinced, or there is potential for disagreement among the panel? Such occurrences should most likely occur when ideological consistency on the panel is low and the bench is diverse, which will diminish the polarization within the group (for more on group polarization on judicial panels, see Sunstein 2003; cross and Tiller 1998; Hettinger, Lindquist and Martinek 2003; 2006). With a few qualifications, we expect judicial decisions to be made based on a judge's policy preferences. As such, written dissent acts as a challenge to this policy preference on the part of the minority. Such dissents stem from ideological disagreements but are most likely triggered when judges attempt to overtly convince audiences to their decision, utilizing persuasion as a strategic tool in order to build coalitions. If this is the case, then we should expect that authentic language, as it attempts to convey sincere, moral righteousness and judgement, will be more likely to trigger dissent when others on the bench disagree. These opinions therefore invite "conflicts of values, conflicts that have the power to influence both outcomes in individual cases and the shape of law's development" (Hettinger, Lindquist, and Martinek 2006). Persuasive language, put simply, is likely a signal that the decision may not be as absolute as the majority would like to believe.

- Hypothesis 2: As the language authenticity of the majority opinion increases, the likelihood of a dissent should likewise increase.

Reacting to the Dissent

Once we have determined how use of justification and persuasion impact the likelihood of a dissent, our next step is to evaluate whether and how majority opinion language *itself* changes in the presence of such events. To this end, we examine the language of the majority opinion itself, and specifically focus on testing whether the existence of a dissent will impact the justificative power (measured specifically by examining the readability of the document) and its persuasive ability (measured by focusing on integrative complexity). The release of a dissenting opinion is part of the strategic game played by judges when crafting law. As the dissent is designed to rebuke the majority and their reasoning, we should expect that the majority opinion author will be impacted by the issuance of a contrasting opinion. Discussions of the impact of a dissent are varied as to whether the existence of secondary opinions will lead the majority to accommodate in an attempt to persuade the minority or solidify their stance in order to firmly reject alternative explanations, shoring up their language in order to provide greater justification. One common contention amongst judges is that issuing a dissent can serve to strengthen the majority opinion by forcing them to consider the alternatives (Urofsky 2017). Justice Ruth Bader Ginsburg refers to this as the "in-house impact" of the dissent, believing that "there is nothing better than an impressive dissent to lead the author of the majority opinion to refine and clarify her initial circulation" (from Urofsky 2017, 17). What this stronger reasoning will appear as is unclear. On the one hand, in order to act as a "unified front" against the dissent, the majority opinion may need to strengthen its resolve by taking a firm policy stance. If this is the case, one alternative is to expect the presence of a dissent to significantly decrease the integrative complexity of the majority opinion, indicative of a failure or capitulation in persuasion resulting in the majority reframing its judgement using a clearer, stricter justification to pose as a firm rejection of the minority's opinion. Perhaps judges will focus more time on clarifying their statements and making them as accessible as possible.

Alternatively, a written dissent may trigger the majority opinion author to work to "accommodate" the dissenter, to answer concerns and perhaps win back an outlying judge. This standpoint corresponds to what Roscoe Pound referred to as the "reconnaissance dissent," since we assume that dissenting authors "look forward with the hope that the majority opinion will be altered to reflect new conditions" (in Peterson 1981, 413). Thus, a written dissent may have the effect of forcing the majority opinion author to consider alternative dimensions and perspectives when developing their opinion, creating an opinion with greater integrative complexity and persuasive power as a means to accommodate the views of the dissenter. From this perspective, attempting to accommodate the dissenter's argument is valuable as it should provide greater clarity as to why the majority rejected the dissenter's arguments. This ultimately leads to a more complex, though less comprehensible opinion, though the trade-off may be warranted as it increases the persuasive power of the argument. From the dissenter's standpoint, writing an independent opinion provides a strategic advantage by forcing the majority to answer questions in greater depth. In contrast, the appearance of a vocal minority may cause the majority to "publicly acknowledge the validity of positions that they do not believe are correct in hopes that it will make a positive impression," (Gruenfeld 1995, 138; see also Tetlock et al. 1984). Taken together, the inclusion of a dissent could theoretically increase the persuasive power of the majority's opinion by providing it a counterargument. This would result in an opinion that is more cognitively complex in the presence of a dissent but also more difficult to read. That is, as the majority now has to argue against an explicit alternative, they will be unable to write in simple, accessible terms, and will thus have to find a new balance between simple justification and persuasive language in an effort to accommodate concerns belayed by the minority.

We are undoubtedly faced with an interesting puzzle concerning how the dissent will ultimately impact the reasoning and language of the majority. If judges seek to accommodate, we should expect to see judges writing less clearly but more persuasively. If, on the other hand, the dissent forces the majority to "dig in their heels," and cement their decision firmly, we should expect the final opinion to be written using less complex, firmer decision rules and greater written clarity. We suspect that the dissent triggers accommodation, and particularly that by forcing the majority to consider an alternative explanation, the existence of a dissent will lead to less comprehensible, more complex final opinions. Specifically, when a dissent is present, we expect it to trigger greater accommodation, ultimately diminishing the reading clarity in the majority decision, as judges attempt to trade off stronger justification power, acknowledging that there may be a reasonable alternative.

- Hypothesis 3: When a dissent is triggered, the reading clarity of the majority opinion will decrease.

Following this, we likewise suspect that by switching strategies and attempting to accommodate the dissenting minority, judges will necessarily shift to writing in a more persuasive style; taking more time to discuss alternatives (particularly those raised by the minority) in order to strengthen their rationale for the decision. We expect that this will lead to greater consideration of multiple alternative explanations in the majority opinion, specifically increasing the cognitive complexity of the majority opinion as judges must differentiate between multiple explanations as well as integrate them in order to successfully show why their decision is the correct one. Additionally, we expect that the language of the dissent itself will have an impact on the majority opinion writer and their strategy in accommodation. Particularly, we argue that dissents that are written in a fashion than maximizes persuasion, and thus show greater cognitive complexity, will have an inverse effect on the majority opinion writer. Persuasion in a dissent triggers the majority to cement itself in its decision, taking a firm stance against the minority in order to ensure that its decision has the strength of law. This should lead the majority inevitably to accommodate less, writing in a manner that is decidedly more certain in its choice.

- Hypothesis 4: When a dissent occurs, the cognitive complexity of the majority opinion should increase.
- Hypothesis 5: In the presence of a dissent, as the cognitive complexity of the dissenting opinion increases, the complexity of the majority will decrease.

A judge's decision to respond to a dissent may be strongly influenced by the institution they reside in, as this retention institution, as we have seen in Chapter 3, may condition particular types of behavior. Essentially, our argument here is that judges will balance justifying their decisions with attempting to persuade audiences dependent on the insulation they have from external audiences – particularly their retention audience. When a dissent is issued along with the majority opinion, we expect judges that are shielded from an ideological public, namely those serving in retention election and appointment-based systems, will strike a balance between complexity (and persuasion) and readability as they attempt to provide a counterargument to the dissent. Since judges in these states do not have to rely actively on external audiences, the focus of their opinions should inevitably be on primary audiences such as their colleagues and the immediate legal community. As the audience focus changes, these judges should write opinions that are framed with clearer rules (thus, less cognitively complex), but which at the same time will likely be less readable, since the inclusion of a dissent forces the opinion author to expend more energy justifying why their choice is the correct one. Thus, rather than attempting to accommodate the dissent, we believe in this situation judges are more likely to "dig in their heel"; pushing back against the dissenting opinion rather than attempting to bring the dissenter into the fold. This effect may be mitigated by the length of a judge's term, however, as judges who face retention more frequently should be more likely in a manner that is more cognitively complex and less readable.

- Hypothesis 6: When a dissent is present, judges in traditionally publicly insulated institutions (appointment and retention systems) will write opinions with greater accessibility and lower complexity.
- Hypothesis 7: When a dissent is present and judicial term lengths increase, judges in insulated institutions will write opinions that are less accessible and more complex.

In order to examine these hypotheses, we break the analysis into two parts. First, we focus generally on whether the publication of a dissent is affected by the tonal qualities of the majority opinion and whether the majority is engaging in justification or persuasion. For this, we utilize a nested logistic mixed-effect regression. When modeling the remaining hypotheses (three through seven), we take the results from part one of our analysis and perform a modified Heckman selection model that accounts for these random parts. We choose to extend our analysis beyond the simple use of the linear model because we believe that the presence of a dissent itself contextualizes the discussion present in the majority opinion. According to Dunn and Neumann (2016), the implications of this viewpoint necessitate a two-step process of analyzing discourse. In the first part, we must examine what leads to a particular communicative event to expose what factors lead to an attempt to reshape the discourse. Following this, we can examine how the presence of an event (in this case the dissent) directly affects the degree at which the discourse is changed. In our model below, we calculate the effect of the selection step in part one by manually calculating the inverse Mills ratio to include in the second step.[3] In both models, the intercept is assumed to vary among years, and among judges within years as well as states within years. Including random intercepts in this way tells the model to expect different baseline levels of the dependent variables for each year and to nest these within the states and for each judge.[4]

Results

We begin by first examining how the tone and focus of the majority opinion might affect the likelihood of a dissent. Starting with salient (death penalty) cases, we find that focusing solely on persuasion and authenticity or justification and analysis have distinctly opposing effects on the likelihood of a dissent in our death penalty cases. In Figures 4.1 and 4.2, we see that our measures for authenticity and analysis in opinions conform to our first two hypotheses, with analytic language decreasing the likelihood of a dissent and authentic language increasing the likelihood. Focusing first on analytic tone, we find death penalty cases with only a minimum level of analysis (in our data, the minimum level of analytic tone is 48.28%) have a predicted probability of including a dissent of 48.46%. In overtly analytic opinions, conversely, we see this probability decrease by 21.02%, to just 27.44%. As opinions tend to rely heavily on analytic language (which we discussed in Chapter 3), we find that textual analysis can go a long way toward decreasing the probability of a dissent. In stark contrast, greater authenticity in majority opinions (indicative of greater persuasive language use) greatly increases the likelihood that a dissent will be issued. When authentic language is low (1.00% at minimum), the probability of a dissent being included with the majority is roughly one in four, with a predicted probability of dissent equaling just 27.36%. In contrast to analytic tone, when authentic language is at its highest (in our data, the maximum level of authentic

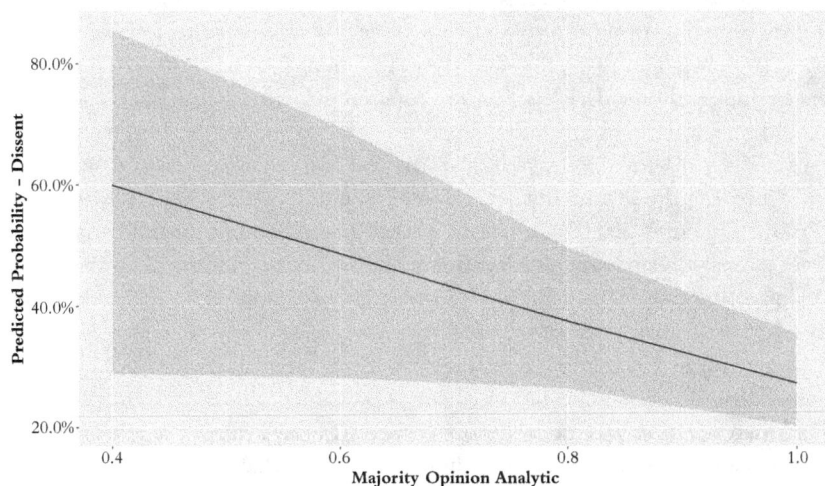

FIGURE 4.1 Predicted Probability of Issuance of a Dissent in Death Penalty Cases by Majority Opinion's Analytic Tone

Figure Created by Authors

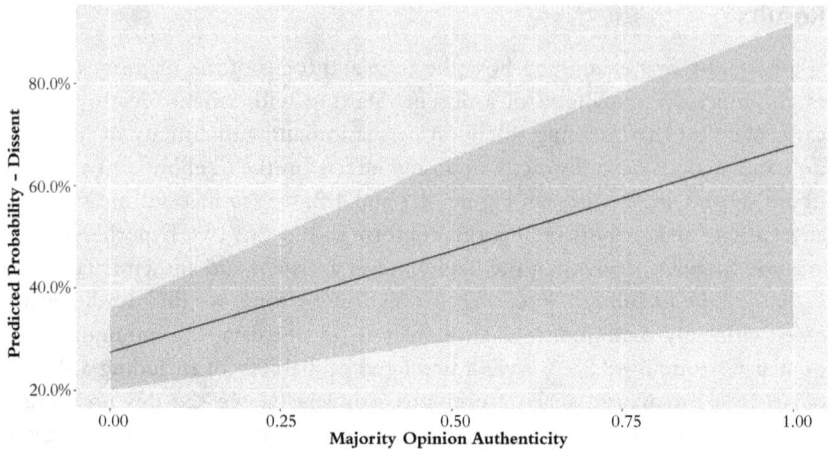

FIGURE 4.2 Predicted Probability of Issuance of a Dissent in Death Penalty Cases by Majority Opinion's Authentic Tone

Figure Created by Authors

tone was 66.51%), we find the probability of a dissent being issued is 48.20%, an increase of 20.84%.

In non-salient cases, we do find support for Hypothesis 1 concerning analytic language, however we do not find similar results for Hypothesis 2 concerning authentic language. We find this interesting, as it does help support our overarching theory concerning the role of case saliency with regard to judicial writing style. In non-salient cases, the stakes tend to diminish concerning external audiences. Judges should feel less pressure to attempt persuasion in such cases, and should therefore focus greater emphasis on clear, strong justification (and therefore analysis) in order to ensure legal clarity and opinion compliance. As we show in Figure 4.3, the probability of a dissent is slightly higher when analysis is low (Prob. | Dissent = 59.80%), however it is notable to point out that the minimum level of analytic language in education cases is 82.37%, compared to 48.28% in death penalty cases. When analysis is highest, the probability of a dissent decreases by 33.91% (Prob. | Dissent = 25.89%).

As we turn to examining how a dissent affects the majority decision, we recognize that the decision to issue a dissent is probably nonrandom. We estimate a Heckman selection bias model for our second set of hypotheses, where the selection equation uses the issuance of a dissent to predict what opinions are observed. We believe that this subset model will provide additional evidence that, among institutional factors significant to the crafting of a decision, the issuance of a dissent fundamentally changes the priorities of the majority opinion author, leading them to attempt greater accommodation while strengthening their rationale for their decision. To determine the extent to which this occurs, we examine the impact of institutional and linguistic factors on our variables for cognitive

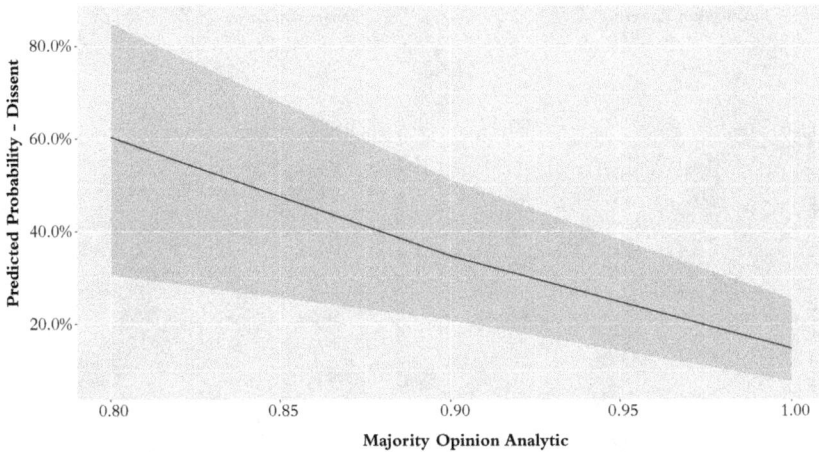

FIGURE 4.3   Predicted Probability of Issuance of a Dissent in Education Cases by Majority Opinion's Analytic Tone

Figure Created by Authors

complexity (in order to examine the effects on persuasion) and comprehensive clarity (to examine justification). It is worth noting at the outset that our findings are limited here only to salient cases. We found no statistically significant results for our nonsalient education cases, based on identical modeling strategies to account for the likelihood of a dissent. Dissents occur at a fairly co-equal frequency in both death penalty cases and education cases in our data, with education cases having only a slightly higher rate of occurrence (31.35% of education cases included a dissent, vs. 29.89% of death penalty cases). The null findings concerning non-salient cases is a frequent trend we will return to in this book. We believe that this is because non-salient cases, by definition, have a smaller audience than salient cases, so judges do not need to write with as much focus on audiences, as they are perceived as not "tuned in" to the decision. As related to our theoretical construct in Chapter 2, outside the immediate audiences of the other judges on the bench and the litigants in the case, non-salient cases will be of interest to only a small portion of the legal community that directly works with the area. Judges need not consider any other external audiences in non-salient cases, whereas numerous audiences external to the conflict exist when the case is salient.

Focusing directly on salient cases, we find that the circumstances that would lead to the issuing of a dissent have significant and interesting consequences for the linguistic strategies employed by the majority opinion author. Based on an analysis of the inverse Mills ratio, we find that increases in the likelihood of a dissent have a significant effect on both our measures of cognitive complexity and reading comprehension. As displayed in Figure 4.4, for persuasion and complexity, we find that an increase in the likelihood of a dissent has the effect of reducing the complexity of a majority opinion

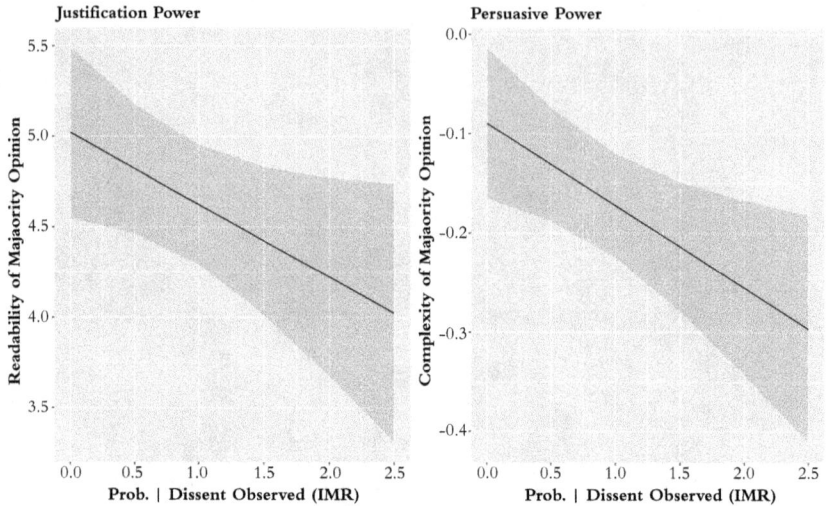

FIGURE 4.4 Impact of Dissent on the Readability and Cognitive Complexity of Majority Opinions in Death Penalty Cases

Figure Created by Authors

by -0.08, contrary to what we initially expected in Hypothesis 4. Even more notably, a similar increase in the likelihood of a dissent reduces the readability of the majority opinion by -0.40 points, which conforms to our expectations in Hypothesis 3. What we see then, and what the visualizations show in Figure 4.4, is that when dissents are issued judges struggle with how they will accommodate their colleagues. On the one hand, judges present a firmer, more rigid defense of their choice, adhering to stricter rules and trading persuasive power and collegial accommodation for stronger greater precision in justification. The dissent, however, fundamentally changes the ability of a judge to state that the answer is clear and obvious, and as a result must spend more time distinguishing itself from the minority dissent, reducing the readability of the document as a result. We believe that this finding conforms to our expectations, as judges placed in such situations engage in attempts not to persuade their colleagues *necessarily*, but to ensure that those *watching* the debate unfold in the opinions agree with the majority opinion once presented. As such, majority opinions that include a dissent attempt to find a line between persuasion *and* justification not to convince their colleagues, but to reach out to external audiences for support.

But what about the attributes of the dissent itself? Interestingly, in our models we find no evidence that a dissent is necessarily triggered by ideological distance between the majority author and the dissenter. We do find that as the dissent attempts to engage in persuasion, it does have an effect on how the

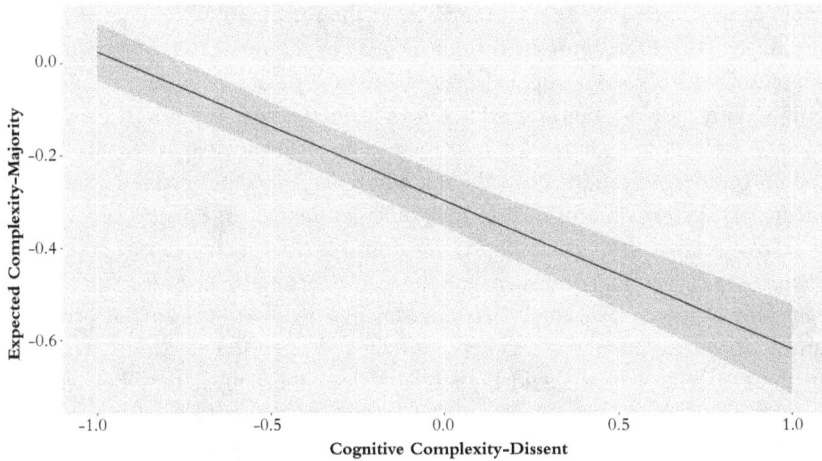

FIGURE 4.5 Expected Cognitive Complexity of Majority Opinion by Cognitive Complexity of the Dissent in Death Penalty Cases

Figure Created by Authors

majority opinion is written, though perhaps not in the direction that the dissenter intended. Based on our analysis, the persuasive power of the dissent itself (measured by calculating the complexity of the dissent using a method similar to the calculation used for the majority opinion) does not have a significant effect on the readability of the majority opinion, but it does have a significant and substantive effect on the persuasive power and complexity of the majority opinion. As Figure 4.5 indicates, as the complexity of the dissenting opinion increases, and the dissenting author attempts to show greater persuasion by differentiating and integrating alternatives into their decision, the majority opinion's complexity diminishes by -0.32.

Our findings thus far seem to indicate that judges have an eye to external audiences when writing the opinion, particularly in the presence of the dissent when the issue is salient, though this may still be a function of the institutions in which the judges exist. As a final test to this model, we focus attention on whether the method of retention will indicate greater justification or persuasion in the presence of dissenting opinions. Our results, as shown in Figure 4.6, are interesting; particularly as it pertains to the interaction between methods of retention and term length in the states. Focusing first on the differences in effects between readability and complexity, we note that we find the exact opposite effects again with regard to the impact of method of retention on language in the majority opinion. It is notable first to point out that we do not find significant differences in non-partisan systems compared to partisan systems. Appointment systems and retention election systems see significant increases in their readability when a dissent is present and holding the conditions for a dissent constant. For appointment systems, we find an increase in the readability of 5.97 points comparatively, whereas retention elections increase by 2.06 points. In contrast, using appointments to retain judges decreases the complexity of opinions by -0.35 points. There are no significant differences in the complexity in non-partisan or retention election systems. We find these differences notable, as it means that the institutional variation across the states in how judges are retained conditions judges in different systems to prioritize different audiences. Functionally, judges who are retained through contested elections consider their external audiences, namely their electoral constituency as their primary audience. A dissent does not cause these judges to change their behavior, as these systems do not prioritize unanimity in the same way that appointment and retention election systems do. In these systems which shield their judges from the public, they behave in a fashion which the primary audience they consider is the audience internal to the court: their fellow judges.

An interesting caveat to these findings, however, is just how these retention institutions interact with term length for judges. As judicial term length increases, we find that the readability of opinions decreases significantly in all but non-partisan elections. We find a similar opposing effect for appointment systems specifically for the complexity of opinions. Coupled with our other findings for salient cases, we believe that this shows that judges pay particular attention to just how frequently they may have to explain themselves to external audiences when writing opinions. Independently, judges value clear, concise, and readable opinions. However, as judges become more insulated from the public in the mechanisms not only of *choice* but also *time*, they trade this value and begin to deviate from this

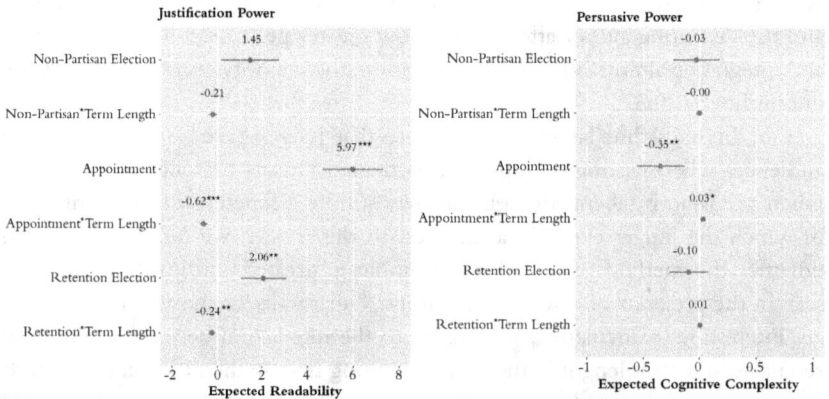

FIGURE 4.6 Expected Readability and Cognitive Complexity by Method of Retention and Term Length

Figure Created by Authors

behavior. This is much more likely for judges who are retained by elite actors, as they recognize that the retention audience may be more cognizant of the policy repercussions of legal decisions.

Conclusion

Does issuing a dissent affect the majority opinion on state courts? Existing studies have examined the strategic considerations judges evaluate when choosing to dissent, often coming to contradictory conclusions about their significance and impact (Blackstone and Collins 2014; Cross and Tiller 1998; Hettinger, Lindquist, and Martinek 2004; 2006; Kim 2009). Our purpose in this chapter was not specifically to refute or demonstrate that judges act strategically when choosing to dissent, but rather to examine what impact such actions have over the majority opinion. As Maltzman, Spriggs, and Wahlbeck (2000) indicate, the choice to dissent is not one that judges choose lightly and is often performed in order to gain some accommodation from the majority. In this way, dissents are inherently a part of the strategic game, but our question throughout is just how *effective* is this strategy?

Our findings add some clarity to this question and the impact that dissents have on the linguistic game that occurs when crafting the majority opinion. Dissents change the playing field for the majority opinion author, and thus require judges to consider more thoroughly how they will interact with their colleagues and what this will mean for interpretation with external audiences. The choice to dissent is a nonrandom event and is generally based on its own unique circumstances. As such, when a judge chooses to dissent, that choice sets into motion a series of behavioral considerations by the majority author. Dissents are found to change the cognitive considerations made by the majority opinion author when crafting a legal decision. Dissents are issued in cases where analysis and justification are low, and persuasion and authenticity are high. When a dissent is issued, the majority opinion is generally found to adhere to a stricter cognitive decision pattern; adhering more strongly to strict rules and discounting multiple perspectives in favor of exclusivity and "black and white" choices.

We also find that the dissent has differential effects depending upon how the judges on the court are retained. The dissent does not have a functional effect on judges who are retained through contested elections, either partisan or nonpartisan. We believe this is because opinion authors in contested electoral systems consider the internal audience of the court to a lesser degree than those in appointment and retention election systems. Ultimately, the majority opinion author in a contested election system is balancing two considerations with their majority opinion. First, they need to retain a majority from the conference vote so that their opinion indeed remains the majority opinion, but a majority simply means a minimum-winning coalition. Second, the majority opinion author is also writing for secondary audiences, primarily the legal community and their electoral constituency. It may be the case that when judges are at more risk of removal (Curry and Hurwitz 2016), majority opinion authors in salient cases will use their platform for prioritizing electoral success rather than considering other members of the court.

This finding is juxtaposed with the reality for judges in appointment and retention election systems, two systems in which judges are at significantly less risk of removal. In each of these systems, majority opinion authors do consider judges who publish a dissent and augment their writing accordingly. We believe that is because these systems prioritize consensus, their retention audiences being more likely to notice individual authors when they are writing for strongly divided courts. If a judge is writing in dissent, or consistently authoring majority opinions for minimum-winning coalitions, they increase their likelihood of being targeted for removal. That is why we find within these systems that judges who work within institutions which have long term lengths are less likely to consider dissents when drafting the majority opinion. When a judge is facing a six-year term in a system that prioritizes consensus, they will be more likely to cater to those in dissent than will a judge in a similar system with a twelve-year term.

This chapter confirms our general theoretical assumption that the audience of the judges and their variation dependent upon retention systems is one of the most important factors in determining how they will write the majority opinion. While this chapter attempts to turn our inquiry inward, towards the influence that other members of the court may have upon the majority opinions, it seems that the external audience to the courts still has a story to tell. In the following chapter, we examine this balancing of internal and external audiences through the use of a per curiam opinion, a tool that can shield individual opinion authors from external accountability.

Notes

1 Even if this is not true, importantly for us, judges believe it to be true (see Maltzman, Spriggs and Wahlbeck 2000).
2 Maltzmann, Spriggs, and Wahlbeck (2000) note that out of the 12,651 observations where a justice cast a conference vote with the majority in their data, only 616 – or 4.9% – were changed to dissents later.
3 To our knowledge, there are no packages that automatically calculate the inverse Mills ratio in R at the present time. However, an examination of the theoretical assumptions of the Heckman model, and formal theory considering its extension to multi-level models indicate that a manual correction is sufficient. An alternative Heckman model without accounting for multi-level effects was run and provides similar conclusions for direction and significance.
4 Specifying the model in this way allows us to produce more conservative estimates and decrease the rate of Type I errors in the model (Barr et al. 2013).

References

Barr, D. J., Levy, R., Scheepers, C., & Tily, H. J. (2013). Random Effects Structure for Confirmatory Hypothesis Testing: Keep It Maximal. *Journal of Memory and Language*, 68(3), 255–278.

Baum, L. (1994). What Judges Want: Judges' Goals and Judicial Behavior. *Political Research Quarterly*, 47(3), 749–768.

Baum, L. (2006). *Judges and Their Audiences: A Perspective on Judicial Behavior*. Princeton: Princeton University Press.

Blackstone, B., & Collins, P. M. (2014). Strategy and the Decision to Dissent on the U.S. Court of Appeals. *Justice System Journal*, 35(3), 269–286.

Brace, P. & Hall, M. G. (1990). Neo-Institutionalism and Dissent in State Supreme Courts. *Journal of Politics*, 52(1), 54–70.

Brace, P., & Hall, M. G. (1993). Integrated Models of Judicial Dissent. *The Journal of Politics*, 55(4), 914–935.

Caldeira, G. A., Wright, J. R. (1988). Organized Interests and Agenda Setting in the U.S. Supreme Court. *American Political Science Review*, 82(4), 1109–1127.

Caldeira, G. A., Wright, J. R., & Zorn, C. J.W. (1999). Sophisticated Voting and Gate-keeping in the Supreme Court. *Journal of Law, Economics, and Organization*, 15(3), 549–572.

Collins, P. M., & Martinek, W. L. (2011). The Small Group Context: Designated District Court Judges in the U.S. Courts of Appeals. *Journal of Empirical Legal Studies*, 8(1), 177–205.

Cross, F. B., & Tiller, E. H. (1998). Judicial Partisanship and Obedience to Legal Doctrine: Whistleblowing on the Federal Court of Appeals. *Yale Law Journal*, 107(7), 2155–2176.

Douglas, W. O. (1948). The Dissent: A Safeguard of Democracy. *Journal of the American Judicature Society*, 32(1), 104–107.

Dunn, K. C., & Neumann, I. B. (2016). *Undertaking Discourse Analysis for Social Research*. Ann Arbor: University of Michigan Press.

Epstein, L., Landes, W. M., & Posner, R. A. (2010). Why (and When) Judges Dissent: A Theoretical and Empirical Analysis. (John M. Olin Program in Law and Economics Working Paper No. 510).

George, T. (1999). The Dynamics and Determinants of the Decision to Grant En Banc Review. *Washington Law Review*, 74(April), 213–274.

Gibson, J. L. (1978). Judges' Role Orientations, Attitudes, and Decisions: An Interactive Model. *American Political Science Review*, 72(4), 911–924.

Gibson, J. L. (1983). From Simplicity to Complexity: The Development of Theory in the Study of Judicial Behavior. *Political Behavior*, 5(1), 7–49.

Giles, M. W. Walker, T. G., & Zorn, C. (2006). Setting a Judicial Agenda: The Decision to Grant En Banc Review in the U.S. Courts of Appeals. *Journal of Politics*, 68(4), 852–866.

Ginsburg, D. H. & Falk, D. (1991). The Court En Banc: 1981–1990. *The George Washington Law Review*, 59(June), 1008–1053.

Gruenfeld, D. H. (1995). Status, Ideology, and Integrative Complexity on the U.S. Supreme Court: Rethinking the Politics of Political Decision Making. *Journal of Personality and Social Psychology*, 68(1), 5–20.

Hall, M. G., & Brace, P. (1989). Order in the Courts: A Neo-Institutional Approach to Judicial Consensus. *Western Political Quarterly*, 42(3), 391–407

Hall, M. G., & Brace, P. (1992). Toward an Integrated Model of Judicial Voting Behavior. *American Politics Quarterly*, 20(2), 147–168.

Hall, M. G., & Brace, P. (1999). State Supreme Courts & their Environments: Avenues to General Theories of Judicial Choice. In Clayton, C. & Gillman, H. (eds.). *Supreme Court Decision-Making: New Institutionalist Perspectives.* Chicago: University of Chicago Press, 281–300.

Hettinger, V. A., Lindquist, S. A., & Martinek, W. L. (2004). Comparing Attitudinal & Strategic Accounts of Dissenting Behavior on the U.S. Court of Appeals. *American Journal of Political Science*, 48(1), 123–137.

Hettinger, V. A., Lindquist, S. A., & Martinek, W. L. (2006). *Judging on a Collegial Court: Influences on Federal Appellate Decision Making.* Charlottesville: University of Virginia Press.

Johnson, C. A. 1979. Lower Court Reactions to Supreme Court Decisions: A Quantitative Examination. *American Journal of Political Science*, 23(4), 792–804.

Kim, P. T. (2009). Deliberation and Strategy on the United States Courts of Appeals: An Empirical Exploration of Panel Effects. *University of Pennsylvania Law Review*, 157(5), 1319–1381.

Klein, D. E. (2002). *Making Law in the United States Court of Appeals.* Cambridge: Cambridge University Press.

Leonard, M. E., & Ross, J. V. (2016). Understanding the Length of State Supreme Court Opinions. *American Politics Research*, 44(4), 710–733.

Lindquist, S. A. & Martinek, W. L. (2009). Psychology, Strategy, & Behavioral Equivalence. *University of Pennsylvania Law Review*, 158(1), 75–81.

Maltzman, F., Spriggs, J. F., & Wahlbeck, P. L. (2000). *Crafting Law on the Supreme Court: The Collegial Game.* Cambridge: Cambridge University Press.

Owens, R. J. & Wedeking, J. (2012). Predicting Drift on Political Insulated Institutions: A Study of Ideological Drift on the United States Supreme Court. *Journal of Politics*, 74(2), 487–500.

Peterson, S. A. (1981). Dissent in American Courts. *Journal of Politics*, 43(2), 412–434.

Posner, R. A. (2008). *How Judges Think.* Cambridge: Harvard University Press

Scalia, A. (1994). The Dissenting Opinion. *Journal of Supreme Court History*, 19(1), 33–44.

Scalia, A. (1997). *A Matter of Interpretation: Federal Courts and the Law.* Princeton: Princeton University Press.

Songer, D. R. (1986). Factors Affecting Variations in Rates of Dissent in the U.S. Courts of Appeals. In Goldman, S. & Lamb, C. M. (eds.) *Judicial Conflict and Consequences: Behavioral Studies of American Appellate Courts.* Lexington: University of Kentucky Press, 117–138.

Tausczik, Y. R. & Pennebaker, J. W. (2010). The Psychological Meaning of Words: LIWC & Computerized Text Analysis Methods. *Journal of Language & Social Psychology*, 29(1), 24–54.

Tetlock, P. E., Hannum, K. A. & Micheletti, P. M. (1984). Stability & Change in the Complexity of Senatorial Debate: Testing the Cognitive Versus Rhetorical Style Hypothesis. *Journal of Personality & Social Psychology*, 46(5), 979–990.

Urofsky, M. I. (2017). *Dissent and the Supreme Court: Its Role in the Court's History and the Nation's Constitutional Dialogue.* New York, NY: Vantage Books.

Van Winkle, S. (1997). Dissent as a Signal: Evidence from the U.S. Courts of Appeals. *Presented at the Annual Meeting of the American Political Science Association*, Washington, DC.

5

EFFICIENCY OR STRATEGY

Per Curiam Usage on State Supreme Courts

"[When] nobody knows what opinion any individual member gave in any case, nor even that he who delivers the opinion concurred in it himself, [a justice's reputation] is shielded completely."

Thomas Jefferson to Justice William Johnson (Oct 27, 1820)

POSNER THOUGHTS
@Posner_Thoughts

PER CURIAM IS FOR COWARDS.

8:24 AM - 27 Oct 2017

Source: @Posner_Thoughts (Jack Metzler), Oct 27, 2017

In the preceding chapters we have focused our attention on understanding what goes into determining judicial language and how judges craft opinions. Our primary focus has been on understanding how a judge's opinion is constrained by the various environmental and institutional factors that permeate throughout the states. The preceding chapter expanded on our understanding by examining how internal debate – particularly the presence of dissenting opinions – affects the contention of the majority opinion. All of these findings have been focused on understanding judicial opinion-writing generally, and how the opinion author is constrained or compelled by their surroundings. In this chapter, we remove many of the constraints experienced by majority opinion authors by examining opinions which are unsigned.

Generally, majority opinions are drafted by and attributed to an individual judge. When audiences evaluate these cases, the opinion is critiqued not only as the "voice of the court," but also based on personal considerations of the opinion writer. As noted by Markham (2006: pg. 926), "The individually signed opinion has become such a cornerstone of American appellate judicial practice . . . that one rarely stops to consider its origin, much less its costs and benefits in the administration of justice." Per curiam opinions, the focus of this chapter, are fundamentally different. Per curiam opinions are unsigned opinions "by the court." While few researchers have detailed the history of per curiam opinions (Ray 2002) and have provided some detailed examinations of their use by the U.S. Supreme Court (Wasby et al. 1992), little empirical research has examined whether they are different linguistically from signed majority opinions. Common knowledge contends that per curiam opinions are used either when the case decided is a straightforward application of precedent, or when the opinion would benefit from multiple viewpoints and the expertise of the panel. Because per curiam opinions are unsigned, however, they may also be used as a strategic device to avoid backlash, particularly in controversial decisions.

It may not be obvious why we choose to dedicate an entire chapter of this book to per curiam opinions. Per curiam opinions are generally viewed as unimportant, especially in the federal judiciary where they are thought of as a functional way to dispose of simple, uncomplicated cases. In state judiciaries, however, there may be another motivating reason to use unsigned opinions. Nearly all state supreme courts judges have to face retention, with the goal of keeping them accountable. Per curiam opinions mask the author, thus making it more difficult to hold a particular judge accountable.

This chapter examines two different aspects of per curiam opinion-writing to assess whether the common knowledge is correct. First, we ask: are per curiam opinions systematically different in their use of language from regular, signed opinions? Second, are systems that use public elections as a means of judicial retention more likely to engage in the drafting of per curiam opinions, and are those opinions systematically different from per curiam opinions from non-elected courts?

The Point of Per Curiam: A Legal History

Readers of the contemporary judicial opinion have grown accustom to documents that span the rhetorical gambit; presenting views of a singular justice with the approval and disapproval of their colleagues added to the end in the form of a concurrence or dissent. It is somewhat interesting, therefore, to note that such publications are a fairly recent development for courts in the United States.

The practice of the single-authored, sometimes contentious opinion largely breaks from the presentation of the "monolithic solidarity" of the branch, as Judge Learned Hand emphasized, instead highlighting the balance a judge makes between personal ideology and institutional integrity (Ray 2002). The unsigned per curiam is one of a court's most basic tools (Wasby et al. 1992), lauded by some to epitomize consensus on the court (Markham 2006; Black's Law Dictionary 2018). The use of such opinions – signed "by the Court" and thus left intentionally anonymous when presented to the public – has a long legal history which links distinctly to institutional developments that have shaped and changed the role of the courts in the United States.

Courts in the United States have traditionally written opinions in one of three distinct ways, following patterns and institutional practices first established and developed in the United States Supreme Court. Originally, expectations for judicial opinions (if the decision was written down at all) was for judges to present their views *seriatim*, with each judge writing separately to explain their individual vote in a case. These opinions were then organized by seniority, sometimes followed by a brief "Summary of the Court," that determined the overall disposition in a case. This practice, linked to the British model of judicial decision-making, was most often utilized to indicate how judges decided in common law courts. Furthermore, it was prioritized by proponents of judicial accountability to the democratically selected branches of government in order to assure that ideological judges could be curbed and controlled.[1] In the early post-revolutionary period, the per curiam[2] was utilized primarily in order to dispose of the most "impersonal" of decisions: those cases in which the law was so obviously clear and without debate that judges could easily dispense with a decision without much depth or legal reasoning (Li et al. 2013; Ray 2002; Robbins 2012; Wasby et al. 1992). As an institutional practice beginning at the Supreme Court, Urofsky (2017) notes that a good majority of such cases saturated the early dockets of the Court. During the pre-Marshall era, approximately 71% of cases heard by the Court were decided in the per curiam fashion, dealing mostly with broad legal matters that today would "never get beyond a local or state tribunal or possibly a federal district court" (Urofsky 2017, 41).

Starting in 1801, courts in the United States began to shift from the presentation of opinions *seriatim* to a practice of issuing a single judgment, an "opinion of the Court," as a way of institutionalizing consensus within the branch (Popkin 2007; Urofsky 2017). The reason for this change, according to Popkin (2007), was to assist in emphasizing the role and place of the judiciary within the broader context of American democracy, and to develop the judiciary into an insular, independent branch of government. The singular opinion, written "for the Court," provided an outlet for judicial power by emphasizing the consensus of the bench over the interpretation of law. Perhaps the strongest proponent of the practice, Chief Justice John Marshall, recognized that consensus was a way to develop power for the judiciary in order to influence public policy; using the practice to bring the branch on equal footing with the more democratically elected branches. The advent of the single opinion written and signed by one person (generally Marshall himself) emphasized institutional integrity and firm agreement among judges, downplaying and often silencing disagreement between members of the bench (Urofsky 2017). In lauding the practice and disseminating it as standard practice in the broader judiciary, Marshall crafted an institutional legacy for courts in the United States to rely upon in order to argue for a co-equal place in the political process; one that required strong "disciplined leadership," and "valued collective institutional power over the independent voices of [a court's] members" (Ray 2002, 182).

It was in this vein of balancing institutional power with the ability to cultivate consensus that the contemporary "mythos" of the per curiam opinion took shape. The third, and current, period of judicial writing features the now ubiquitous "single-authored" judicial opinion, wherein judges mix elements of the older *seriatim* practice with elements of Marshall's institutional legitimacy strategy. Since Marshall, the path of judicial opinions at both the state and federal level has taken shape around the dual sentiments of collegiality and individualism amongst members of the bench. Historically, as consensus broke down and judges found advantages in writing separately, either in concurrence or dissent, the rationale for the continued use of a singular opinion emphasizing consensus became questionable. Coupled with this, the debate taking shape in state courts over accountability and independence led some states to explicitly demand judges provide written testaments of their legal reasoning (Radin 1930). "Public accountability through the disclosure of votes and opinion authors," as Justice Ginsburg (1990, 140) relates, "puts the judge's conscience and reputation on the line."

Given these institutional developments, the per curiam opinion served a unique role for the Court, acting as both a device for protecting the institution and assuring that their rulings would maintain the force of law. When the contemporary per curiam took shape in the 1862 case of *Mesa v. United States* (67 U.S. 721), the Court established the practice as way to efficiently resolve cases without much explanation. As the original purpose of the per curiam was to dispose of "easy" cases, it follows that its development as a strategic tool is linked to attempts by the judiciary to signal institutional agreement, even in the absence of unanimity or consensus. Proponents of unsigned per curiam opinions argue that their use depoliticizes the judiciary and removes the ability of "activist judges" to dictate policy. As evidence of a per curiam opinion's effectiveness, proponents ironically tend to point to the series of per curiam briefs issued by the US Supreme Court in the wake of *Brown v. Board of Education*. In the years after *Brown*, the Court systematically struck down segregation in a series of other public accommodations, the best known of which occurred in 1956 when the Court struck down segregation in public housing by simply stating, "The judgment is affirmed," citing no precedent and providing no further rationale (*New Orleans*

City Park Improvement Ass'n v. Detiege, 358 U.S. 891 (1955)). Their ability to do this was due to the fact that *Brown* was decided unanimously by the Supreme Court in 1954. Had Chief Justice Warren not gained full consensus, the issuance of per curiam opinions for future decisions would have likely carried very little weight as precedent. In this vein, the per curiam was able to reduce the broader debate by subtlety invoking the consensus that surrounded *Brown*. "By eliminating legal discussion and allowing the per curiam form to carry its message of unstoppable progress, the Court communicated its constitutional position more effectively and *less provocatively* than a sequence of fully developed opinions could have done" (Ray 2002, pg. 189, emphasis added).

Thus, the initial reasoning and the subtext of the per curiam was clear. As Ray (2002, 177) points out, per curiam were reserved for opinions where "the case is so easily resolvable, so lacking in complexity or disagreement among the justices, that it requires only a brief, forthright opinion that *any member of the court could draft and that no member of the court need sign*." This rationale for the practice would persist for a number of years, with per curiam opinions making their regular appearance in a great many non-controversial cases until the year 2000, when the presidential election between George W. Bush and Al Gore made it to the chambers of the U.S. Supreme Court.

Far from an uncontroversial opinion, *Bush v. Gore* (2000) was likely the first time most Americans became aware of the per curiam as a tool of the judiciary. Of the two issues in this case, a 7–2 majority agreed that the recount violated the 14th Amendment's Equal Protection Clause, and a 5–4 majority ruled that no constitutionally adequate method could be developed in a reasonable time. The opinion was unsigned, though the divisions on the Court were readily apparent. Instead of being protected by unanimity, three judges (Chief Justice Rehnquist and Justices Scalia and Thomas) concurred in writing with the per curiam and discussed at some length the dissents in the case, of which there were four, authored by Justices Stevens, Souter, Ginsburg, and Breyer. With such a public and ideological divide evident to any observer, why was a per curiam opinion used? Traditionally, per curiam opinions have been used for legally easy cases or cases that have high levels of agreement across the judges. Nevertheless, by the very virtue of the fact that the opinion is unsigned, it makes accountability and criticism of the opinion author exceedingly difficult.

The Per Curiam as a Strategic Device

Despite the conventional view that per curiam opinions exist to dispose of simple cases, because they lack a signed author they provide courts with the ability to engage in strategic behavior. The question for us is, just what strategic benefit does the per curiam have for state courts?[3] Legal and political analysis of the per curiam, predominantly focused on the federal courts, have determined that the power of per curiam comes from its ability to effect institutional factors that may constrain the court. As a strategic device, the per curiam has been viewed as a tool for increasing the efficiency of the court, or for obfuscating the court's decision by hiding the author, thus attempting to ensure the decision's legitimacy is not questioned, by emphasizing that it is not the biased opinion of one author but the view of the full "unbiased court."

Fundamentally, as the previous discussion about the origins of the opinion indicates, the per curiam opinion is a device for efficiently disposing of cases that might otherwise slow down a court (see Masood and Songer 2013; Ray 2002; Wasby et al. 1992). Expediency can be valuable to a court for several reasons; however, it is most closely tied to the ability to diminish the workload of a court, particularly those with mandatory dockets or no intermediate appellate court. Cases that can be decided based on procedural disposition rather than substantive law can quickly be taken care of without much presumed disagreement among members of the court; fulfilling the standard mentioned by Ray (2002) previously of a decision "any judge" would find reasonable and would write. If this were the case, we should expect to find some correlation between the existence of discretionary jurisdiction and/or intermediate appellate courts and the occurrence of a per curiam brief.[4]

Efficiency may have a separate meaning, however, and one that links more directly to the language used in the opinion, and thus our primary interest in understanding the use of language by the judiciary. According to Ray's (2002) analysis of the history of per curiam usage on the U.S. Supreme Court, the use of the opinion was not just to affect the simple alacrity of decision disposal, but to ensure that cases of *high priority* were decided quickly. This is reasonable when discussing the U.S. Supreme Court, as the decision in some cases can have substantial and immediate impact on the lives of citizens. We might likewise translate this to the state high courts as well, particularly as it pertains to deciding salient cases over non-salient cases.[5] Linguistically, we believe that this means that the prioritization of the opinion's frame (as examined in Chapter 3) may significantly impact the occurrence of a per curiam. Particularly, we expect that cases which may have significant audience repercussions – in the form of audience backlash or major policy change – will be more likely than other cases to be written per curiam. To test this in our models, salient case frames are grouped together as a single dichotomous variable, based on whether the opinion is dominated by these frames. Table 5.1 displays how we organized case frames by salience. We suspect that opinions where the dominant frame has the potential to pique external audience interest (such as death penalty cases involving questions of mental illness, or education cases focused on school funding) will be more likely to be delivered per curiam compared to those with less salient, and thus less "political" implications.

- Hypothesis 1: Salient opinion framing should increase the likelihood of writing per curiam.

TABLE 5.1 Frame Salience by Case Type

	Salient Frame	*Non-Salient Frame*
Salient Cases	Case Facts; Jury Challenges; Jury Instructions; Mental Illness; Physical Evidence; Questioning; Sentencing	General Attorney Issues; General Trial Issues; Ineffective Counsel; Legal Factors; Precedent; Procedural Issues; Prosecution Errors; Witness Issues
Non-Salient Cases	Constitutional Requirements for Education; School Funding; Student Performance	Administrative Issue; Complaints; Employee Relations; Injury Case

Source: Table Created by Authors

Alternatively, a second strategic use for per curiam may focus less on efficiently deciding "easy" cases while ensuring that high-profile cases have adequate institutional cover. As a strategy, per curiam may be best suited in state courts for those cases where judges have a greater fear of accountability for their actions. A common starting point for the consideration of judicial legacy and judicial ideology is the analysis of a judge's written opinion, presumed to be intended not just for the litigants but for external audiences as we have argued (see also Baum 2006; Markham 2006; Posner 1995). The problem with the per curiam is they lack an opinion author and thus eschew any notion of accountability. This is especially problematic for state courts where there is a general expectation of accountability for judicial decisions. As Ray (2002, 187) notes, "With no Justice signing the opinion, there [is] no individual to be blamed for evading the tough questions. The choice had been made by a faceless entity." The lack of an author removes agency that is associated with the signing of an opinion, thus allowing a judge to "wash their hands" of an issue without suffering consequences for their decisions. Li et al. (2013) note that this lack of accountability has led critics to complain about poor quality of opinions, evasion of difficult issues, lack of transparency to the public, and others (see also Robbins 2012). As *Bush v. Gore* should remind us, not all per curiam opinions are brief, or procedural, or mechanical applications of the law. Sometimes, per curiam opinions contain highly important issues, and have significant impact.

Judges may use the per curiam strategically in order to accomplish a different goal: make *new* law. That is to say, judges may craft per curiam in order to institutionalize new precedent and practices, even despite disagreement among members of the branch. As such, we argue that attempts to use the per curiam to make new law are inherently linked to language crafting, as judges recognize the power of the opinion to legitimize their choices, independent of the methods of accountability used to retain judges. Much like how dissents can lead judges to write in a way that cements justification and attempts to consider external audiences with regards to persuasion, per curiam opinions can be utilized to eschew persuasion altogether by relying on the belief that the court is speaking with "one voice."[6] As the per curiam is strongest when all judges on the bench are in agreement (Ray 2002), we should expect that the opinion itself will be crafted in an attempt to accommodate all judges in order to maintain group cohesion. We expect that per curiam decisions will be written using a greater level of analysis compared to single-author opinions and should likewise be written in a way that emphasizes readability in order to appear deterministic in their argument. We suspect that there will be limits to when judges will find it advantageous to sign their name to a clearly written opinion, however, and as such we also test to determine whether a curvilinear relationship occurs between readability and the likelihood of per curiam opinions.

- Hypothesis 2: As analytic language increases, the likelihood of a per curiam opinion increases.
- Hypothesis 3: The likelihood of a per curiam opinion should be at its highest when readability is at its highest or lowest, indicating a curvilinear relationship.

As we argue that the per curiam works systematically through the use of justification in the opinion, we presume that judges will need to emphasize such language to a greater degree, and thus likely not attempt persuasion too heavily. The logic behind this is simple: as the opinion already obfuscates the name of the opinion author and thus appears to be the voice of a "singular court," to external audiences, judges should see less need to persuade these audiences by displaying breadth of argument or emphasizing authentic language. This is to say that judges writing per curiam will likely recognize that, even if the opinion is not singular in voice, the fact that it appears "by the court" provides enough institutional leverage to avoid sparking substantial backlash from external audiences. Following our assumptions concerning justification and language clarity specifically, it may be the case that the relationship between cognitive complexity and the likelihood of per curiam is curvilinear; indicative that judges may find it advantageous to sign their name to opinions when the decision strikes a balance between integrating multiple arguments and making a clear, distinctive choice between alternatives. In such situations, we suspect that the likelihood of a per curiam should decrease.

- Hypothesis 4: As authentic language use increases, the likelihood of a per curiam opinion will decrease.
- Hypothesis 5: The likelihood of a per curiam opinion should be at its highest when cognitive complexity is at its highest or lowest, indicating a curvilinear relationship.

There exist some institutional reasons why we would expect the use of per curiam opinions to vary across states based upon which method is used to retain judges. As we have discussed in previous chapters, accountability to the public is not equal across judicial retention systems. It is clear that contested elections (and to a lesser extent, retention elections) prioritize public accountability in how they retain their judges. However, the key to winning re-election in these systems is, in large part, name recognition. For a strategic opinion author, this means you want your name attached to an opinion when the decision is popular, and not attached when the decision is unpopular or controversial.

- Hypothesis 6: Judges retained by a form of public accountability will be less likely to utilize per curiam opinions.

From a communicative standpoint, the use of per curiam may provide useful cover to judges when both the issue and the decision itself will prove controversial. As previously determined in Chapter 3, judicial decisions may take on a variety of frames as they are presented to the public, and these frames may likewise vary with regard to salience within specific audiences. As such, it is not difficult to surmise that judges may utilize per curiam opinions in cases where the framing of the decision itself may bring about controversy or outright scorn from retention audiences specifically. In this case, having the protection of partisanship is likely key to ensuring a judge can ensure their retention when the case's framing is salient. In order to test this directly, we interact methods of retention with frame salience, as determined above. We presume that in instances where the decision frame is salient, judges in states where the ideological congruence between retention audiences and judges is lower will be more likely to employ the per curiam to provide cover, using institutional integrity in order to shield judges from backlash.

- Hypothesis 7: States that insulate judges from representative politics through their method of retention will increase the likelihood of writing per curiam when the decision frame is salient.

Choosing to Write Per Curiam

An empirical examination of per curiam opinions offers a unique opportunity for us to understand what factors lead judges to anonymize their decisions. Studies of per curiam usage at the federal level have provided some unique insight into the role and purpose of such opinions; therefore, our analysis of the per curiam's usage at the state level requires careful consideration of the unique circumstances in which they arise. As Figure 5.1 shows, per curiam opinions are exceedingly rare in the dataset.[7] As such, to account for the low frequency of per curiam occurrences, we switch our modeling strategy in this chapter and use a pooled

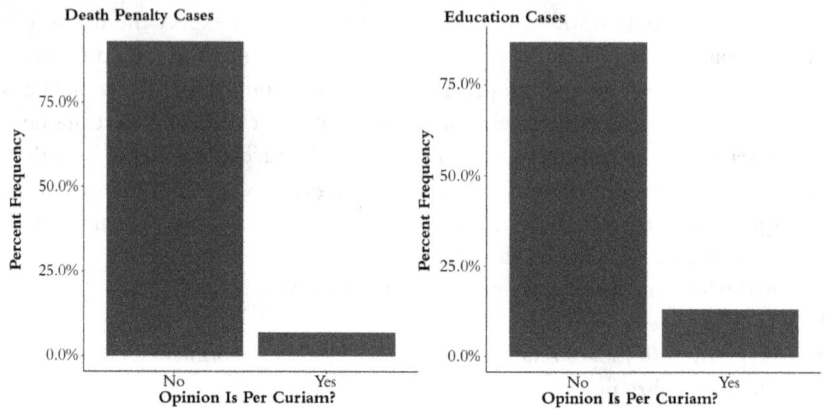

FIGURE 5.1 Frequency of Per Curiam Opinions in Death Penalty and Education Cases before State Supreme Courts

Figure Created by Authors

penalized logistic regression using the Firth transformation to account for bias due to rare events. In death penalty cases, judges utilized per curiam opinions 6.92% of the time, while in education cases per curiam opinions were delivered 13.07% of the time.

Looking first at how per curiam usage varies by method of retention, we find that systems that emphasize public accountability are significantly less likely to write opinions per curiam, however case type does play an important role in determining which methods are significantly affected. We do not find a significant effect when we interact method of retention with the salience of the opinion frame, and so we can conclude that retention mechanisms do independently cause judges to consider their position when deciding a case. The impact of method of retention on the likelihood of writing per curiam is shown in Figure 5.2. Consistent with Hypothesis 6, in death penalty cases we find that judges in states that use elite appointment to retain their bench are more likely to write opinions per curiam compared to states that retain using some kind of electoral mechanism. While substantively small overall, the difference in the likelihood of writing per curiam between elite reappointment states and all other methods of retention is exceedingly greater, with a predicted probability of writing per curiam of 11.90%, approximately 5% higher than methods that utilize election.[8] In contrast, we find that retention election courts are significantly less likely to publish per curiam in non-salient (education) cases. According to Figure 5.2, retention election systems are far less likely to use per curiam compared to other methods of retention, elite appointment or other electoral methods. The likelihood of writing per curiam in retention election systems is just 8.52%. Retention elections are notoriously low salient events, with a high degree of ballot roll-off. That

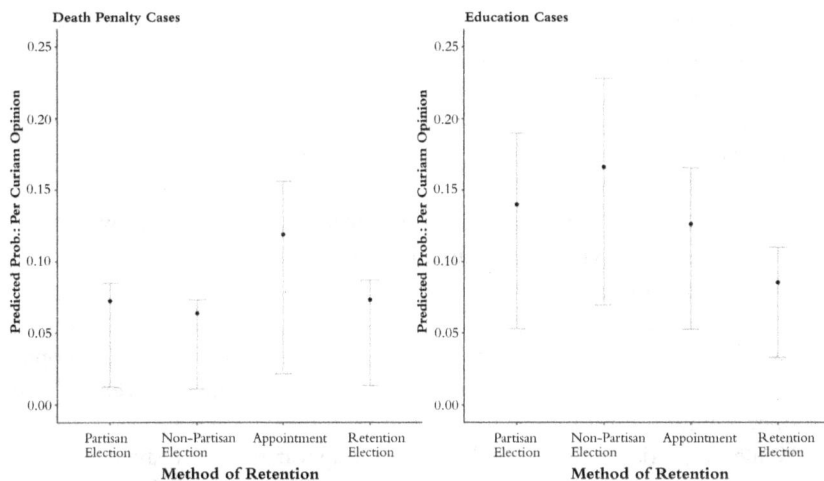

FIGURE 5.2   Predicted Probability of Per Curiam Opinions by Method of Retention in the State

Figure Created by Authors

judges within this system seem to eschew writing per curiam in both salient and non-salient cases may be because authoring an opinion is one of the easiest (and cheapest) ways for judges to gain name recognition.

Considering that individual death penalty cases are likely not salient to elite audiences, and that education cases are not ones that the public in retention election systems will be distinctly aware of or consider when voting, we are left with a puzzle as to why these systems impact the likelihood of writing per curiam. We argue that judges in these situations choose to write per curiam (or not) precisely because of their secondary audience. When elected courts choose not to write per curiam it is likely because they feel that the increase of name recognition which comes along with an authored opinion is important. Judges in retention election systems are consistently less likely to use per curiam across both types of cases, which is consistent with the lower salience of more retention election contests. For elite reappointment judges, this means using the per curiam to dispose of simple cases costs them nothing, as those charged with their retention are political elites, familiar with the judges and the work of the court.

In our data, judges in elite reappointment systems decided only 9.10% of death penalty cases (391 cases total). Of those cases, only 8.18% (32 cases total) were decided per curiam. Examining these specific cases, our assumption that these judges are disposing of simple cases in a per curiam fashion has some merit. The median length of a per curiam from elite reappointment states was just over 2,500 words, about three times lower than the median for all death penalty cases observed. Content-wise, these cases appear fairly simplistic in their arguments as well.[9] For example, in one case from the Delaware Supreme Court, the appellants request for post-conviction relief was denied as moot, and easily decided based on procedural grounds from the lower court.

The electoral protection provided to judges by the method of retention used in the state is a reasonable starting point for understanding why a court may write per curiam. Our interests, however, primarily lie in whether language use can predict the likelihood of a per curiam opinion, and what this might mean about the internal machinations of a court. Unlike previous chapters, we find no evidence that judges writing per curiam are any less analytic in their reasoning (Hypothesis 2), nor are they any less authentic (Hypothesis 4). Thus, we can at least conclude that, at the very least, judges in state courts do not appear to be explicitly changing the way that they write per curiam compared to signed opinions, as the level of effort and enthusiasm is arguably the same between different types of opinions.[10]

While per curiam opinion authors do not appear to modify their language overtly by focusing heavily on authenticity or analysis, we do find some evidence to indicate that more implicit measures of persuasion and justification are present and significantly impact the likelihood of a per curiam opinion being issued. Particularly, we find that in death penalty cases judges are more likely to issue per curiam opinions when the level of complexity in a case increases. As we show in Figure 5.3, per curiam opinions are more likely to be issued in death penalty cases as the cognitive complexity of the opinion increases; a finding that is non-existent for education cases. This finding is most interesting as it does not conform with our initial expectations in Hypothesis 5, which argues for a curvilinear relationship. According to our findings, when judges write clear, strictly decided opinions using "black-and-white" arguments, the probability of a per curiam opinion is roughly 4.49%. In contrast, opinions that display a wide array of arguments, and attempt to integrate these arguments to various degrees in order to reach a conclusion, have a predicted probability of being decided per curiam of 14.48%, increasing the likelihood of a per curiam by roughly ten percent. We believe that this is an indication that judges carefully decide when it is best to write anonymously, and that the type of the case may be a dominant factor, particularly when the court needs to consider multiple lines of argument in order to reach a decision.[11] Our findings indicate that when judges find it necessary to write persuasively in order to reach their conclusion, they may also grow concerned that their writing – or they themselves – may be scrutinized to a greater degree. As a result, using the anonymity of the per curiam is worthwhile in order to provide a judge with cover when making difficult decisions or shifting the precedent for death penalty cases; a finding similar to what Ray (2002, 187) refers to as "working through indirection."

While judges may use the per curiam as institutional coverage when trying to persuade external audiences to their opinion, the "common belief" is that the per curiam is frequently executed in order to justify "simple decisions." As Figure 5.4 displays, the relationship between writing per curiam and the clarity of the judicial

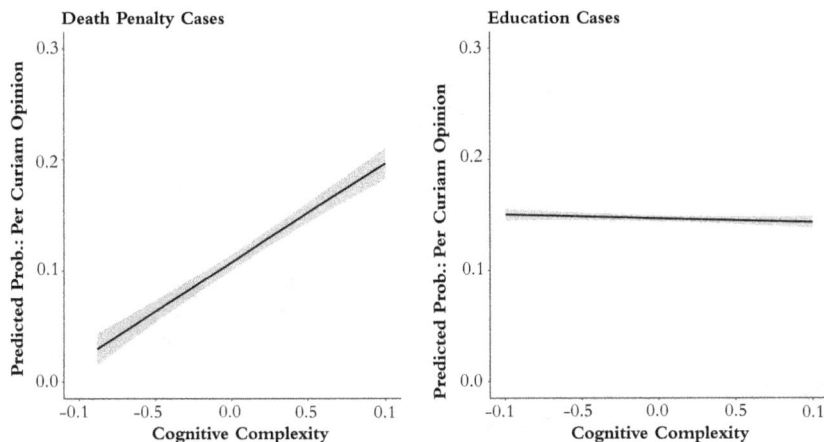

FIGURE 5.3   Predicted Probability of Per Curiam Opinion by Cognitive Complexity in Death Penalty and Education Cases

Figure Created by Authors

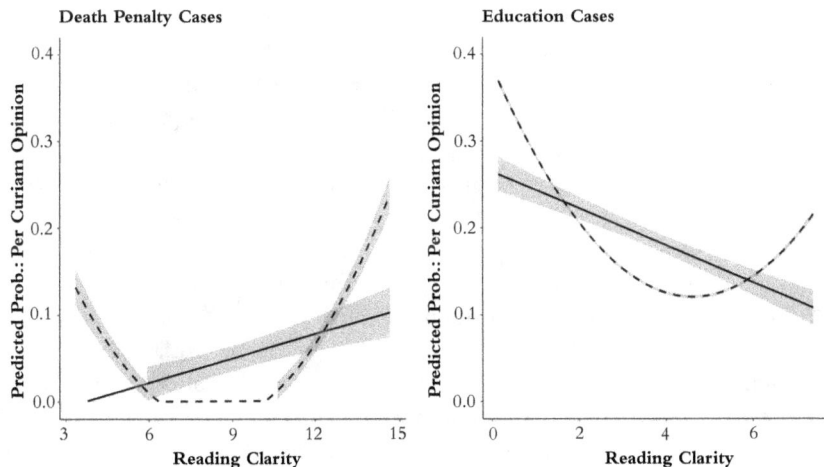

FIGURE 5.4   Predicted Probability of Per Curiam Opinion by Reading Clarity in Death Penalty and Education Cases

Figure Created by Authors

opinion is a fairly complex one. Particularly, in death penalty cases, there appears to be a distinct and substantively impactful curvilinear relationship between the reading clarity of an opinion and the likelihood of an opinion being submitted per curiam. When opinions are written using complicated language that might confuse external audiences and potentially serve to diminish the understanding of the opinion of the court, the likelihood of writing per curiam is 15.67%; however, as the clarity of the opinion shifts toward the median expected readability for such cases, this likelihood essentially drops to zero. Cases written with the average level of readability, within a standard deviation, have practically no likelihood of being written per curiam according to our findings for death penalty cases, indicating that judges writing for salient cases such as these find greater value in making their stances known to external audiences. We presume that the value in eschewing the option to write anonymously in these cases comes from the fact that judges see the value of attaching their names to what would otherwise be considered a "standard opinion" for the court and ensures that the court maintains accountability with retention constituencies by not attempting to hide behind anonymity. As the left-hand graph in Figure 5.4 shows, however, when judges go outside the standard expected margin for readability, the likelihood that the decision will be announced per curiam increases to a striking and substantially higher likelihood, increasing to a maximum of 24.60% when clarity is at its peak for death penalty cases. Thus, when opinions are written simply – indicative of an "easily disposed of" case with very little exposition on the meaning of law or the value of precedent – the attitude toward delivering opinions per curiam changes drastically according to our results. Judges in these circumstances appear to find little value in attaching their name to such an opinion, as the decision (in their minds) is so clear that little to no argument needs to be made, exemplifying the trade-off between persuasion and justification we have been arguing is inherent in judicial decision-making.

Comparatively, education cases take on a similar – thought not nearly as dramatic – curvilinear relationship. The most difficult to read cases have a substantially greater likelihood of being written per curiam when compared to the most clearly written education cases, with a maximum predicted probability of 37.93% for cases with the greatest amount of reading clarity. As opinions increase in the clarity of their language, the likelihood of writing per curiam decreases to a minimum of 12.71% for cases written with an average level of readability; however, the likelihood does trend upward in a similar fashion to what we find with death penalty cases, increasing to 23.35% for the most clearly written education opinions in our data.

Conclusions

The per curiam opinion can be thought of as the "multi-tool" of the judicial tool box: it has a lot to offer, with relatively few drawbacks. When used in conjunction with unanimous opinions, it further enforces the perception that it is *the* opinion of the court. When used in controversial topics, it provides anonymity to the author, and reduces the likelihood of retention-based retaliation. When used in relatively simple cases, it allows for brief, simple opinions that do not need significant exposition. As the per curiam opinion has a lot to offer not only opinion authors, but courts as a whole, it may seem shocking that they aren't utilized significantly more than they are.

Part of the reason why, as is a consistent finding of this book, has to do with the effect of external audiences. Judges in courts retained by public elections (partisan, non-partisan, or retention) are often at a battle for name recognition. Signed judicial opinions are among the few ways, outside of campaigning, that a sitting judge can increase name recognition. Even in salient cases, where having your name attached to an unpopular decision may have consequences, our data demonstrate that neither the direction of a decision, nor the salience of the issue has any effect on the likelihood of a per curiam opinion. A judge's external audience does.

Language choices also have an independent role to play in the likelihood of a per curiam opinion. In a salient policy area, such as the death penalty, as the decision in the case gets more complex, considering more and varied arguments, judges find the need to shield the majority opinion author in the cloak of anonymity. As the court works through complicated arguments in a salient policy area, a per curiam offers them protection from external audiences. Furthermore, we find a consistent relationship across death penalty and education cases regarding reading clarity. Texts that are very readable and texts that are exceedingly difficult are more likely to be published as per curiam opinions than those that are close to the median of reading clarity. In death penalty cases, the probability of a per curiam opinion at the median level of reading clarity is nearly zero.

The story of the per curiam opinion is not as easy as Thomas Jefferson would have you believe. They are not just "convenient for the lazy, the modest, and the incompetent" (in Markham 2006). They are a strategic tool which can be useful in numerous situations, and in an institution where every policy choice needs to be justified in writing, blinding the author of the opinion from the relevant external audience is a highly effective tactic. While per curiam opinions may mask dissensus behind a shield of institutional legitimacy, however, not all cases are decided in this way, and many cases are likely to end in bargaining breakdown. In the next chapter we consider this possibility more directly, particularly focusing on how opinions change when consensus fails, and judges vote non-unanimously.

Notes

1 Thomas Jefferson, most notably, emphasized a return to the practice of seriatim after the Marshall Court did away with the practice as a way to keep a "vigilant eye" on the Court. His contention against the practice of singular opinions written "by the Court" may have primarily been due to his loathing of John Marshall, however (see Urofsky 2017).

2 Technically, while these cases were decided and written in a fashion similar to that of the per curiam, the first "official usage" of the practice does not occur until the

mid-19th century. This correlates with changes in the practices and procedures of the courts in the United States, particularly as it pertains to collegiality and consensus on the bench.

3 We exclude the state of Florida for the analysis here and in the rest of this chapter, as it has an institutional tradition of writing all death penalty cases per curiam. Florida accounts for 911 cases in our death penalty dataset, with 96.71% of those opinions being coded as per curiam. As this substantially reduces the variability within the state, and significantly biases our dependent variable by artificially inflating the number of occurrences, we remove the state from our analysis. We do not find any significant impact from removing Florida from the analysis.

4 While we do find there is a significant correlation between the existence of an intermediate appellate court and the issuing of a per curiam opinion, the direction of the correlation is the opposite of what we would expect if the type of opinion was meant to increase efficiency. Theoretically, having an intermediate appellate court (IAC) should reduce the occurrence of per curiam opinions, however we find that the existence of an IAC is correlated with an increase in the use of per curiam opinions by the state high court (Chi^2 test = 57.479, p > .001). We find no significant correlation between per curiam opinions and discretionary jurisdiction in our data. Thus efficiency, from a workload perspective, may not be achieved by relying on the anonymous opinion per se. In the full models below, we control for discretionary jurisdiction and court professionalism in order to account for the potential for per curiam to act as a tool for efficiency nonetheless.

5 In this sense, we do find a correlation that we would expect. Death penalty cases do appear to have a significant, positive correlation with the use of per curiam opinions (Chi^2 = 51.192, p > 0.001), indicative that efficiency may be based more on priority than quick disposal.

6 While per curiam opinions certainly do see a diminished likelihood of secondary opinions (either concurrences or dissents) compared to authored opinions in our data subset, 30.35% of per curiam do still include secondary opinions along with the court's opinion.

7 While some states (such as Nevada in death penalty cases) have a fairly even distribution of signed and per curiam opinions, most have very few instances, and some states have zero instances of per curiam opinions in our data. Currently, to our knowledge there is no reliable method of accounting for rare events in multi-level models. While penalized multi-level logistic regressions show some promise for accounting for rare events, the computational requirements in order to train and test such a dataset is beyond the scope of our current data and will have to be considered by future work studying per curiam at the state level.

8 To ensure our findings were not being skewed due to decision direction in the case, we control for whether a judge is reversing the death penalty, and for robustness interacted decision direction with method of retention to determine if there was an effect. In the primary model, decision direction does not significantly impact the likelihood of writing per curiam, and the interaction has no substantive effect on the model.

9 On average, per curiam opinions do tend to be shorter in length compared to authored opinions in both death penalty and education cases. The average length for authored opinions in death penalty cases was 10,211 words, whereas per curiam opinions averaged 6,121 words. Authored education cases, on average, were 5,512 words in length, and decreased to 3,241 for per curiam opinions.

10 Per Curiam are often derided as being the "handmaiden of law clerks" (Nygaard 1994, pg. 50) and are generally assumed to be a symptomatic of increased workloads and an overburdened court docket; critiqued as a savvy shortcut to dispense with a case without giving it much thought or attention (Murray 2000). Based on our initial findings for writing style here, these accusations appear to be unfounded. We do find,

however, that as professionalism in the court increases, the likelihood of writing per curiam likewise increases in both death penalty and education cases. In contrast, having a discretionary docket decreases the likelihood of per curiam opinions in death penalty cases.

11 It is worth noting that these findings are robust, and not contingent on whether the case reverses a death penalty decision, nor on the salience of the frame being used in the decision. We find that the decision to reverse the death penalty does not independently affect the choice to write per curiam and interacting a reversal of the death penalty with our measure for complexity does not have a significant effect.

References

Baum, L. (2006). *Judges and Their Audiences: A Perspective on Judicial Behavior*. Princeton: Princeton University Press.

Bush v. Gore (2000), 531 U.S. 98.

Garner, B. A., & Black, H. C. (2014). *Black's Law Dictionary*. 10th ed. St. Paul: West.

Ginsburg, R. B. (1990). Remarks on Writing Separately. *Washington Law Review*, 65(1), 133–150.

Li, W., Azar, P., Larochelle, D., Hill, P., Cox, J., Berwick, R. C., & Lo, A. W. (2013). Using Algorithmic Attribution Techniques to Determine Authorship in Unsigned Judicial Opinions. *Stanford Technology Law Review*, 16(3), 503–534.

Markham, J. (2006). Against Individually Signed Judicial Opinions. *Duke Law Journal*, 56(3), 923–952.

Masood, A. S., & Songer, D. R. (2013). Reevaluating the Implications of Decision-Making Models: The Role of Summary Decisions in U.S. Supreme Court Analysis. *Journal of Law and Courts*, 1(2), 363–389.

Mesa v. United States (1862), 67 U.S. 721.

Murray, P. L. (2000). Maine's Overburdened Law Court: Has the Time Come for a Maine Appeals Court? *Maine Law Review*, 52, 43–80.

New Orleans City Park Improvement Ass'n v. Detiege (1955), 358 U.S. 891

Nygaard, R. L. (1994). The Maligned Per Curiam: A Fresh Look at an Old Colleague. *Scribes Journal of Legal Writing*, 5, 41–50.

Popkin, W. D. (2007). *Evolution of the Judicial Opinion: Institutional and Individual Styles*. New York: New York University Press.

Posner, R. A. (1995). *Overcoming Law*. Cambridge, MA: Harvard University Press.

Radin, M. (1930). The Requirement of Written Opinions. *California Law Review*, 18(5), 486–496.

Ray, L. R. (2002). The History of the Per Curiam Opinion: Consensus and Individual Expression on the Supreme Court. *Journal of Supreme Court History*, 27(2), 176–193.

Robbins, I. P. (2012). Hiding Behind the Cloak of Invisibility: The Supreme Court and Per Curiam Opinions. *Tulane Law Review*, 86(6), 1197–1242.

Urofsky, M. I. (2017). *Dissent and the Supreme Court: Its Role in the Court's History and the Nation's Constitutional Dialogue*. New York, NY: Vantage Books.

Wasby, S. L., Peterson, S., Schubert, J., & Schubert, G. (1992). The Per Curiam Opinion: Its Nature and Functions. *Judicature*, 76(1), 29–38.

6

THE POLITICAL RAMIFICATIONS OF OPINION CONTENT

Unanimity and Strategic Writing

"The course of every tribunal must necessarily be, that the opinion which is delivered as the opinion of the court, is previously submitted to the judges; and, if any of the reasoning be disapproved, it must be so modified as to receive the approbation of all, before it can be delivered as the opinion of all."

Chief Justice John Marshall (1819)

The written opinion is a device that serves multiple purposes when it is published, but our interest in this chapter places primacy on what takes place just before publication. Within the study of judicial politics, it is well demonstrated that bargaining occurs on high courts as the majority opinion takes shape and all the way to the announcement of a decision (Cross and Tiller 1998; Hettinger, Lindquist and Martinek 2006; Kim 2009; Maltzman, Spriggs and Wahlbeck 2000; Murphy 1973; Van Winkle 1997). Judges debate what points of law should be focused on, elaborated, and even removed. Furthermore, we know such bargaining influences how likely an individual judge will be to join the majority opinion, and whether judges choose to write separately in the form of concurrences or dissents. It can influence the pivotal member to remain with the majority opinion, or, more central to our inquiry, entice even more judges to sign on.

In the previous chapters we examined what causes justices to focus on certain frames, how a dissent effects the majority opinion's language, and if per curiam opinions are written in a different fashion than signed opinions, but this chapter does not attempt to predict differences in the written word. Here, we switch gears and instead use the written word to predict unanimity. We believe that variations in majority opinions are interesting in their own regard, as this book is dedicated to understanding them, but this chapter examines a perennial topic in judicial politics: what influences the likelihood of a unanimous decision.

We believe that as individuals bargain over opinion language, the number of viewpoints considered in the opinion should increase, leading judges to write in more complex ways and compelling judges to focus specifically on writing persuasively, rather than simply justifying their choices to the rest of the bench. As a result of this focus and the added complexity of bargaining, we expect that opinions that exhibit greater bargaining should likewise be longer and thus require stronger reading comprehension on the part of peripheral audiences compared to opinions that have a minimum winning coalition. The trade-off here is that by prioritizing indicators of persuasiveness in the opinion over justification, judges may increase the size of the winning coalition, which should better insulate them from backlash from retention audiences. We assume that this bargaining will result in more complex opinions, and this added degree of complexity should increase the likelihood of a unanimous decision.

While this at first blush, may seem contradictory to our findings in Chapter 4 recording the likelihood of a dissent, they are consistent. Complexity increases when bargaining occurs. A published dissent represents a failure in bargaining, but the effects should still be present in the majority opinion. We know that dissents are more likely to occur when the opinion is complex, and this is a signal of when bargaining has failed. However, bargaining that doesn't fail should produce a unanimous opinion as well. In this chapter, we focus on predicting unanimous cases, which means by definition, the bargaining was successful. Still, the causal factor in both Chapter 4 and here is the increased likelihood of complexity because of the nature of linguistic bargaining over the content of the majority opinion.

To this point, we have primarily focused on the individual attributes that may impact the language of the opinion, and particularly how linguistic choices are affected by changes and affect formal decisions in judicial opinions. While some strategic motivations have received attention (such as the role of dissents and choice to publicly defect from the majority), we have yet to fully uncover how the bench itself may impact majority authors and their writing. Judges wish to see their opinions hold the weight of law (Baum 2006; Murphy 1973; Segal and Spaeth 1992, 2002), though in order to successfully translate their thoughts and ideas into precedent they must have the backing of their colleagues as well. As our theory dictates, the strength of a judicial opinion is, in part, based upon just how firmly the Court acts as a cohesive bloc in both voting and agreement on the language of the opinion. As the other judges on a court are the first degree of separation in our model of judicial target audience dispersion (see Chapter 2), any division that occurs should invite further disagreement as the opinion of the court disseminates through other layers. In the worst case, such divisions eventually make their way to external audiences responsible for retaining judges, inviting controversy in the next retention phase. We believe that this will lead some judges, dependent upon the methods by which they are retained and the issue being decided, to engage in greater collective bargaining within the branch in order to ensure protection, and this bargaining will become apparent within the language of the opinion itself.[1]

The Importance of Unanimous Decisions

Our inquiry to this point has focused on understanding variations in the content of majority opinions. Connected with the opinion, however, is the decisional output represented by the direction of the decision and the size of the majority coalition. While research on state courts has discovered several interesting findings concerning how judges make decisions (Langer 2002; Hall 1998; Hall and Brace 1992; Leonard 2014), very little theory has focused on coalition building (but see Leonard and Ross 2014). Studies of coalition building at the federal level have yielded some findings that will help to motivate how we think judges on state supreme courts should behave in this arena.

Early research on the Supreme Court argued that majority coalition size was merely a function of the ideology of the members of the Court (Prichett 1948; Segal and Spaeth 1992). It was thought that justices of the Court would have little motivation to engage in strategic behavior, preferring to behave attitudinally, because their institution was shielded by the Constitution. Murphy (1964) counters this line of thinking by noting numerous situations where justices might behave strategically, voting against their sincere ideology because they desire to maximize other goals (see also Baum 2006; Spriggs, Maltzman, and Wahlbeck 1999; 2002). Some of the most convincing evidence that justices would actively attempt to court a majority coalition larger than a minimum winning coalition comes from Ulmer (1971) which documents the extensive lengths Chief Just Earl Warren went to in order to maintain a unanimous decision in *Brown v. Board of Education* (1954). According to Justice Harold H. Burton's papers, after oral arguments, Warren faced a 6–3 vote coming out of conference. Chief Justice Warren desperately wanted a unanimous decision because of the importance of the issue being considered, and actively lobbied members of the Court in the minority. Furthermore, and central to our inquiry here, he *purposely* wrote the opinion in such a way as to convince those who were initially in dissent to join the majority coalition.

What exactly impacts the size of the majority coalition? Previous studies of judicial voting behavior have posited several theories to explain coalition formation, all of which emphasize bargaining over content of the opinion as the primary motivation. Underlying judicial decision-making, according to Spriggs, Maltzman, and Wahlbeck (1999), is the simple fact that no judge may act unilaterally, and thus all judges must engage in strategic behavior and bargaining to some degree in order to achieve their goals while on the bench. Many scholars argue that there is considerable institutional pressure at work to foster greater unanimity within the judiciary (Baum 1997; Caldeira and Wright 1988; Lax 1996; Rhode 1972). Chief among these pressures is the role of institutional integrity and legitimacy. Institutional legitimacy is vital to American courts in particular, as it assures the court may wield the force of law and achieve the policy goals of the individual justices despite the court's shaky foundation in representative democracy. This means courts are conscious of their position within the greater governmental structure and undertake very specific behaviors to maintain their legitimacy in the eyes of the public.

What is often confounding within discussions of coalition formation on the court is attempting to reconcile occurrences of unanimous decisions with bare minimum majorities. Unanimous opinions by their very nature act as a signal of consensus to the public. While it may not be the case that the decision was ideologically sincere or the result of bargaining, unanimous opinions tend to invoke the mechanical nature of the law rather than any type of ideological decision-making. This, it is assumed, should insulate the Court from backlash. If there is a low likelihood of backlash, however, opinion authors may not pursue anything beyond a minimum winning coalition. If the decision in the case will alter precedent on a salient issue, it should be to the opinion author's benefit to consider the desire of those in the conference minority and modify how the opinion is written.[2] Because of this, courts may engage in more opinion language bargaining when either 1) they want the decision to have more weight and thus be more likely to have the desired effect, 2) the issue is salient and the justices want to prevent backlash or, 3) they are facing an external threat (Rehnquist 1996, Mason 1956, Seddig 1975).

At the state level, evaluations of the role of institutional integrity, coalition formation, and judicial decision-making are often subsumed by the debate over accountability and independence (but see Leonard and Ross 2014). Implicit in the arguments made by authors debating the importance of these concepts is a normative belief that the integrity of the judiciary is in some way tied to how judges are selected and retained. The literature on judicial selection has paid particular attention to whether retention systems – specifically merit selection – are better able to produce "quality judges," able to make legal decisions without succumbing to political pressure (Gill 2010; Gill, Lazos and Waters 2011; Goelzhauser 2014; Hall 2011). Empirical study of institutional variation tends to come up short in stating definitively that any single system is able to produce a "quality judge," and there is still substantial debate over what this term might imply (see Goelzhauser 2014 in particular for further discussion). Evidence does indicate, however, that judges are likely to exhibit strategic behavior in different ways depending on how they are retained (Curry and Hurwitz 2016). Competitive elections have been shown to impact the judicial ideology of the bench (Curry and Romano 2018), as well as the rationale for vote choice in salient cases (Brace and Boyea 2008; Brace and Hall 1997; Hall 1987; 1992; 2007). Judges in elite appointment systems are less likely to use judicial review to overturn laws (Langer 2002), while judges in both elite appointment systems and retention election systems are more likely to retire when they can be replaced with an ideologically similar judge (Curry and Hurwitz 2016).

As the central tool of the majority, it makes sense that another logical place where strategic behavior will be apparent is within the majority opinion. The crafting of the opinion is shaped through the deliberative process (Spriggs, Maltzman and Wahlbeck 1999; Maltzman, Spriggs and Wahlbeck 2000). We should expect, therefore, that the final resulting language of the opinion will show traces of this process when it is presented to the various legal, public, and political audiences who may come into contact with the court's ruling and are important for judicial retention at the state level. Judges must be conscious of these audiences and their colleagues as they write and refine the majority opinion, which should inevitably lead to trade-offs in language and the emphasis on particular arguments. As Murphy (1964, 57) notes, "a justice must learn not only how to put pressure on his colleagues but how to gauge what amounts of pressure are sufficient to be 'effective' and what amounts to overshoot the mark and alienate another judge." Scholars have noted that judges struggle with balancing the desire to institute clear, coherent policy via the opinion when faced with the diverse ideological preferences of the bench (Staton and Vanberg 2008; see also Cray 1997; Schwartz 1983; Ulmer 1971). This process should be even more complex in the absence of life tenure which is the environment in which most state court justices exist. By bargaining with the opinion content, judges may therefore find a way to balance institutional pressure and prestige with the desire to achieve policy goals (Staton and Vanberg 2008).

Collegial Bargaining and Language Choice

At the heart of understanding collegial bargaining in the judiciary or other collective bodies responsible for decision-making is understanding just how multiple voices are translated into a singular opinion or choice. The language used to set precedent is often viewed as a cohesive statement of all the judges involved. By signing on to an opinion, judges essentially state "I have nothing more to add" to the language used to persuade and justify a judicial choice; however, we know that the process of crafting opinions is not so simplistic. Along with being a strategic body, courts are also a deliberative one, and as such we should expect that the language of an opinion and the final majority coalition to be affected by deliberative bargaining as well. Deliberative bargaining is an expectation of democratic politics generally, and the structure of the judiciary makes it a necessary requirement in order for a decision to be reached. As Benhabib (1996, 69) notes, governing institutions are arranged so that "what is considered in the common interest of all results from processes of collective deliberation conducted rationally and fairly among free and equal individuals." The emphasis in deliberation is often on the coming to agreement between individuals as a result of the presentation of arguments and ideas. Implicitly in these accounts is the process by which parties come to agree. Judges, attempting to reach a decision, engage in this process through the opinion writing and opinion sharing process, which results in a final written document presented by the court. According to Cohen (1996, 100), in political deliberation such as this, "participants regard one another as equals; they aim to defend and criticize institutions and programs in terms of considerations that others have reason to accept . . . and they are prepared to cooperate in accordance with the results of such deliberation treating those results as authoritative." Descriptions of this process in the judiciary abound (Baum 2006; Hettinger, Lindquist and Martinek 2006; Murphy 1973; Maltzman, Spriggs and Wahlbeck 2000; Popkin 2007; Rhode 1972), all of which detail in some way how the crafting of opinions is dependent in part on bargaining and compromise. To achieve some modicum of agreement, therefore, we should generally expect individuals participating in deliberation to engage in bargaining in order to get the most favorable outcome to their preferences. This is what separates "deliberation" and decision-making, from simple "argumentation."

We question what this process of deliberation might look like, and what we should expect from the ends of such deliberation (in this case, the majority opinion). We start with the general belief that crafting judicial opinions is an iterative and deliberate processes, wherein a group of judges are tasked with making a moral choice between alternatives in order to resolve a dispute. According to Guttman and Thompson (1996), deliberation and the act of deliberative decision-making requires that the group itself exercise reciprocity in laying claims to arguments; or rather to "appeal only to reasons or principles that potentially can be shared by others" (Walhof 2005, 156). This exercise in reciprocity is important to understanding the role of coordination in majority opinion crafting, as it is an indicator of how judges as authors find compromise amongst often ideologically distinct cohorts. Deliberative procedures like the collegial "game", believed by scholars to be the heart of judicial opinion crafting, emphasize such reciprocity by following what Benhabib (1996) describes as "practical rationality." Beyond free contestation and deliberation of issues, central to practical rationality is the ability of actors to freely express multiple arguments in order to evaluate what judgements and opinions may need revision, and that decisions made can be challenged publicly. In the judicial system, as cases climb through the appellate process the focus and level of disagreement between parties intensify, the stakes get higher, and the precedent's shadow longer compared to the trial or intermediate appellate level. The role of the final opinion is to find resolution to this conflict, while striking a balance regarding the legitimacy of the claims from both parties.

In his ground-breaking work on majority coalitions on the U.S. Supreme Court, Rhode (1972) found that while justices engage in bargaining at the opinion writing stage of the process, they are generally concerned only with gaining a minimum-winning coalition. This, however, can be modified by the presence of an external threat to the Court's decision-making. For the U.S. Supreme Court, the nature of these external threats generally comes in the form of court curbing legislation. When these threats exist, the Court will be increasingly likely to make decisions with a larger majority coalition size. Generally, however, the only threats which the Court faces are legislative attempts to restrict their jurisdiction in certain types of cases. Members of the U.S. Supreme Court are exceedingly insulated because of the constitutional protections that shield them from most external threats.

State courts of last resort, however, exist in an environment with varying external threats, largely as a function of their degree of judicial independence. While justices on the U.S. Supreme Court are institutionally protected and thus must only truly fear jurisdictional restrictions from the legislature, Leonard (2016) notes that state courts with a high degree of judicial independence, namely courts that retain their judges either through retention elections or elite appointment, will experience a higher likelihood of court curbing legislation. Within these institutions, we should expect judges to be more likely to engage in opinion bargaining to increase the size of the majority coalition towards unanimity to insulate them from institutional attacks. This makes sense, as we have previously found in Chapter 5 that judges will consider the method by which the opinion is delivered, with judges in retention election states being much more likely to submit opinions per curiam compared to other systems when deciding death penalty cases in particular; a finding that is only increased when we consider how the opinion is framed. Judges residing on courts that are retained by contested elections must consider an entirely different audience when they decide cases. Their audience does not reside in the governor's mansion or the state legislature but are legal practitioners and the electorate. When the majority opinion author is writing for this audience, they will be less likely to engage in language bargaining beyond what is needed to maintain a majority coalition. Indeed, Leonard and Ross (2014) find that judges retained via contested elections are much more likely that those in retention election systems or elite reappointment systems to write separately through a dissent or concurrence.

- Hypothesis 1: States that utilize contested elections to retain their judges will be more likely to decide cases non-unanimously.

The institutional components of the court should go a long way toward motivating judges to seek larger coalitions based upon their desired goals. With these institutional components in mind, we believe that the communicative components of the opinion should likewise have a direct impact on the likelihood of the court reaching consensus. Particularly, following our findings in Chapter 3 and based upon previous discussions of coalition building thus far, we believe that opinion framing is impacted by the desire to form consensus and appease members of the court as well as external audiences. As such, we assume that this desire to accommodate should affect the consistency with which a frame is applied relative to other communicative and institutional elements that may drive coalition formation and increase the probability of a unanimous decision. As we found in previous chapters, there exist several options when framing decisions. While some frames may be dependent on contextual components of the case, we believe that given the broad nature of the most common frame types we find in judicial opinions, judges have a wide range to accommodate others when crafting the opinion. As a result, judges must consider which of the available frames will be most likely to be accepted by their colleagues, while simultaneously considering how broader audiences may react to a chosen frame. We argue that the consistency with which a judge adheres to a single, dominant frame (as calculated in Chapter 3) will therefore substantively impact the likelihood of seeing a non-unanimous decision. Specifically, greater frame dominance is indicative that the opinion author feels strongly that their choice is the correct choice, and as such will likely increase the likelihood of seeing a non-unanimous decision.

- Hypothesis 2: Single frame dominance, measured by frame consistency used by the majority, will increase the likelihood of a non-unanimous decision.

Along with frame dominance in the majority opinion, we believe that the emphasis placed on *particularly salient frames of argument* should likewise have a substantial effect on the ability of the opinion to form a cohesive majority and avoid a non-unanimous decision. As we discovered in our analysis of per curiam opinions in Chapter 5, the salience of an opinion frame can have consequences for the way in which the majority opinion is delivered to various audiences within the states. Judges, we assume, ought to be more willing to sign on to majority opinions that avoid frames that may seem controversial in order to avoid backlash by external audiences such as the greater legal community, the public, or other branches of government. Opinions which therefore rely on frames that might stoke the flames of debate should cause other judges on the bench to disassociate themselves from the majority by either writing a concurrence or dissenting. While this may at times be unavoidable, we nevertheless believe that the use of salient case frames will impact the likelihood of a non-unanimous decision. Particularly, salient frames that have the potential to result in some kind of backlash from external audiences should increase the likelihood of a non-unanimous decisions, whereas the reliance on more technical, less salient frames should be more likely to generate broader consensus amongst members of the court. As a control, we also interact the use of a salient frame with the consistency of its use in the majority opinion. While the use of a salient frame should increase the chances of a non-unanimous decision on its own, we believe that greater dominance of such frames should have the opposing effect of decreasing the likelihood of a non-unanimous decision. We argue that this is likely an indication of judges rallying around the institution in particular cases where the decision's future relies heavily on utilizing the court's institutional integrity in order to wield judicial power effectively. Thus, we break our hypotheses for frame salience and its interaction with frame dominance as follows:

- Hypothesis 3: Salient opinion frames will be more likely to occur in non-unanimous cases.
- Hypothesis 4: Consistent use of a salient frame will decrease the likelihood of a non-unanimous decision.

Finally, frame salience may also be based upon the expectations that judges have concerning external audiences within the state. Judges in states that have a closer connection to audiences outside of government, primarily through the use of contested elections, should be more likely to defect when the majority chooses controversial or otherwise salient frames in the writing of the opinion. Judges in state courts who rely on maintaining some connection with the audiences responsible for their retention are more likely to exhibit greater ideological congruence when making decisions. This should likewise translate to the framing of a decision as well. We suspect that judges in states that make maintaining ideological congruence between the judiciary and the public more difficult, such as states that utilize non-partisan, elite reappointment or retention elections, will be more likely to have judges defect from the majority when the case frame is considered salient (Curry and Romano 2018). In order to test this assumption, we interact frame salience with method of retention used in the state. Like our assumptions in Hypothesis 1, we presume that judges in states that utilize mechanisms which interrupt the representational link between judges and the electorate will be more likely to write non-unanimously when the majority focuses specifically on salient or controversial case frames.[3]

- Hypothesis 5: States that insulate judges from representative politics through their methods of retention will increase the likelihood of non-unanimous decisions when the majority writes using salient frames.

Language choices should also be indicative of broader coalition-building and could be a key indicator of strategic bargaining over the content of the decision. There is no doubt that the judicial opinion is a titular tool in the exercise of judicial power, and it follows that judges will attempt to work strategically to manipulate the language in the opinion in order to meet their goals. While the opinion is generally highlighted as being the legal thought of the singular opinion author, this does not mean that their words are theirs alone. Other judges must sign off on the rationale, and this allows non-writing judges to insert themselves into the opinion-writing process by making requests for particular language to be included by the opinion author (see Maltzman, Spriggs, and Wahlbeck 2000). We believe that this will inevitably lead to trade-offs in the use of justification and persuasive language in the opinion, as judges work to hold together coalitions through their word choice. Writing in this way is not as simple as it may appear at first glance, however, and presents a unique "Goldilocks problem" for judges writing for the court. We suspect that judges work diligently to maintain just the right balance between justifying their decisions to both their colleagues and external audiences and attempting to persuade these groups into agreeing with their rationale. Thus, we presume that there exist curvilinear relationships for the primary mechanisms of justification (specifically language clarity measured through readability) and persuasion (measured by the cognitive complexity of the argument presented). We feel that prioritizing mechanisms of justification in language – strong analytic writing and increased language clarity – is a signal that judges are attempting to control for coalition breakdown in the absence of a unanimous decision. Clear, simple language should be most likely in a non-unanimous opinion, where the author must attempt to explain that their rationale is the only legitimate choice, as discussed in Chapter 2. This effect should be mitigated, however, by instances when all judges agree that the institutional integrity of the branch may be damaged if consensus is not reached in a unanimous decision. In these cases, we expect that the use of justification in the language of the majority opinion will result in a decreased likelihood of a non-unanimous decision.

- Hypothesis 6: As linguistic mechanisms of justification (analytic language and language clarity) increase, the likelihood of a non-unanimous decision will increase.
- Hypothesis 7: The likelihood of a non-unanimous decision will be at its lowest when readability is at its lowest or highest, indicative of a curvilinear relationship.

The Goldilocks dilemma inherent in writing the majority opinion may not extend only to attempts to justify decisions. We suspect that judges will also attempt to strike a balance in their use of persuasion while writing the final opinion in an attempt to draw in their colleagues and bolster institutional support. Following this, when judges shift from justification to persuasion, we believe that this is an indication that the opinion author is attempting to reach out and build greater support in order to protect the decision and the court from any potential backlash from external audiences. Such attempts will likely strain the majority opinion author as they attempt to work through the different perspectives in their decision and try to integrate the request of their colleagues into a cohesive statement. This should inevitably lead to greater emphasis on authentic language signals, as well as increased cognitive complexity as judges attempt to integrate different arguments into a cohesive whole. Judges must be careful not to alienate more ideologically distinct judges on the bench, which should inevitably lead to a curvilinear relationship, similar to what we suspect to be present with justifying language as well.

- Hypothesis 8: As persuasive indicators (authentic language and cognitive complexity) increase, the likelihood of a non-unanimous decision will decrease.
- Hypothesis 9: The likelihood of a non-unanimous decision will be at its lowest when cognitive complexity is at its lowest or highest, indicating a curvilinear relationship.

Language Bargaining and the Breakdown of Unanimity in Majority Opinions

We are particularly interested in examining the intricacies of coalition-building in state courts. As such, we begin our analysis by examining why unanimity may dissolve and how institutional factors such as method of retention and the language of the majority opinion may mitigate or exacerbate coalition breakdown. To examine such events, we model the data using a multi-level logistic regression, using the occurrence of non-unanimous opinions as the dependent variable. We choose to model the likelihood of a non-unanimous opinion in this chapter because our assumptions are based on how majority authors put forward some strategic effort in order to maintain the majority coalition. While not necessarily a rare event, non-unanimous decisions are less likely to occur in our data compared to unanimous decisions, as show in Figure 6.1. For death penalty cases, non-unanimous decisions occur in 31.62% of the data, and 28.11% of the time in education cases.

Beginning with our hypotheses concerning methods of retention, we find that retention mechanisms affect the likelihood of unanimous decisions in salient (death penalty) cases. As we see in Figure 6.2, in education cases the method of retention does not substantively impact the likelihood of a non-unanimous decision directly. Interestingly, this finding and our findings for death penalty cases provide some evidence to indicate that systems that seek to depoliticize the judiciary by masking partisanship are most likely to decide cases non-unanimously. As the results for death penalty cases in Figure 6.2 show, states using partisan elections to retain judges have the lowest likelihood of writing non-unanimous decisions, with a predicted probability of 21.86%. Simply masking partisanship through the use of non-partisan elections increases the predicted probability that the court will decide a case non-unanimously to 41.22%, an increase of 19.36% in our model. On the opposite end of the spectrum, states that utilize elite appointment to retain the bench are 57.89% likely to decide cases non-unanimously. Finally, retention elections likewise increase the probability that the court will decide cases non-unanimously compared to partisan systems, though not nearly as substantially as non-partisan elections or elite appointments. For retention

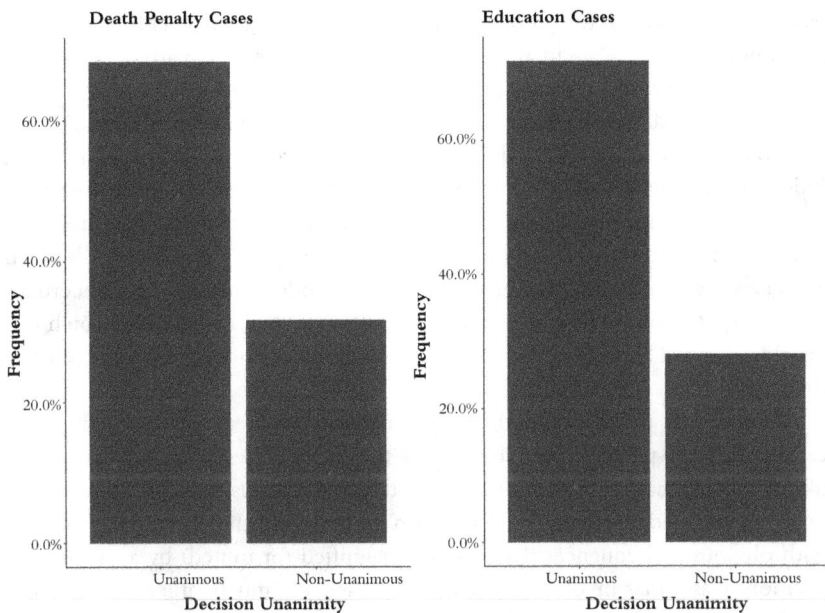

FIGURE 6.1 Frequency of Unanimous and Non-Unanimous Decisions in Death Penalty and Education Cases

Figure Created by Authors

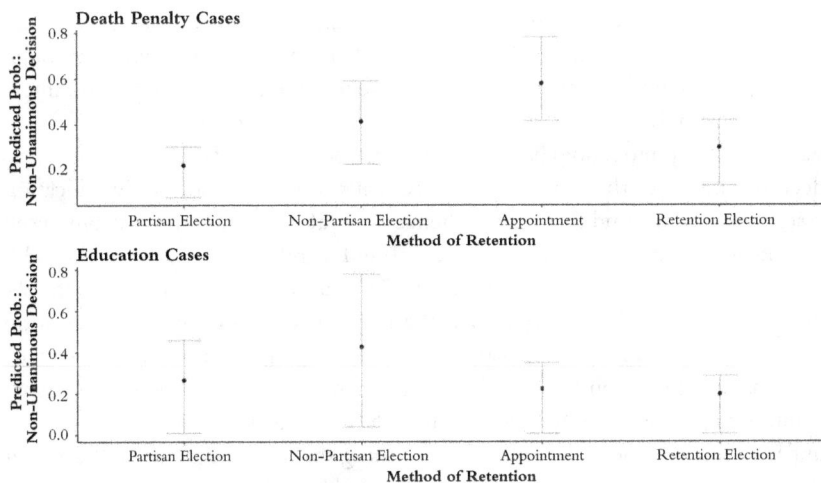

FIGURE 6.2 Predicted Probability of Non-Unanimous Decision in Death Penalty Cases based on Method of Retention

Figure Created by Authors

elections, we find that the predicted probability the court will decide a case non-unanimously is 29.67%, an increase of 7.81% compared to partisan elections. This finding is interesting and cannot be overstated. In death penalty cases, when controlling for ideology, the system which is most likely to have non-unanimous decisions is a system in which the public plays no direct role: elite appointment. Judges in states where the connection with the electorate is less strong are much more likely to engage in debate, which leads to non-unanimous decisions. This can be problematic, particularly for institutional integrity. Decisions can be seen as signals that the court is at best unable to provide clear answers concerning policy disputes, or at worst is symptomatic of ideological in-fighting, which can provide external audiences with an outlet to rationalize removing a judge from the bench.

We feel that there is something systematically different between education cases and death penalty cases that mutes the effect of selection system on the likelihood of unanimous opinions. The death penalty is a highly salient, and relatively consistent area of law. A decision for or against the death penalty comes with obvious consequences that may be magnified (or muted) by a unanimous decision. Cases that involve education range across a much larger area of jurisprudence: they include budget concerns to tenure decisions. This means that not only are the vast number of opinions salient to very few, the law is less settled and less consistent. If the area of law is not salient to a retention constituency, then there is less of a reason to pursue a unanimous decision. While certain types of education decisions may be salient to particular constituencies, that we find no effect across the methods of retention likely speaks to the overall lack of salience to any specific retention audience.

The method of retention modifies who the external audiences are, for whom the opinion is written, and judges are more likely to attempt bargaining through the majority opinion in cases where issue salience and method of retention intersect. Interestingly, we find that case issue salience, measured by the use of salient frames in the opinion, does have an impact on the likelihood of a non-unanimous decision, however this is present only in *non-salient cases* (specifically education cases). That is, we find that frame salience is significant when the case type itself is non-salient, and results in a substantial and significant decrease in the odds of receiving a non-unanimous decision. This amounts to an approximate 5% decrease in the predicted probability of a non-unanimous decision in education cases where the framing of the case may be salient. While this finding is substantively small and in contrast with our initial expectations in Hypothesis 5, what is interesting is how frame salience interacts with other variables that may also impact non-unanimous decisions. Our running theory throughout has been that writing style and language choice are predicated by judges attempting to appease explicitly or predict implicitly what external audiences want to hear. If that is the case, then variations in the framing of decisions ought to be conditioned by the methods of retention used to maintain the bench, as this will be the best, most constant constraint placed upon a judge when writing a decision. It follows, given the unique findings for frame salience on its own, that we should expect that judges rallying around a majority opinion many be affected not only by the salience of the case itself (that is, whether it is a death penalty case or education case in our data), but also by the salience of the opinion frame as well. As Figure 6.3 shows, we find that taking frame salience into account in this way has a distinctly unique effect on the likelihood of a non-unanimous decision in both death penalty and education cases. In death penalty cases, we find that frame salience actually increases the odds of deciding non-unanimously in all methods except partisan elections, which follows from our initial hypothesis. Judges in states that utilize partisan elections recognize that they must speak to passionate publics when making decisions. When the court must not only decide a salient case but also must decide using a salient frame for their decision, we should expect that judges will rally around the bench in order to protect institutional integrity, thus decreasing the likelihood the court will decide non-unanimously. We find that, in partisan election systems, the predicted probability that the court will decide non-unanimously when the majority opinion focuses on a salient case frame decreases by 3.93% compared to non-salient frames. For all other methods of retention, utilizing a salient frame in order to reach a decision has the effect of increasing the predicted probability the court will decide

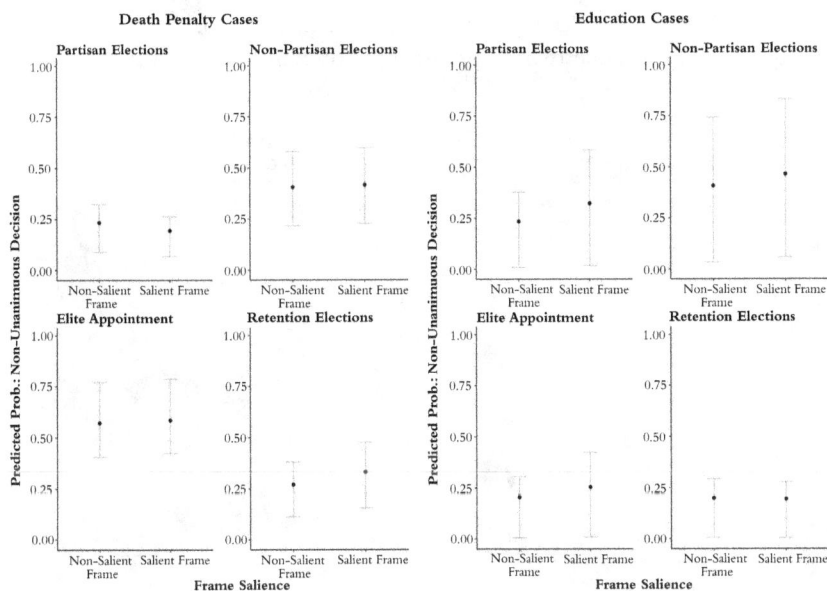

FIGURE 6.3 Predicted Probability of Non-Unanimous Decisions in Death Penalty and Education Cases by Method of Retention and Frame Salience

Figure Created by Authors

non-unanimously; increasing by 1.15% in states that use non-partisan elections, 1.32% in states using elite appointments, and 6.10% for retention election systems. That the effect is so pronounced in states which use retention elections is not shocking. Judges are very rarely removed from office in retention elections, even when they are ideologically out of step with their constituency. Interestingly, when we look at the differences between salient and non-salient cases themselves, we find that the only method of retention to significantly impact the likelihood of a non-unanimous decision when interacted with opinion frame salience is retention elections, although the finding is substantively small in magnitude, resulting in a decrease in the predicted probability that the court will decide non-unanimously of 0.40%.

As previously discussed in Chapter 3, judges may utilize multiple frames when writing an opinion in order to account for case complexities. While the dominant frame of the opinion may act as a signal to external audiences and may assist or hinder the ability of the majority to rally, the consistency with which the majority opinion adheres to the frame will show how resolute the majority is that their decision is based on a singular, distinct set of circumstances. Frame consistency, however, is a double-edged sword as it allows the majority to firmly justify their choice as the singular, correct choice, but also risks alienating judges who may view things differently, increasing the chances of concurrences and dissents. As we see in Figure 6.4, increasing the dominance of a frame on its own has a strong and positive effect on the likelihood of the court deciding non-unanimously. For death penalty cases, cases that did not extensively utilize a single dominant frame (where a single opinion frame was actively utilized in

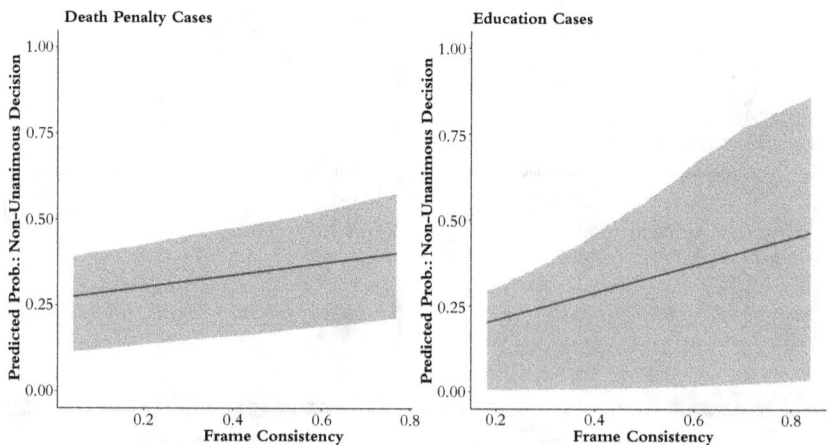

FIGURE 6.4 Predicted Probability of Non-Unanimous Decision by Frame Use Consistency in Death Penalty and Education Cases

Figure Created by Authors

below 22% of the total opinion), the predicted probability of a non-unanimous decision was 30.56%. When the opinion maximized the use of a singular frame (in our data, the maximum frame consistency was 76.91%), the predicted probability of a non-unanimous decision went up to 40.31%, an increase of 9.75%. Death penalty cases, due to their salience with external audiences such as interest groups, the media, and the public, are likely to exhibit greater levels of conflict from the bench, as judges attempt to work within various institutional and ideological constraints. Education cases, in contrast, provide judges with more freedom to disagree without risking clear ideological signals to external audiences. As a result, as we see in Figure 6.4, the magnitude of the effect for frame consistency on the likelihood of a non-unanimous decision is much greater for these non-salient cases. When the majority only uses the dominant frame a bare minimum of the time (in our data, the minimum frame consistency for education data was 18.12%), the likelihood of a non-unanimous decision was 20.71%. Utilizing the dominant frame to an average degree (40.44% in our data) increased the predicted probability to 33.28%. When the court's opinion was determined almost solely on the basis of a single frame (the maximum for our data was 84.02% frame consistency in education cases), the likelihood of a non-unanimous decision increased to a total of 45.75%, an increase of 25.04% from the minimum and 12.47% from the average.

Recall that we initially assumed that frame consistency may interact with frame salience in ways that will cause judges to trade off between ideological goals and institutional integrity. Given our findings so far, we suspect that these trade-offs will vary in death penalty and education cases, as judges may find unique opportunities to satisfy policy goals without being troubled by claims of ideological bias dependent on how the opinion is framed and on the salience of the case itself. As such, we suspect that in education cases, using a single, salient frame will likely increase the probability of a non-unanimous decision; a signal that judges are utilizing the opinion to push a distinctive policy goal with external audiences. Alternatively, in death penalty cases single frame dominance when interacted with frame salience should have the opposing effect, decreasing the likelihood of a non-unanimous decision as judges attempt to rally around the institution in order to protect its legitimacy by standing with the majority opinion. Figure 6.5 confirms these beliefs. The most striking difference between death penalty and education cases, based on our analysis, is the differential effect of salience on frame dominance and the likelihood of a non-unanimous decision. In death penalty cases, as judges utilize non-salient frames more consistently, the marginal effect on the predicted probability of a non-unanimous decision increases by 0.24%. This indicates that when judges believe that external audiences will be less likely to notice a death penalty decision being made, they are more likely to disagree with one another as they sort out their decision. When a single non-salient frame is used exclusively over others in an opinion, the likelihood of a non-unanimous decision is 44.31%, whereas diminishing the overall

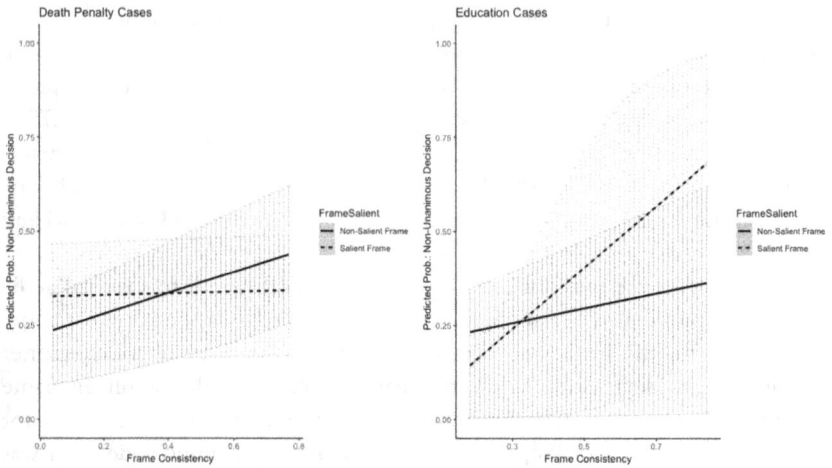

FIGURE 6.5   Predicted Probability of Non-Unanimous Decision by Frame Use Consistency and Frame Salience in Death Penalty and Education Cases

Figure Created by Authors

reliance of a single frame in a decision decreases this probability to a minimum of 24.20%. In contrast, consistent opinion framing for death penalty cases when the decision frame is salient does not appear to have a substantial effect on the probability of a non-unanimous decision. As we argue, this is likely due to the recognition by the court that when external audiences are more likely to pay attention to the decision, judges tend to be reticent about appearing to disagree with their colleagues. When frame consistency is minimized in these cases, the probability of a non-unanimous decision is 32.73%. When a single frame dominates such cases, however, the probability of a non-unanimous decision increases only to 34.34%, an overall increase of just 1.61%. We find almost the exact opposite effect occurs when we examine education cases, however. According to our findings, when judges use non-salient frames in deciding an education case, an increase in the frame consistency increases by one unit the predicted probability of a non-unanimous decision increases by just 0.161%. When frame consistency is at its greatest in such cases, the probability of a non-unanimous decision is 36.48%. As Figure 6.5 shows, we find a dramatic difference between non-salient and salient framing of decisions. As frame consistency increases by approximately 1% in saliently framed education cases, the predicted probability of non-unanimous decisions increases by 0.51%, going from a minimum probability of 15.72% to a maximum of 66.44% overall.

Setting the proper frame is not the only way that judges attempt to corral their peers, and the language chosen to discuss the facts of a case can have marked effects on the likelihood of losing support for a decision. Interestingly, focusing on persuasion versus justification in writing the majority opinion can lead to some varying and significant effects dependent on the salience of the case. Particularly, we find that writing authentically, which is indicative of the language of persuasion, has a significant effect only in death penalty cases. The use of authentic language in the majority opinion has the effect of increasing the likelihood of a non-unanimous decision, as we display in Figure 6.6. When the validity of a judicial choice is questioned by others on the bench, judges should be expected to attempt to write more persuasively, but this strategy may emphasize and strain relationships among judicial colleagues. We find that an approximate one-point increase in the use of authentic language in the majority opinion increases the predicted probability of a non-unanimous decision being reached by 0.54%. When judges use the average level of authenticity in their language (33.76% in our data), the likelihood of a non-unanimous decision being reached is 43.19%. Reducing authenticity to its minimum (1.00% in our data) reduces this predicted probability by 14.68%, while emphasizing persuasion explicitly by maximizing the use of authentic language increases the probability by 15.85%.

As we have argued previously, the cognitive complexity of a decision goes a long way toward attempting to persuade others on the bench to agree with the majority's reasoning. The logic behind this is simple: by including the thoughts and opinions of other judges while crafting the majority opinion, judges necessarily write and think in a more complex way while strategically appeasing these audiences, which can help in reducing the potential that external audiences will

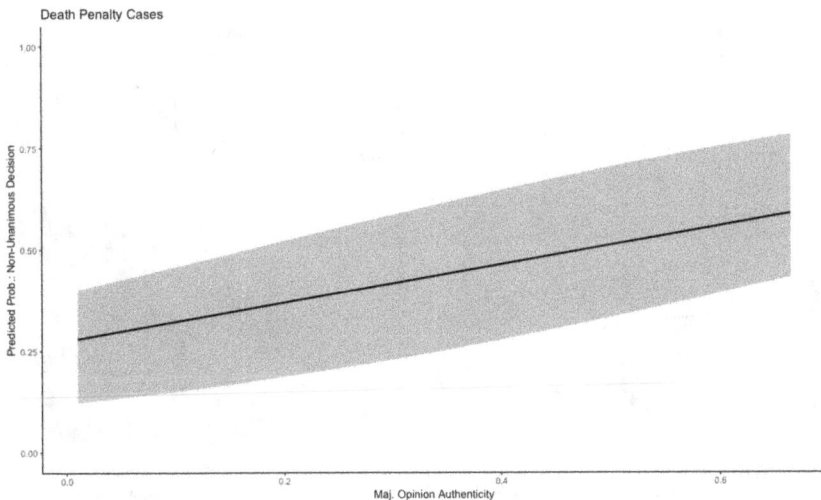

FIGURE 6.6   Predicted Probability of Non-Unanimous Decision by Authenticity of Majority Opinion Language in Death Penalty Decisions

Figure Created by Authors

disagree with the majority. Similar to previous findings discussed above, this strategy of persuasion can have mixed results depending on whether the case in question will be salient to external audiences. As Figure 6.7 shows, greater cognitive complexity in the majority decision decreases the likelihood of a non-unanimous decision in death penalty cases, however the effect is reversed for cases focusing on education. For death penalty cases, minimal cognitive complexity – cases where the majority opinion author writes in firm "black-and-white" rationales and does not attempt to engage with alternative lines of reasoning or argument – results in the likelihood of a court reaching a non-unanimous decision of 35.80%. By striking a balance between differing opinions, integrating some and rejecting others, the probability of a non-unanimous decision decreases by approximately 5% (predicted probability = 30.74%). When judges are most open to differing opinions and attempt to integrate various lines of reasoning into a singular, cohesive statement, the predicted probability of a non-unanimous decision decreases to just 25.86%. Alternatively, for education cases firm rationale with little attempt at integrating alternative opinions results in a probability of a non-unanimous decision of 20.35%, whereas open integration of differing opinions increases the probability of a non-unanimous decision to 40.05%. Most interesting is that, contrary to some of our initial expectations, we do not find evidence that complexity and persuasion exhibit traits of a "Goldilocks" effect, as tests of the curvilinear relationship for cognitive complexity were non-significant in both death penalty and education cases.

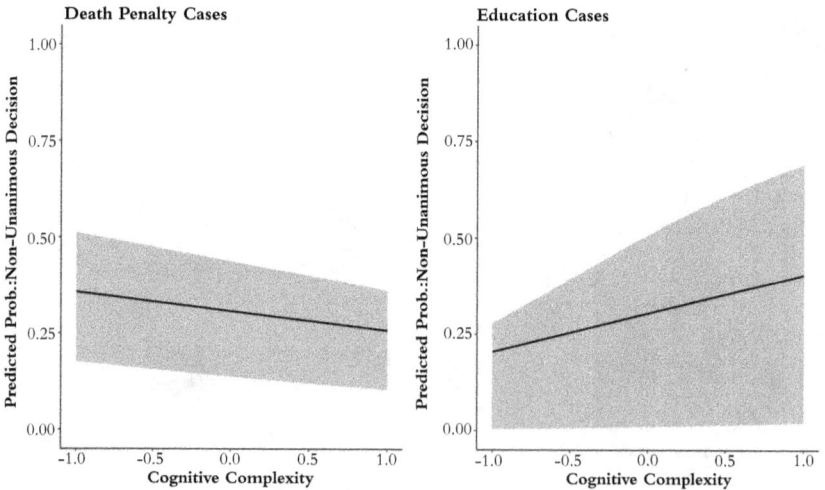

FIGURE 6.7 Predicted Probability of Non-Unanimous Decision by Cognitive Complexity of Majority Opinion in Death Penalty and Education Cases

Figure Created by Authors

While judges may mitigate the effects of attempting authentic persuasion by including a healthy dose of analysis in their opinion, we find that this has a significant effect only when judges are deciding non-salient cases. As we show in Figure 6.8, as judges focus on analysis when writing an opinion, the likelihood of a non-unanimous decision being reached decreases by 0.75%. While judicial opinions focus heavily on analysis on average, as the x-axis in Figure 6.8 shows, we find that stronger focus can have a marked impact on the likelihood of consensus. When analysis is at its lowest (82.37% in our data), the predicted probability of a non-unanimous decision being reached is 41.30%. By focusing exclusively on analysis in an opinion (99.00% in our data), the majority can reduce the likelihood of a non-unanimous decision to 26.79%, a reduction of 14.51%. Substantively, education is one of those areas where each state has a significantly unique and largely independent jurisprudence from the federal government and the other states. Because of this, analysis plays an important role in educating justices about the case law and convincing them the majority opinion is correct. In a salient area that is well known and well trod like death penalty jurisprudence, analytic language appears to be less important.

In order to rally support for their opinion, judges may also rely on writing in simple, easy to understand language when justifying their choices in the opinion. If this is the case, then we should expect that clearer, "plain English," language will have a distinct impact on the likelihood of a non-unanimous decision being reached. Judges recognize that there is a fine line to be drawn when writing

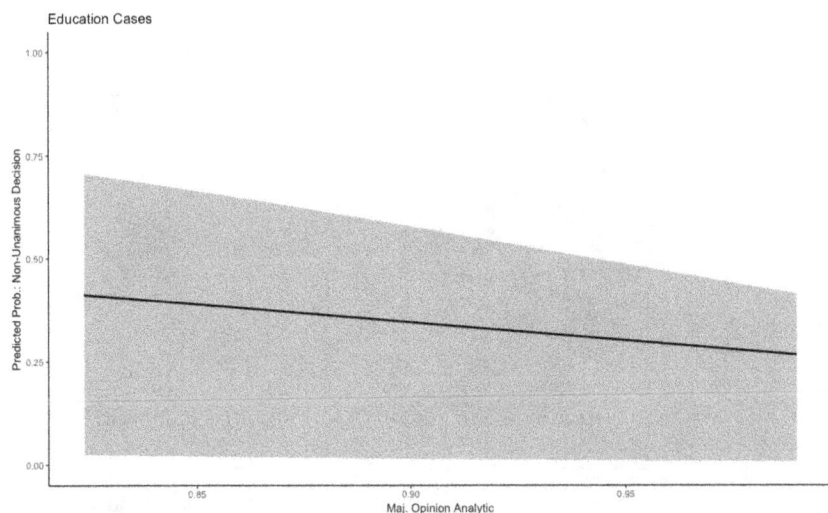

FIGURE 6.8   Predicted Probability of Non-Unanimous Decision by Use of Analytic Language in Majority Opinion in Education Cases

Figure Created by Authors

plainly, however, as there is a strategy behind obfuscation in order to protect the bench from backlash (see Fix and Fairbanks n.d.; Romano and Curry n.d.; Stanton and Vanburg 2008). In order to explore whether justification in this way leads to a Goldilocks dilemma for judges, in Figure 6.9 we also examine both the linear and curvilinear relationships between readability and the probability of a non-unanimous decision. We find that both death penalty and education cases exhibit similar patterns when we include the squared versions of readability in the model. As we can see, the probability of reaching a non-unanimous decision is relatively low when the opinion is complex and difficult to comprehend for both death penalty and education cases. While increasing the reading clarity of the opinion has a marginal, slowly steeping curve for education cases based on an analysis of the curve in Figure 6.9, in death penalty cases increasing the readability of an opinion greatly increases the likelihood of a non-unanimous decision until reaching the approximate average for readability in these decision (the average readability for death penalty cases in our data was 9.175, and 3.774 for education cases), after which both types of case reach an asymptote and then decline. This makes sense, as we should expect the use of simple language is a signal from the bench that they are disregarding alternative arguments in order to make a clear, "plain" statement concerning their decision. While such statements have the benefit of clarity, they risk alienating judges who may disagree or believe the case should be decided on different grounds, thus diminishing support for the majority opinion. Looking specifically at the curvilinear predictors for death penalty cases, we find that when the majority writes in complex, obfuscating language, the likelihood of a non-unanimous decision is at its

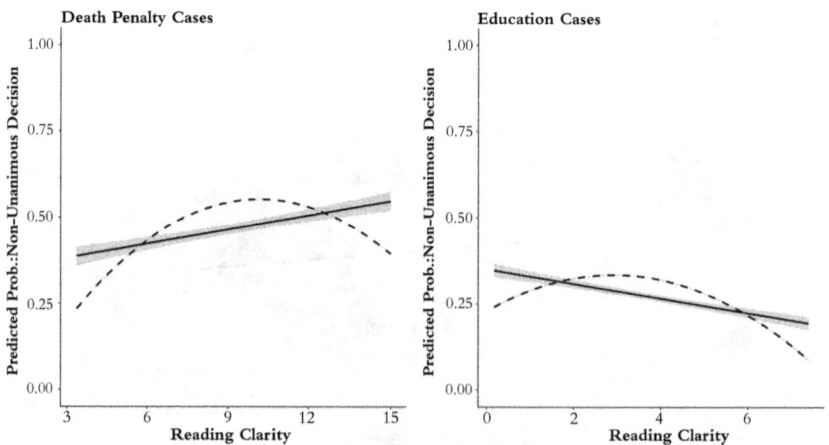

FIGURE 6.9 Predicted Probability of Non-Unanimous Decision by Language Clarity of Majority in Death Penalty and Education Cases

Figure Created by Authors

lowest, with a predicted probability of 24.51%. As judges write more plainly, the predicted probability of a non-unanimous decision being reached should increase by approximately 7.00%, to a maximum probability of 55.41% at its peak. For education cases, opinions written with difficult language and thus lower reading comprehension scores have a predicted probability of reaching a non-unanimous decision of 23.37%, which increases to a 29.03% likelihood of a non-unanimous decision when language clarity is at its median. Interestingly, in contrast to death penalty cases, education cases see a steeper decline in the predicted probability of a non-unanimous decision after reaching its asymptote, with the clearest, simplest decisions in our data having a predicted probability of a non-unanimous decision of just 11.20%. While this seems unexpected at first, given the differences between salient and non-salient decisions we have found thus far, it is not all that surprising. For non-salient decisions, judges have no clear motivation to strongly obfuscate, and using simple language should be more likely to gain greater support.

Conclusions

Without collegial support, judges cannot transform their written opinion into law. Contentious decisions, as they signal dissensus, are more likely to draw attention from outside audiences, as these will likely become the battleground for policy debates in the broader public sphere. As the basic power of the court is to settle disputes, the ability of a judge to firmly state their rationale and gain the support of their colleagues is vital to this end. This chapter has demonstrated that this is a difficult task, as opinion authors must walk a tightrope between justifying their choices and attempting to persuade others that they are right in their decision. Teetering too heavily on one strategy over another can have adverse consequences on the likelihood that the opinion will receive the institutional support it needs in order to be accepted by external audiences, and judges also must keep in mind how these external audiences, especially those involved in the retention process, will perceive their decision.

This chapter has focused directly on how language and external audiences may affect the likelihood of a court being unanimous. We have found that judges are particularly influenced by language choices when deciding whether or not to join the majority opinion, and that different strategies are utilized in order to gain institutional support and maintain institutional legitimacy depending on the salience of both the case itself, and the selected case frame used in the opinion. Interestingly, persuasion can be an effective strategy in salient (death penalty) cases when a judge attempts to identify and integrate alternative opinions and explanations into the opinion. Judges can likewise increase support by ensuring that their final decisions are justified clearly, as we find that judges who write in clear "plain English" are most likely to avoid a non-unanimous decision. We find that judges strike a balance between justifying their decision and attempting to gain allies, and that this strategy can go a long way toward convincing external audiences toward the court's decision.

Ultimately, the method of retention serves functionally as a proxy for the external audience. As judges in these state supreme courts must be retained, the method of retention makes explicit whom the external audience is. As we find effects concerning method of retention, what we are discovering is how these judges perceive their audience. When we discover a null effect when we theorize that an effect should exist, we learn that judges don't think the audience cares. Further research should examine these audience effects more thoroughly. When Baum says judges care about their audiences, his commentary is about an institutional environment with little variation. Federal judges have life tenure, which means everyone may be writing for different audiences. At the state level, judges face a varying array of pressures, that are affected by the institutions in which they work. We can learn a significant amount about how judges perceive their audiences by examining how they write judicial opinions.

Notes

1 Dissents and special concurrences are hard indicators of disagreement with the language and legal choices made in the majority opinion, but they can also be indicators of when opinion bargaining failed. A great number of dissents and special concurrences claim that, if the majority had not included a specific portion of the opinion, the disagreement would been resolved and the author could have joined the majority. While these statements explain the reason for the opinion, they are also a signal to the author as to how easy it would have been to accommodate the dissent/concurrence. Because of this, we observe only when language negotiations fail, not when they are successful.

2 Lobbying other judges not in the majority alone, without any significant language bargaining, is unlikely to change how an individual judge will vote. The majority opinion author will likely need to compromise on their draft.

3 We recognize implicitly that the size of workload that a court has should also affect their likelihood of unanimity. Across our time line, not all courts report consistently their yearly workload. This would mean dropping entire years of states from our analysis and could significantly bias our findings.

References

Baum, L. (1997). *The Puzzle of Judicial Behavior*. Ann Arbor: University of Michigan Press.

Baum, L. (2006). *Judges and Their Audiences: A Perspective on Judicial Behavior*. Princeton: Princeton University Press.

Benhabib, S. (1996). Toward a Deliberative Model of Democratic Legitimacy. In Benhabib, S. (ed.) *Democracy and Difference: Contesting the Boundaries of the Political*. Princeton: Princeton University Press, 67–94.

Brace, P. A. & Hall, M. G. (1997). The Interplay of Preferences, Case Facts, Context, and Rules in the Politics of Judicial Choice. *Journal of Politics*, 59(4), 1206–1231.

Brown v. Board of Education (1954), 347 U.S. 483.

Caldeira, G. A., & Wright, J. R. (1988). Organized Interests and Agenda Setting in the U.S. Supreme Court. *American Political Science Review*, 82(4), 1109–1127.

Cohen, J. (1996). Procedure and Substance in Deliberative Democracy. In Benhabib, S. (ed.) *Democracy and Difference: Contesting the Boundaries of the Political.* Princeton: Princeton University Press, 187–217.

Cray, E. (1997). *Chief Justice: A Biography of Earl Warren.* New York: Simon & Shuster.

Cross, F. B. & Tiller, E. H. (1998). Judicial Partisanship and Obedience to Legal Doctrine: Whistleblowing on the Federal Court of Appeals. *Yale Law Journal,* 107(7), 2155–2176.

Curry, T. A. & Hurwitz, M. S. (2016) Strategic Retirement of Elected & Appointed Justices: A Hazard Model Approach. *Journal of Politics,* 78(4), 1061–1075.

Curry, T. A. & Romano, M. K. (2018). Ideological Congruity on State Supreme Courts. *Justice System Journal,* 39(2), 139–154.

Epstein, L., Segal, J. A., & Spaeth, H. J. (2001). The Norm of Consensus on the U.S. Supreme Court. *American Journal of Political Science,* 45(2), 362–377.

Fix, M. P. & Fairbanks, B. (2018). Does Obfuscation Breed Obscurity? The Relationship Between Opinion Readability and Citations from State High Courts. *Unpublished Manuscript.*

Gill, R. (2016). Do Judicial Performance Evaluations Influence Retention Election Results? In Bonneau, C. W., & Hall, M. G. (eds.) *Judicial Elections in the 21st Century.* New York: Routledge.

Gill, R., Lazos, S. R., & Waters, M. (2010). Sacrificing Diversity for 'Quality': How Judicial Performance Evaluations are Failing Women & Minorities. *Paper presented at the Annual Meeting of the Western Political Science Association,* Las Vegas, NV.

Goelzhauser, G. (2014). *Choosing State Supreme Court Justices: Merit Selection and the Consequences of Institutional Reform.* Philadelphia: Temple University Press.

Gruenfeld, D. (1995). Status, Ideology, and Integrative Complexity on the U.S. Supreme Court: Rethinking the Politics of Political Decision Making. *Journal of Personality and Social Psychology,* 61(1), 5–20.

Guttman, A., & Thompson, D. (1996). *Democracy & Disagreement.* Harvard: Harvard University Press.

Hall, M. G. (1987). Constituent Influence in State Supreme Courts: Conceptual Notes and a Case Study. *Journal of Politics,* 49(4), 1117–1124.

Hall, M. G. (1992). Electoral Politics and Strategic Voting in State Supreme Courts. *Journal of Politics,* 54(2), 427–446.

Hall, M. G. (2007). Voting in State Supreme Court Elections: Competition and Context as Democratic Incentives. *Journal of Politics,* 69(4), 1147–1159.

Hall, M. G. (2015). *Attacking Judges: How Campaign Advertising Influences State Supreme Court Elections.* Stanford: Stanford University Press.

Hall, M. G. & Brace, P. (1992). Toward an Integrated Model of Judicial Voting Behavior. *American Politics Research,* 20(2), 147–168.

Hettinger, V. A., Lindquist, S. A., & Martinek, W. L. (2006). *Judging on a Collegial Court: Influences on Federal Appellate Decision Making.* Charlottesville: University of Virginia Press.

Kim, P. T. (2009). Deliberation and Strategy on the United States Courts of Appeals: An Empirical Exploration of Panel Effects. *University of Pennsylvania Law Review,* 157(5), 1319–1381.

Langer, L. (2002). *Judicial Review in State Supreme Courts: A Comparative Study.* New York: SUNY Press.

Lax, J. & Rader, K. (2015). Bargaining Power in the Supreme Court: Evidence from Opinion Assignment & Vote Switching. *Journal of Politics,* 77(3), 648–663.

Leonard, M. E. (2014). Elections and Decision-Making on State High Courts: Examining Legitimacy and Judicial Review. *Justice System Journal*, 35(1) 45–61.

Leonard, M. E. (2016). State Legislatures, State High Courts, and Judicial Independence: An Examination of Court-Curbing Legislation in the States. *Justice System Journal*, 37(1), 53–62.

Leonard, M. E., & Ross, J. V. (2016). Understanding the Length of State Supreme Court Opinions. *American Politics Research*, 44(4), 710–733.

Maltzman, F., Spriggs, J. F., & Wahlbeck, P. L. (2000). *Crafting Law on the Supreme Court: The Collegial Game.* Cambridge: Cambridge University Press.

Mason, A. T. (1956). *Harlan Fiske Stone: Pillar of the Law.* New York: Archon Books.

Murphy, W. F. (1973). *Elements of Judicial Strategy.* Chicago: University of Chicago Press.

Popkin, W. D. (2007). *Evolution of the Judicial Opinion: Institutional and Individual Styles.* New York: New York University Press.

Pritchett, C. H. 1948. *The Roosevelt Court.* New York: Macmillan.

Rehnquist, W. H. (1996). The Supreme Court: The First Hundred Years Were the Hardest. *University of Miami Law Review*, 42, 475–490.

Rhode, D. (1972). Policy Goals and Opinion Coalitions in the Supreme Court. *Midwest Journal of Political Science*, 16(2), 218–224.

Schwartz, B. (1983). *Super Chief: Earl Warren and His Supreme Court? A Judicial Biography.* New York: New York University Press.

Seddig, R. G. (1975). John Marshall and the Origins of Supreme Court Leadership. *University of Pittsburgh Law Review*, 36, 785–833.

Segal, J. A., & Spaeth, H. J. (1992). The Supreme Court & the Attitudinal Model. Cambridge: Cambridge University Press.

Segal, J. A., & Spaeth, H. J. (2002). *The Supreme Court & the Attitudinal Model Revisited.* Cambridge: Cambridge University Press.

Spriggs, J. F., Maltzman, F., & Wahlbeck, P. J. (1999). Bargaining on the U.S. Supreme Court: Justices' Responses to Majority Opinion Drafts. *Journal of Politics*, 61(2), 485–506.

Staton, J. K. & Vanberg, G. (2008). The Value of Vagueness: Delegation, Defiance, & Judicial Opinions. *American Journal of Political Science*, 52(3), 504–519.

Ulmer, S. S. 1971. Earl Warren and the Brown Decision. *Journal of Politics*, 33(3), 68–702.

Van Winkle, S. (1997). Dissent as a Signal: Evidence from the U.S. Courts of Appeals. *Presented at the Annual Meeting of the American Political Science Association*, Washington, DC.

Walhof, D. R. (2005). Bringing the Deliberative Back In: Gadamer on Conversation and Understanding. *Contemporary Political Theory*, 4(2), 154–174.

7

CONCLUSION

It seems obvious to us that judges write for specific audiences. Through reading many opinions, we have found that sometimes this behavior is rather overt. The best example of this comes from Justice Harold G. Clarke of the Georgia Supreme Court and graduate of the University of Georgia. He said of a juror's response to a question during voir dire, "A fuller response would have been required if the juror had been asked that all-important question, 'How 'bout them Dawgs? (276 S.E.2d 1)'" Of course, not all evidence of audience pleasing behavior is as clear as Justice Clarke's. This book seeks to investigate the when and how of this audience-pleasing behavior. Building upon the ground-breaking work of Larry Baum in *Judges and Their Audiences* (2006), we develop a theory of judicial behavior that treats judges as representatives of various internal and external audiences that may be invested in the outcome or impact of a judicial decision. We focus specifically on the recognition that the institutions of retention used in state courts of last resort prioritize different audiences; and that judges, depending on the type of case being decided, should write in a specific fashion in an attempt to please, or at a minimum placate, their retention constituency. While retention audiences are arguably secondary spectators for these opinions (the primary audience are the other judges on the court and the litigants in the case), they are of significance because nearly all state supreme court justices have limited terms and must be retained by this constituency to remain in power.

Unlike the federal judiciary, most judges at the state level do not enjoy life tenure and there is a significant amount of variance in how states retain their judges. Some states utilize contested elections, either partisan or non-partisan, in which two individuals face off for the judicial seat. For these retention systems, the retention audience for the judges' opinions will be their electoral constituency. Another subset of states retain their judges through elite reappointment, either by the governor or legislature. For judges in these elite reappointment systems, their retention audience are the members of that elite institution charged with their retention. The last institution used in the states to retain judges is uncontested public confidence votes, known generally as retention elections. While the retention audience in these systems is the same as contested elections (the electorate), we contend that the connection between these judges and the electorate will be less vibrant. Using all death penalty and education majority opinions written in state supreme courts from 1995 to 2010, we examined whether the primary audience (other judges on the courts) and also the secondary audience (the retention constituency) have predictable effects on the content, form, and coalition size of the court's opinion.

We identify two different types of language that judges may use in their opinions: the language of justification and the language of persuasion. An opinion that exhibits a high degree of justification will focus on a small number of reasons why the decision reached is the only possible conclusion given the facts and the application of the law. For our purposes, the language of justification is operationalized as readability and analytic language/reasoning, where an easily understood text with a high degree of analysis exhibits higher degrees of justification. In contrast, an opinion that utilizes a higher amount of persuasive language should include numerous viewpoints and apply logic to determine which one is correct and why. Thus, we operationalize persuasion as cognitive complexity, where opinions which have a high degree of cognitive complexity exhibit a high degree of persuasive language. Such opinions are likely to be written using a greater amount of authentic, belief-based reasoning as well, and thus we fortify our measure of complexity by including a measure of authenticity in reasoning in order to more fully capture how judges persuade within an opinion. As we highlight in Chapter 2, we believe that the language of persuasion and justification exist as trade-offs.

In Chapter 3, we find that the framing of an opinion is substantively affected by whether judges wish to prioritize persuasion in an attempt to influence external audiences or seek to justify their choice and provide a deterministic answer to legal disputes. Salient cases tend to be more complex in their decisions. Furthermore, when examining the effect of method of retention on frame consistency, we find that judges in institutions where the retention audience is provided with more information (partisan elections and elite appointment) will frame decisions differently from those where information is limited. In cases of limited information systems, judges tend to write opinions that are less consistent in their use of frames and generally longer in their explanations, which we argue is indicative of the presence of strategic considerations when crafting opinions and deciding law. Likewise, we find that judges are very careful in their choice of language when developing the initial frames in salient and non-salient cases; choosing their words carefully to ensure that their arguments can be understood broadly.

In Chapter 4, we turn our attention inward and question how dissents impact the opinion and the language used by judges writing for the majority. As numerous judges, jurists, and scholars of the law have argued, the dissent is a peculiar part of judicial rhetoric, as it allows judges to speak unconstrained about their view about a decision (see Urofsky 2017). We find that, when faced with a dissent, judges will fundamentally shift the way in which they write when speaking for the majority, often writing in firmer, more deterministic justifications to strengthen their argument against a contrasting opinion. Likewise, we find that the method of retention used to maintain the bench has a substantive impact over this process, with retention audiences having a direct effect over the language of the majority opinion when a dissent is present.

In Chapter 5, we ask a unique question for judicial research, focusing on the decision to write per curiam and how language and audience dynamics may impact the likelihood that the court writes anonymously. We find that, when faced with an elite audience, judges are more likely to write anonymously in order to provide some institutional shielding against possible backlash. This is particularly true in salient decisions such as death penalty cases. We also find that this has a dynamic impact on the language used in the opinion itself, with per curiam opinions generally eschewing attempts at persuasion, and trying to find equilibrium for writing clear, "plain language" decisions so that the court may better defend itself.

Finally, in Chapter 6, we examine whether the findings in the preceeding chapters, concerning language choices in the majority opinion, have any impact on the decisional output in the case. We find that judges are more likely to vote unanimously when the opinion is crafted in a way that strongly and clearly dictates the rationale of the opinion; however, in salient cases judges must also bargain with and persuade their colleagues that their opinion is correct, and as such must write decisions that incorporate greater complexity in their legal arguments. This inevitably leads to a balancing act for judges when attempting to write to maintain a majority coalition, while also keeping in mind that retention audiences may be watching and waiting to reprimand a court that goes against their wishes.

This book is an attempt to bring the richness of the field and methodologies of political communications together with the institutional richness and theories of state high courts. We examined numerous aspects of opinion writing on state supreme courts and found numerous audience effects dependent upon how the judges were retained. Judges modify how they write majority opinions depending upon the relevant retention constituency. Furthermore, judges also consider their colleagues when drafting opinions, though these effects are also dependent upon how judges are retained. The task of opinion writing is significantly complex, and we provided a means to understand it, through the lens of the language of justification and the language of persuasion.

Future Research Directions

That we have discovered significant audience effects in opinion-writing leads us to believe this is a useful theory to motivate other studies that examine judicial behavior. As these judges engage in audience representation during opinion writing, there is a significant likelihood they do so in other arenas as well. Furthermore, even though we find less evidence of secondary audience effects in judges retained by elite reappointment, we still believe the theory of audience representation applies equally to this institution. There are other types of cases, and still other types of behavior, that audience representation may theoretically explain.

Judge Don Willet of the Fifth Circuit Court of Appeals joined the social media platform Twitter in October of 2009. He quickly amassed a significant number of followers, in part due to his humor and focus on family. On September 28th, 2017, the day Justice Willet (then serving on the Texas Supreme Court) was nominated by President Trump to become Judge Willet, the tweets dried up. In his wake, many other state judges began to join the medium, with judges like Chief Judge Stephen Louis A. Dillard of the Georgia Court of Appeals engaging in a widespread call for other judges to use social media to engage with the public (Dillard 2017). But when examining which judges are joining and using Twitter, it appears that not all methods of retention are equally represented (Curry and Fix n.d.). The judges who populate Twitter are overwhelming judges who face contested elections. Curry and Fix surmise that this is largely a function of audience representation. Being active on Twitter provides two interrelated benefits for judges. First, it confers legitimacy upon the institution of the state supreme court. Gibson and others (Gibson 2008, 2009; Gibson, Gottfried, Carpini and Jamieson 2011) demonstrate that the more individuals know about the judicial system, the more they support it, and interacting with judges on social media should have that effect. Second, there are obvious electoral benefits to engaging with an electoral constituency on social media. That judges in retention election and elite reappointment states are so significantly unrepresented on Twitter is likely a function of a collective action problem. As the public is not an important audience for them, because either they are less connected (retention elections) or because they are retained by another institution (governor or legislature), individual judges are less likely to take individual action to benefit the institution of the court.

This should mean that the judges on courts that are retained through methods other than contested elections will engage in other types of legitimacy-conferring events. Leonard (2016) notes that judges with more judicial independence are more likely to experience attempts at court-curbing by the legislature. Beyond making decisions (and writing opinions) that please the legislature, justices can attempt to garner a high degree of public legitimacy. There are only a few ways courts can engage in legitimacy-conferring events if the individual justices are likely to shirk when they gain no individual benefit, or when the need for such benefit is low. Observationally, some courts that have experienced external attacks on their legitimacy have engaged in public education campaigns in different forms to increase their general good will with the public. Courts such as the Iowa Supreme Court and Kansas Supreme Court have taken their chambers on the road, hearing cases in community centers and schools across the state to educate the public about the process of judging and demystify the institution more generally. These institutionally organized attempts to increase legitimacy may be more likely to occur in courts that are more independent of the public, whereas Twitter usage, or engaging with the public on an individual basis, may be more likely to occur in institutions that are more accountable to the public. Examining this possible variance could provide us more insight into how audience representation shapes judicial behavior at the state level.

Over ten years ago Baum (2006) reminded us that nearly all people engage in approval-seeking behavior, even judges. We are not the first scholars to use this theoretical motivation to examine judicial opinion writing, primarily at the US Supreme Court (see Black, Owens, Wedeking and Wohfarth 2016), but we believe the concept of audience representation applies even more fully to the courts of last resort in the states. As the institutions of retention vary across the states, we believe different audiences will become salient to the judges in predictable fashions. We found significant, and varied, audience effects in opinion writing dependent upon the method of retention and the topic being written about. We hope future scholars will use the concept of audience representation to provide a more robust picture of judges and judging at the state level, focusing not just on the final vote in cases, but on all aspects of judicial behavior.

References

Baum, L. (2006). *Judges and Their Audiences: A Perspective on Judicial Behavior*. Princeton: Princeton University Press.

Black, R. C., Owens, R. J., Wedeking, J., & Wohlfarth, P. C. (2016) *U.S. Supreme Court Opinions and their Audiences*. Cambridge: Cambridge University Press.

Curry, T. A., & Fix, M. P. (n.d.). May It Please the Twitterverse: The Use of Twitter by State High Court Judges. *Unpublished Manuscript*.

Dillard, S. L. (2017). #Engage: It's Time for Judges to Tweet, Like, & Share. *Judicature*, 101(1), 11–1.

Gibson, J. L. (2008). Challenges to the Impartiality of State Supreme Courts: Legitimacy Theory and 'New-Style' Judicial Campaigns. *American Political Science Review*, 102(1), 59–75.

Gibson, J. L. 2009. 'New-Style' Judicial Campaigns and the Legitimacy of State High Courts. *The Journal of Politics*, 71(4), 1285–130.

Gibson, J. L., Gottfried, J. A., Delli Carpini, M. X., and Jamieson, K. H. (2011). The Effects of Judicial Campaign Activity on the Legitimacy of Courts: A Survey-based Experiment. *Political Research Quarterly*, 64(3), 545–55.

Glennville Wood Preserving Company, INC. v. Riddlespur (1981), 276 S.E.2d.

Leonard, M. E. (2016). State Legislatures, State High Courts, and Judicial Independence: An Examination of Court-Curbing Legislation in the States. *Justice System Journal*, 37(1), 53–6.

Urofsky, M. I. (2017). *Dissent and the Supreme Court: Its Role in the Court's History and the Nation's Constitutional Dialogue*. New York, NY: Vantage Book.

APPENDIX A

Data Collection and Transformations

Throughout this book, we have been motivated by the following question: What factors motivate the writing styles of judges in state supreme courts? To provide empirical insight into this question, we collected data on death penalty and education cases decided by the state courts of last resort in all 50 states (37 states for death penalty cases, including each state where the death penalty was legal in 1995). Opinion collection for death penalty cases was performed using the Lexis legal archive, and we focused on collecting all cases decided by the high court in which a justice wrote a formal, published opinion between the years of 1995 and 2010.[1] We would like to thank Meghan Leonard and Joe Ross for providing us with education cases in the same time frame. The education cases were collected using Westlaw. The full dataset is comprised of 15 years of data from over 400 judges, with a final total of 5,239 death penalty cases, and 1,413 education cases.

Constructing Cognitive Complexity

Cognitive complexity, developed in psychology and cognitive science, is utilized to measure a speaker's ability to evaluate complicated situations and arrive at a decision. Complex thinkers tend to consider an extensive range of issues as they attempt to reconcile different, sometimes contradictory strains of thought, whereas less complex thinking generally adheres to attitudinal decision-making and dogma (Winters 1996). Measures of cognitive complexity have been utilized previously by Owens and Wedeking (2012) to predict ideological drift on the U.S. Supreme Court and are popular when analyzing textual data in political science in order to investigate the behavioral components of political speech (see Tetlock, Bernzweig, and Gallant 1985; Gruenfeld and Presten 2000; Gruenfeld

1995; Tetlock 1986; Gibbons 1990; Romano 2018). To construct our measure of complexity, we run each opinion through the Linguistic Inquiry and Word Count 2015 (LIWC) content analysis program and measure judicial speech on seven indicators commonly associated with greater rhetorical complexity (Gruenfeld 1995; Owens and Wedeking 2012).[2] Specifically, we include measures for the number of negations, use of insight, causation, discrepancy in language use, tentativeness, language that exhibits certainty, and the number of six-letter words used in a document.

Five of dimensions identified were considered to positively affect cognitive complexity based upon the ability of a speaker to clearly differentiate between ideas as well as integrate these ideas into cohesive arguments. The clearest example of how this may occur in speech is through the use of terms associated with *causation*. LIWC measures causation by searching a document for terms such as, "because," "effect," "hence," and other terms that refer to causal processes. Causation focuses on the ability of a speaker to tap into and understand the relationships between various parts or components (differentiation), and particularly how changes in one circumstance may influence changes in another (integration). Increased levels of causation typically correspond with greater cognitive complexity overall. Along with causation, *insight* and *discrepancy* work to indicate the ability of a speaker to provide depth and greater understanding to complex phenomenon. *Insight*, as measured by LIWC, is based on the use of terms such as, "think," "know," and "consider" in speech. Insight captures the degree and depth of an individual's understanding about an experience, as well as capturing how well a speaker understands the underlying nature of an event. Along with this, *discrepancy* measures the use of terms like, "should," "would," and "could" and provides details about the ability of a speaker to identify inconsistencies between different cases. Greater levels of discrepancy are indicative that a speaker is able to differentiate between occurrences or events, while the complimentary insight indicates higher levels of integration between complex events.

The final two indicators included in the measure that are positively associated with cognitive complexity calculate the amount of *tentativeness* a speaker has in their text, and the number of *six letter words* present in the document. A higher degree of tentativeness (terms such as, "maybe," "fairly, "and, "perhaps") indicates how much restraint an individual expresses, or how hesitant they may be to act. One final indicator, the number of words with six or more letters in a speech, is commonly used in linguistics to determine a speaker's level of sophistication. Previous examinations of integration and cognitive complexity have shown that increased numbers of six-letter words in a speech are associated with higher levels of cognitive complexity (Gruenfeld 1995; Owens and Wedeking 2012).

Along with the indices that positively affect cognitive complexity, two indicators were included that are theorized to negatively affect the complexity of a speaker. Specifically, *certainty* is included in the measure by counting the incidents of terms such as, "always," "clearly," or, "absolutely." Certainty is generally associated with the degree of confidence a speaker has in their determination of something, and also tends to be correlated with expressions that paint issues as less complex. As a result, increased certainty tends to diminish a speaker's expressed ability to provide integrative understanding or show clear differentiation between courses of action. Finally, LIWC measures the level of *negation* by searching for terms such as, "no," and, "never." The use of these terms generally is associated with occurrences when a speaker acknowledges the absence of something that is considered positive or affirmative.

Using the scores calculated through LIWC, we construct a measure of complexity by subjecting the indices to an exploratory factor analysis using principle components. Based on an analysis of the variance using both the Guttman-Kaiser and Broken Stick model, the results of the factor analysis returned a two-factor solution for both death penalty and education cases, as showed in Figures A.1 and A.2. According to the Guttman-Kaiser model, factors should be retained based upon the magnitude of their eigenvalues, with the general view being that values greater than the average should be retained. The bar charts of the eigenvalues at the top of Figure A.1 and A.2 both indicate that a two-factor solution is possible for the analysis, though factor two only minimally meet the threshold for retaining. As a second test, therefore, the Broken Stick model was implemented and clearly indicated that a two-factor solution was sufficient. The Broken Stick model is based on an examination of the total percentage of the variance explained by each component. Since the eigenvalue of a PCA represents a measure of each component's variance, components are retained only if the

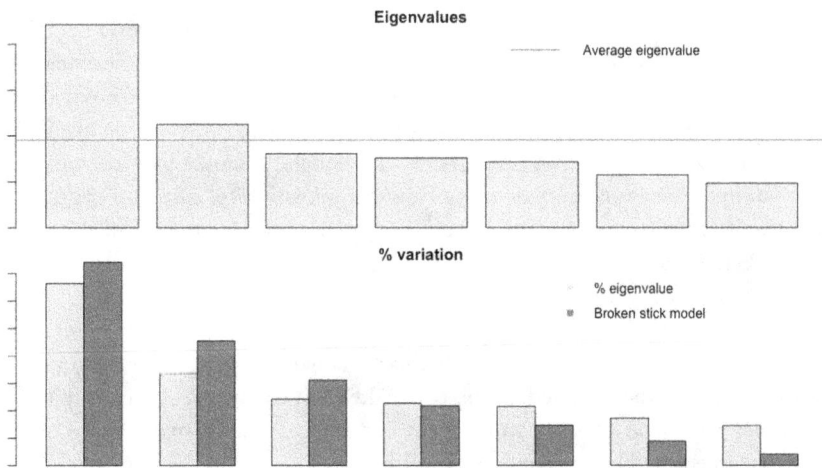

FIGURE A.1   Principle Component Analysis of Indicators of Cognitive Complexity in Death Penalty Cases based on Eigenvector Values Using the Kaiser-Gutman and Broken-Stick Method

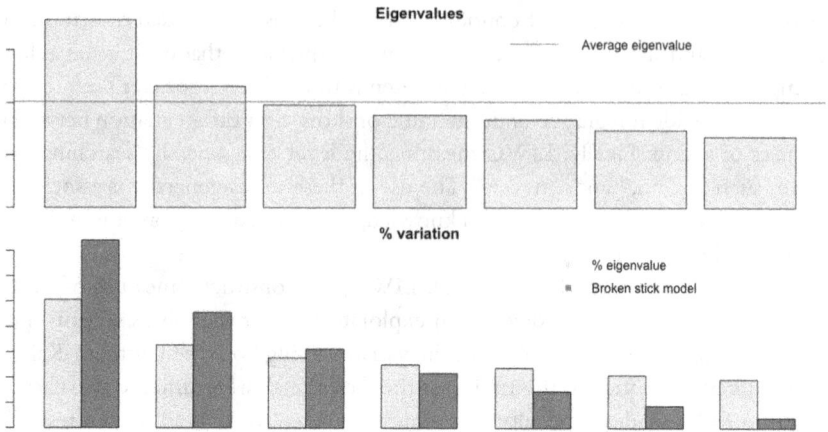

FIGURE A.2 Principle Component Analysis of Indicators of Cognitive Complexity in Education Cases based on Eigenvector Values Using the Kaiser-Gutman and Broken-Stick Method

associated value is larger than the value given by the broken stick distribution (MacArthur 1957; Cangelosi and Goriely 2007).

Based on an examination of the eigenvalues, we find that the covariates load well on two factors, which we term "differentiation," and "integration," based on the previous literature in cognitive political psychology (Gruenfeld 1995; Owens and Wedeking 2016; Tetlock et al. 1984; Winters 1996). Using the values produced by the PCA, we construct two new factor scores for the amount of differentiation and integration we find in each opinion, which we standardize for comparability. As previous examinations of complexity posit an inverse relationship between the two measures, we simply subtract the score for differentiation from the score for integration in order to calculate our initial value for cognitive complexity. Finally, we rescale complexity into a singular measure of bounded between -1 and 1. Table A.1 provides us with a useful example in understanding how complexity works in text. In our low complexity level case, the court uses a fairly simple metric in making their final decision. The sentence, in this case, was upheld because it was determined that the retrospective change to Florida's aggravating circumstances clause when applying the death penalty was not an ex post facto law as it was applied in the case. While this may seem complicated from a readability standpoint, it is fairly clearly framed as a simple question of legal factors and how they applied to the case. Alternatively, in our high complexity example, the Texas court acknowledges and utilizes a seven-part test in order to determine whether the application of the death penalty was reasonable. This inevitably leads to a far more complex set of arguments, as the court must apply several different rationales and integrate them into a cohesive argument in order to explain their decision.

TABLE A.1 Low and High Cognitive Complexity Examples

Low Complexity Example	High Complexity Example
MELVIN TROTTER, Appellant, vs. STATE OF FLORIDA, Appellee. Appellant was convicted of first-degree murder for the stabbing of a grocery store owner during a robbery. The trial court found as an aggravating circumstance that appellant had been on community control at the time he committed the murder. The trial court's sentence of death was reversed by an appellate court because, at the time, aggravating circumstances under Fla. Stat. Ann. β 921.141 had not been found to include community control. At resentencing, the trial court again imposed the death penalty after finding community control as an aggravating circumstance. The court affirmed appellant's sentence because subsequent legislation, specifically β 921.141(5)(a) (1991), had made it clear that community control was an aggravating circumstance. **The court noted that the trial court's use of community control as an aggravating circumstance did not constitute an ex post facto violation because the use of community control as an aggravating circumstance merely constituted a refinement in β 921.141(5)(a)'s sentence of imprisonment factor, not a substantive change in Florida's death penalty law.**	**LONNIE EARL JOHNSON, Appellant v. THE STATE OF TEXAS** Appellant was convicted of capital murder. During the punishment phase the trial court admitted, over appellant's objection, victim impact evidence. The jury was required to answer a special issue that asked about appellant's personal moral culpability. The jury's instructions included language about evidence affecting appellant's moral blameworthiness. Appellant was sentenced to death and review to the Texas supreme court was automatic under Tex. Code Crim. Proc. Ann. art. 37.0711, β 3(j). **The court applied a seven-part test to determine the admissibility of the victim impact evidence.** The court found that appellant's general objection to all victim impact evidence was not specific enough to preserve error on appeal. Rather, a specific objection had to be made to each objectionable statement or group of statements. Appellant did not object during the testimony nor did he cross-examine the witnesses. The court affirmed appellant's conviction and sentence because the trial court did not abuse its discretion when it admitted victim impact evidence over appellant's general objection.
Word Count = 2,444 Readability Score = 3.527 Frame = Legal Factors	Word Count = 45,251 Readability Score = 7.404 Frame = Case Facts

Source: Table Created by Authors

Constructing Readability

Of particular concern when developing a model of textual complexity is how to model the sophistication of political speech. While textual sophistication has grown in prominence and scholarly focus, the development of measures that can sufficiently quantify the concept has remained relatively stagnant since the 1950s (but see Benoit, Munger, and Spirling 2017). The problem with using readability as a proxy for textual sophistication stems from the fact that these measures – such as the commonly known Flesch Reading Ease (FRE) score or the Flesch-Kincaid Grade Level (FKGL) score – were primarily designed to measure early childhood comprehension, *not political sophistication*. Thus, as Benoit, Munger, and Spirling (2017) correctly point out, studies that utilize these measures in order to examine political complexity or comprehension are relying on "out of domain" prediction mechanisms, since such measures were "never intended for the more general task of measuring the 'sophistication' of texts in a given domain such as politics, where abstract conceptual appeals to 'democracy' or 'liberty' might make documents significantly more difficult to follow over and above their sentence structure or average number of syllables" (pg. 7–8).

Thus, for the majority of works interested in measuring reading clarity, determining the *right* measure of textual complexity is important in order to justify the validity of results. As a baseline, such measures focus on the difficulty an individual has assessing a piece of writing by evaluating a variety of factors such as word use, sentence structure, and language complexity, which allow evaluators to better assess whether a piece of prose can be understood by an audience. We recognize that scholars can reasonably disagree over what measure of readability is best suited for examining political texts, and thus choose here to rely on a composite measure of readability by performing a principle component analysis on nine measures commonly used in social sciences and business in order to measure comprehension. These include the commonly used Flesch and Flesch-Kincaid reading scales (Flesch 1948; 2002) – well known for their relative simplicity and accessibility for textual analysis (see Cann, Goelzhauser and Johnson 2014 for an excellent discussion of the value of the Flesch measures) – to more complex measures such as the "Fog" Index developed by Gunning (1952), which has been found to be reliable in determining comprehension of technical documents by a general reader (Aijina, Laouiti, and Msolli 2016; Terblanche and Burgress 2010). To ensure comparability across case type, we started by merging death penalty and education cases into a single dataset. Table A.2 provides a quick summary breakdown of the measures utilized to generate our composite score for readability.

Using a process similar to the one used to generate our complexity scores, we first determine how well various indices scale for readability. Based on the analysis of the eigenvector values using both the Guttman-Kaiser and Broken Stick model, as displayed in Figure A.3, we find that readability measures commonly

TABLE A.2 Descriptive Statistics for Death Penalty Cases

Variable	Mean	SD	SE	Median	Range	Skewness
Automated Readability Index	14.3	1.7	0.02	14.2	16.4 (5.5–21.9)	0.15
Coleman Lau Index	14.17	1	0.01	14.1	11.21 (7.41–18.62)	0.25
Flesch Reading Ease	52.95	6.27	0.09	53.04	59.29 (28.13–87.42)	0.01
Flesch-Kincaid Grade Level	9.58	1.58	0.02	9.5	14.5 (2.1–16.6)	-0.08
FOG Index	8.52	1.17	0.02	8.47	11.17 (4.91–16.08)	0.44
Fucks Index	81.66	16.31	0.23	80.37	159.6 (24.73–184.33)	0.6
Linsear Write Index	7.86	3.55	0.05	7	47 (2.5–49.5)	2.36
SMOG Index	12.84	1.19	0.02	12.82	11.14 (7.52–18.66)	0.09
Word Count	9285.09	8434.09	116.89	7065	93475 (198–93673)	2.77

Descriptive Statistics for Education Cases

Variable	Mean	SD	SE	Median	Range	Skewness
Automated Readability Index	12.12	2.48	0.07	11.92	21.6 (4.41–26.01)	0.8
Coleman Lau Index	10.55	1	0.03	10.53	7.15 (6.67–13.82)	0.07
Flesch Reading Ease	47.29	7.14	0.19	47.65	51.32 (17.05–68.36)	-0.36
Flesch-Kincaid Grade Level	12.31	2.03	0.05	12.15	16.2 (6.61–22.81)	0.77
FOG Index	7.8	1.31	0.03	7.67	10.21 (4.33–14.54)	0.91
Fucks Index	107.05	22.47	0.6	104.65	190.5 (48.42–238.92)	0.97
Linsear Write Index	15.65	4.08	0.11	15.11	29.97 (5.93–35.9)	0.93
SMOG Index	13.75	1.38	0.04	13.65	9.74 (9.67–19.41)	0.43
Word Count	5212.73	5245.14	139.54	3688	57711 (99–57810)	3.97

Source: Table Created by Authors

reduce to a single factor for comparison. This is unsurprising, as readability measures tend to exhibit strong correlations across differing measures.

Using the values produced by the PCA analysis, we generate a new score for readability which we term "reading clarity," which we scale to be between 0 and 15 in order to account for the extent of differences across common scoring types. The benefit of our measure, however, comes from the fact that it allows us to talk about "readability" as a function of clarity, rather than complexity. Often, reading comprehension measures take the form of "grade level" indicators, wherein

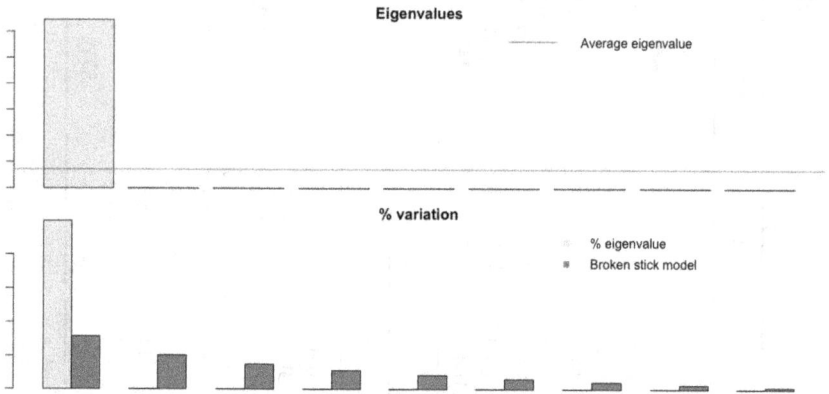

FIGURE A.3 Principle Component Analysis of Indicators of Readability in All Cases based on Eigenvector Values Using the Kaiser-Gutman and Broken-Stick Method

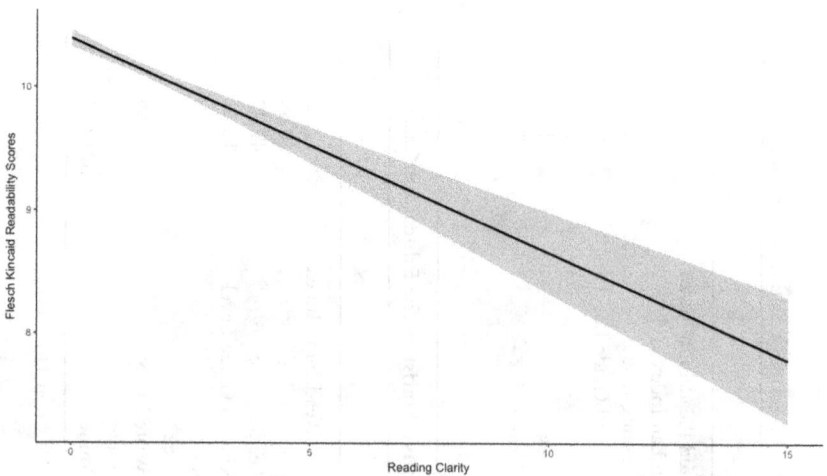

FIGURE A.4 Comparative Analysis of Readability based on PCA vs. the Flesch Kincaid Readability Grading Scale

higher scores indicate a higher level of comprehension needed in order to understand a document. While this makes some intuitive sense at an explanatory level, "readability" is often understood in terms of how *easy* it is to read a text, not how *difficult*. Our measure corrects for this by reversing these scales. As Figure A.4 shows, opinions that would rank *high* on the Flesch-Kincaid readability measure – that is to say, opinions that are significantly *difficult* to understand – rank low on our measure of readability. Thus, as the ease of comprehension increases, so too does the readability of the document. This allows us to specifically focus on the commonly stated refrain that good opinions should be written in "plain English" and specifically that justification will be written clearly so that external audiences have the best chance of understanding the content of an opinion.

Descriptive Statistics

Throughout this text, we have included a number of controls based upon the previous literature. Table A.3 provides summary statistics for the covariates for death penalty cases included in the model. Table A.4 provides similar statistics for education cases. We focus here on describing some of the more complicated variables used in our analysis. Appendix B provides full models for all chapters, including all controls included in the model.

Aside from complexity and readability (discussed above), method of retention is controlled for here using a categorical variable indicating how the court specifically retained judges during the time period under study. Our control category for all chapters was the use of partisan elections (coded as "1" in our data), as this method of retention is often placed under the most scrutiny by critics for being "unjudge-like" in behavior. Thus, we test explicitly whether partisan elections have any substantial effect by comparing them directly to the remaining options for retention in order to get a clearer picture of how retention mechanisms impact opinions. Method of retention ranges from 1 to 4, with "2" indicating a state uses non-partisan elections to retain their judges, "3" indicating elite reappointment systems, and "4" indicating retention elections used to maintain the bench. As Figure A.5 shows, method of retention is dispersed differently based on case type in our data; with most education cases occurring in states with non-partisan elections, whereas death penalty cases occur most frequently in states using retention elections.

While our primary purpose is to understand the role of language in judicial opinions and how institutional factors such as method of retention affect such language, we recognize that several other factors may affect the opinion writing process. We can separate these covariates based on whether they are characteristics of the majority opinion writer, of the court and state more generally, or case-specific circumstances. Along with the methods of retention, we also control for other institutional variations that occur among the states, namely whether the supreme court has discretionary jurisdiction, term length for judges, the number

TABLE A.3 Descriptive Statistics: Death Penalty Cases

Variable	Missing (%)	Mean	SD	SE	Median	Range	Skewness
Institutional Variables							
Method of Retention	0	2.93	1.22	0.02	4	3 (1–4)	−0.5
Term Length	0	7.99	2.83	0.04	8	93 (6–99)	13.02
Discretionary Jurisdiction	0	0.94	0.24	0	1	1 (0–1)	−3.58
Number of Seats	0	7.06	1.19	0.02	7	4 (5–9)	−0.01
Simultaneous Voting	0	1.39	0.49	0.01	1	1 (1–2)	0.44
Opinion Assignment Method	0	2.29	0.91	0.01	2	4 (1–5)	1.06
Professionalism	0	0.76	0.16	0	0.74	0.73 (0.31–1.04)	0.01
Judge Specific Variables							
Ideological Extremism (Maj. Author)	0	0.99	0.96	0.01	0.69	5.8 (0–5.8)	1.68
Female Author	0	0.19	0.39	0.01	0	1 (0–1)	1.62
African American Author	0	0.06	0.24	0	0	1 (0–1)	3.69
Top 14 Law School	0	0.14	0.35	0	0	1 (0–1)	2.02
Prior Judicial Experience	0	0.56	0.5	0.01	1	1 (0–1)	−0.25
State Specific Variables							
Public Mood	0	0.37	0.05	0	0.36	0.27 (0.26–0.52)	0.59
Percent Conservatives (in State)	0	0.36	0.06	0	0.35	0.34 (0.22–0.56)	0.48
Case Specific Variables							
Reversed Sentence	0	1.24	0.43	0.01	1	1 (1–2)	1.23
Dissent Issued	0	0.3	0.46	0.01	0	1 (0–1)	0.88
Concurrence Issued	0	0.31	0.46	0.01	0	1 (0–1)	0.84
Number of Votes in a case	9.3	6.64	1.22	0.02	7	9 (1–10)	−0.26
Non-Unanimous Decision	9.3	1.32	0.47	0.01	1	1 (1–2)	0.79

Opinion Specific Variables

Cognitive Complexity (Maj. Op.)	0	-0.2	0.2	0	-0.21	2 (-1–1)	0.34
Reading Clarity (Maj. Op.)	0.23	4.44	1.01	0.01	4.18	11.65 (3.35–15)	2.77
Analytic Language (Maj. Op.)	0	0.93	0.03	0	0.94	0.51 (0.48–0.99)	-1.98
Authentic Language (Maj. Op.)	0	0.09	0.05	0	0.08	0.66 (0.01–0.67)	2.49
Frame Consistency	0	0.28	0.1	0	0.27	0.73 (0.04–0.77)	0.83
Salient Frame	0	0.41	0.49	0.01	0	1 (0–1)	0.37
Median Court Ideology	0	-0.09	0.58	0.01	-0.1	3.12 (-1.5–1.62)	0.28
Ideological Distance – Maj. Op – Median	0	0.84	0.9	0.01	0.57	5.64 (0–5.64)	1.59
Cognitive Complexity (dissent)	70.25	-0.42	0.16	0	-0.41	2 (-1–1)	0.47
Ideological Distance: Maj Op. – Dissent	73.03	-0.55	2.82	0.08	-0.48	16.01 (-7.91–8.1)	0.01
Inverse Mills Ratio	0	1.29	0.51	0.01	1.33	2.54 (0.08–2.62)	-0.15

Source: Table Created by Authors

TABLE A.4 Descriptive Statistics: Education Cases

Variable	Missings (%)	Mean	SD	SE	Median	Range	Skewness
Institutional Variables							
Method of Retention	0	2.68	1.01	0.03	3	3 (1–4)	−0.03
Term Length	0	14.75	23.5	0.63	8	96 (3–99)	3.27
Discretionary Jurisdiction	0	0.77	0.42	0.01	1	1 (0–1)	−1.3
Number of Seats	0	6.65	1.32	0.04	7	4 (5–9)	0.21
Simultaneous Voting	0	1.38	0.49	0.01	1	1 (1–2)	0.47
Opinion Assignment Method	0	2.1	1.02	0.03	2	4 (1–5)	0.93
Professionalism	0	0.67	0.16	0	0.68	0.73 (0.31–1.04)	0.18
Judge Specific Variables							
Ideological Extremism (Maj. Author)	0	1.01	0.99	0.03	0.63	5.63 (0–5.63)	1.55
Female Author	0	0.21	0.41	0.01	0	1 (0–1)	1.44
African American Author	0	0.04	0.2	0.01	0	1 (0–1)	4.63
Top 14 Law School	0	0.21	0.41	0.01	0	1 (0–1)	1.39
Prior Judicial Experience	0	0.64	0.97	0.03	1	9 (0–9)	6.22
State Specific Variables							
Public Mood	0	0.36	0.05	0	0.35	0.25 (0.26–0.51)	0.45
Percent Conservatives (in State)	0	0.35	0.06	0	0.34	0.36 (0.19–0.55)	0.46
Case Specific Variables							
Liberal Disposition	0	6.17	23.2	0.62	0	99 (0–99)	3.75
Dissent Issued	0	0.31	0.46	0.01	0	1 (0–1)	0.8
Concurrence Issued	0	0.2	0.4	0.01	0	1 (0–1)	1.54
Number of Votes in a case	0	5.96	1.66	0.04	6	9 (0–9)	−0.73
Non-Unanimous Decision	2.05	1.28	0.45	0.01	1	1 (1–2)	0.98

Opinion Specific Variables

Cognitive Complexity (Maj. Op.)	0	−0.15	0.27	0.01	−0.15	2 (−1–1)	0.11
Reading Clarity (Maj. Op.)	0	4.44	1.01	0.03	4.52	7.38 (0–7.38)	−0.53
Analytic Language (Maj. Op.)	0	0.96	0.02	0	0.97	0.17 (0.82–0.99)	−1.59
Authentic Language (Maj. Op.)	0	0.12	0.07	0	0.1	0.59 (0.01–0.6)	1.87
Frame Consistency	0	0.4	0.11	0	0.39	0.66 (0.18–0.84)	0.62
Salient Frame	0	0.32	0.47	0.01	0	1 (0–1)	0.78
Median Court Ideology	0	−0.02	0.48	0.01	−0.04	3.12 (−1.5–1.62)	0.19
Ideological Distance – Maj. Op – Median	0	0.89	0.95	0.03	0.58	5.79 (0–5.79)	1.56
Cognitive Complexity (dissent)	81.6	−0.52	0.18	0.01	−0.52	2 (−1–1)	2.75
Ideological Distance: Maj Op. – Dissent	72.82	−0.26	2.67	0.14	−0.27	15.64 (−8.38–7.26)	−0.09
Inverse Mills Ratio	1.98	1.25	0.49	0.01	1.27	2.61 (0.11–2.72)	−0.04

Source: Table Created by Authors

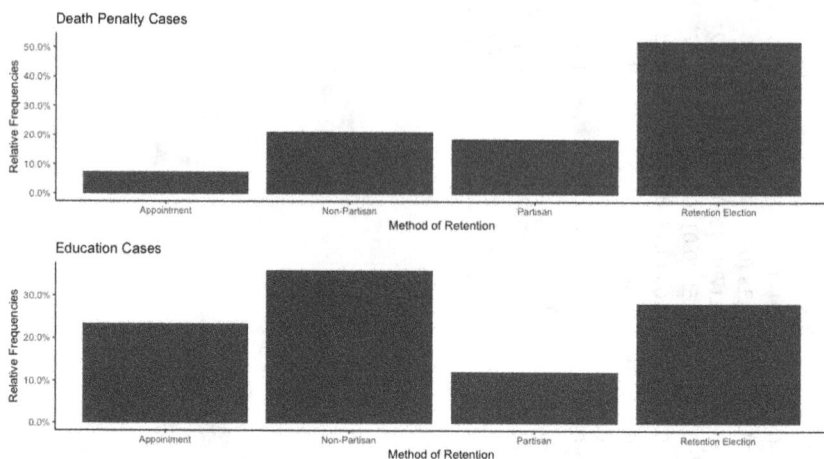

FIGURE A.5 Frequency of Cases by Method Used to Retain Judges in the State

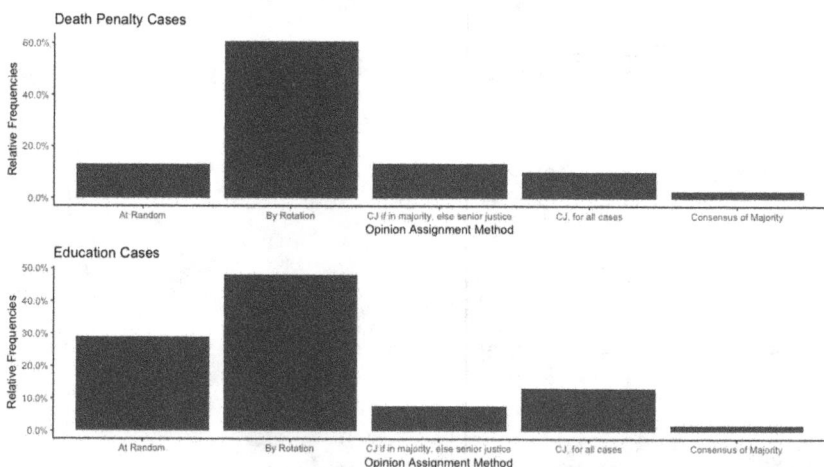

FIGURE A.6 Frequency of Cases by Method of Opinion Assignment Used in the State

of seats on the court and the court's level of professionalism (based on the Squires index), and opinion assignment and voting features of the institution. Specifically, we use Hughes, Wilhelm and Vining's (2015) breakdown of methods of opinion assignment and voting procedures to control for whether or not judges are required to vote simultaneously on a given case, or whether the initial conference vote is performed in some other way. Methods of opinion assignment were organized by categories that ranged from "1" (At Random) to "5" (Consensus of the Majority). The vast majority of decisions were written by courts using rotation as the means by which opinions where assigned. Figure A.6 displays a simple frequency chart for all death penalty and education cases.

Notes

1 Data was scraped from the Lexis Legal Archive utilizing keyword searches of the following phrases: "death penalty," "death sentence," "capital punishment," sentenced to death." The compiled cases were hand coded for their disposition and outcome, and cases that dealt with ancillary matters (such as the constitutionality of the death penalty itself) were removed. The data represent only those in which a criminal defendant's case was reviewed for error, and in which the justices published a written, formal opinion outlining their reasoning for affirming or reversing the death penalty sentence.

2 While previous scholarship working with complexity measures have commonly included measures of *inclusive* and *exclusive* language, as well as language measuring inhibition in calculating their scores, the latest dictionaries from the LIWC team (Pennebaker et al. 2015) removed these measures due to their weak psychometric values. While we do have indicators for these values for death penalty cases, value calculations for education cases were not possible to collect. Thus, for consistency, we drop these values from our variable generation process.

References

Ajina, A., Laouiti, M., & Msolli, B. (2016). Guiding Through the Fog: Does Annual Report Readability Reveal Earnings Management? *Research in International Business and Finance*, 38, 509–516

Benoit, K., Munger, K., & Spirling, A. (2017). Measuring and Explaining Political Sophistication Through Textual Complexity. https://ssrn.com/abstract=3062061 (accessed on May 26, 2019)

Cangelosi, R. & Goriely A. (2007). Component Retention in Principal Component Analysis with Application to cDNA Microarray Data. *Biology Direct*, 2(2), 1–21

Flesch, R. (1948). A New Readability Yardstick. *Journal of Applied Psychology*, 32(3), 221–233

Gibbons, F. X. (1990). Self-attention and Behavior: A Review and Theoretical Update. *Advances in Experimental Social Psychology*, 23(2), 249–303

Gruenfeld, D H. (1995). Status, Ideology, and Integrative Complexity on the U.S. Supreme Court: Rethinking the Politics of Political Decision Making. *Journal of Personality and Social Psychology*, 68(1), 5–20

Gruenfeld, D. H. & Preston, J. (2000). Upending the Status Quo: Cognitive Complexity in the U.S. Supreme Court Justices Who Overturn Legal Precedent. *Personality and Social Psychology Bulletin*, 26(4), 1013–1022

Gunning, R. (1952). *The Technique of Clear Writing*. New York: McGraw-Hill

Hughes, D.A., Wilhelm, T., & Vining Jr., R.L. (2015). Deliberation Rules and Opinion Assignment Procedures in State Supreme Courts: A Replication. *Justice System Journal*, 36(4), 395–410

MacArthur, R.H. (1957). On the Relative Abundance of Birth Species. *Proceedings of the National Academy of Sciences*, 43, 293–592

Owens, R. J. & Wedeking, J. (2012). Predicting Drift on Political Insulated Institutions: A Study of Ideological Drift on the United States Supreme Court. *Journal of Politics*, 74(2), 487–500

Pennebaker, J. W., Booth, R. J., Boyd, R. L., & Francis, M. E. (2015). *Linguistic Inquiry and Word Count: LIWC2015*. Austin, TX: Pennebaker Conglomerates (www.LIWC.net)

Romano, M. K. (2018). Legislators Off Their Leash: Cognitive Shirking and Impending Retirement in the U.S. House. *Social Science Quarterly*, 99(3), 993–1005

Terblanche, M., & Burgess, L. (2010). Examining the Readability of Patient-Informed Consent Forms. *Open Access Journal of Clinical Trials*, 2, 157–162

Tetlock, P. E. (1986). A Value Pluralism Model of Ideological Reasoning. *Journal of Personality and Social Psychology*, 50(4), 819–827

Tetlock, P. E., Bernzweig, J., & Gallant, J. L. (1985). Supreme Court Decision Making: Cognitive Style as a Predictor of Ideological Consistency in Voting. *Journal of Personality and Social Psychology*, 48(4), 1227–1239

Winter, D. G. (1996). *Personality: Analysis and Interpretation of Lives*. New York: McGraw

APPENDIX B

Full Chapter Models

Chapter 3

TABLE B.1 Language and Method of Retention Effects on the Consistency of an Opinion Frame in Death Penalty Cases

Indicators	Frame Consistency
	Estimates
Intercept	−0.064
	(0.159)
Non-Partisan Election	−0.016★★
	(0.006)
Appointment	0.000
	(0.008)
Retention Election	−0.013★
	(0.006)
Term Length	0.001
	(0.001)
Discretionary Jurisdiction	−0.037★★★
	(0.009)
Reversed Sentence	0.013★★★
	(0.003)
Dissent	0.004
	(0.003)
Concurrence	0.001
	(0.003)
Per Curiam Opinion	−0.004
	(0.008)

(Continued)

Indicators	Frame Consistency Estimates
Ideological Extremeness	0.000
	(0.002)
African American Judge	0.003
	(0.007)
Female Judge	0.001
	(0.004)
Top 14 Law School	0.009
	(0.005)
Number of Seats	0.014★★★
	(0.002)
Prior Judicial Exp.	−0.008
	(0.004)
Simultaneous Voting	0.004
	(0.007)
Assign. Method: By Rotation	−0.008
	(0.006)
Assign. Method: CJ if in majority	−0.019★
	(0.008)
Assign. Method: CJ, for all cases	0.043★★★
	(0.009)
Assign. Method: Consensus of Majority	−0.006
	(0.014)
Professionalism	0.020
	(0.018)
Public Mood	0.083★
	(0.035)
Analytic Language Use	0.442★★
	(0.168)
Authentic Language Use	0.178★★★
	(0.036)
Opinion Length	−0.017★
	(0.008)
Cognitive Complexity	−0.021
	(0.013)
Frame: Legal Factors	−0.085★★★
	(0.007)
Frame: Case Facts	−0.095★★★
	(0.007)
Frame: Jury Instructions	−0.034★★★
	(0.010)
Frame: Precedent	−0.047★★★
	(0.010)

| | Frame Consistency |
Indicators	Estimates
Frame: Precedent	−0.047★★★
	(0.010)
Frame: Jury Challenges	−0.050★★★
	(0.007)
Frame: Procedural Issues	−0.117★★★
	(0.007)
Frame: Witnesses	−0.087★★★
	(0.007)
Frame: Questioning	−0.072★★★
	(0.008)
Frame: Mental Illness	−0.035★★★
	(0.007)
Frame: Ineffective Counsel	−0.042★★★
	(0.006)
Frame: Sentencing	−0.071★★★
	(0.007)
Frame: Prosecution Error	−0.097★★★
	(0.007)
Frame: Physical Evidence	−0.075★★★
	(0.007)
Frame: Gen. Attorney	−0.029★★★
	(0.007)
Reading Clarity	0.107★★
	(0.034)
Analytic Language*Reading Clarity	−0.131★★★
	(0.036)
Authentic Language*Cognitive Complexity	0.024
	(0.109)

Random Effects

σ^2	0.01
$\tau_{00\ JID}$	0.00
$\tau_{00\ Year}$	0.00
$\tau_{11\ JID.stcode}$	0.00
$\tau_{11\ Year.stcode}$	0.00
$\rho_{01\ JID}$	−0.97
$\rho_{01\ Year}$	−0.94
ICC_{JID}	0.12
ICC_{Year}	0.01
Observations	5194
Marginal R^2/Conditional R^2	0.179/0.283
AIC	−9978.330

*p < 0.05 **p < 0.01 ***p < 0.001

Source: Table Created by Authors

TABLE B.2 Language and Method of Retention Effects on the Consistency of an Opinion Frame in Education Cases

Indicators	Frame Consistency Estimates
Intercept	0.015
	(0.665)
Non-Partisan Election	−0.001
	(0.011)
Appointment	−0.021
	(0.013)
Retention Election	−0.002
	(0.012)
Term Length	0.000**
	(0.000)
Discretionary Jurisdiction	0.002
	(0.010)
Liberal Disposition	0.000
	(0.000)
Dissent	0.014*
	(0.006)
Concurrence	0.008
	(0.007)
Per Curiam Opinion	−0.003
	(0.011)
Ideological Extremeness	−0.000
	(0.003)
African American Judge	−0.022
	(0.015)
Female Judge	0.002
	(0.008)
Top 14 Law School	−0.010
	(0.008)
Number of Seats	−0.004
	(0.003)
Prior Judicial Exp.	0.001
	(0.003)
Simultaneous Voting	−0.004
	(0.007)
Assign. Method: By Rotation	−0.009
	(0.007)
Assign. Method: CJ if in majority	−0.007
	(0.014)
Assign. Method: CJ, for all cases	0.004
	(0.011)
Assign. Method: Consensus of Majority	0.028
	(0.025)
Professionalism	0.015
	(0.026)

| | Frame Consistency |
Indicators	Estimates
Public Mood	−0.021
	(0.070)
Analytic Language Use	0.341
	(0.686)
Authentic Language Use	0.232★★★
	(0.051)
Opinion Length	0.007
	(0.022)
Cognitive Complexity	−0.007
	(0.020)
Frame: Complaints	0.023★
	(0.010)
Frame: Funding	0.106★★★
	(0.011)
Frame: Employee Relations	0.034★★★
	(0.010)
Frame: Injury Case	0.092★★★
	(0.010)
Frame: Constitutional Requirements	0.008
	(0.011)
Frame: Student Performance	0.030★★
	(0.011)
Reading Clarity	0.069
	(0.137)
Analytic Language*Reading Clarity	−0.073
	(0.142)
Authentic Language*Cognitive Complexity	−0.004
	(0.130)

Random Effects

σ^2	0.01
$\tau_{00 \text{ JID}}$	0.00
$\tau_{00 \text{ Year}}$	0.00
$\tau_{11 \text{ JID.stcode}}$	0.00
$\tau_{11 \text{ Year.stcode}}$	0.00
$\rho_{01 \text{ JID}}$	−1.00
$\rho_{01 \text{ Year}}$	−1.00
ICC_{JID}	0.13
ICC_{Year}	0.00
Observations	1413
AIC	−2184.985

*$p < 0.05$ **$p < 0.01$ ***$p < 0.001$

Source: Table Created by Authors

Chapter 4

TABLE B.3 What Affects the Likelihood of a Dissent in Death Penalty and Education Cases?

Indicators	Death Penalty Model Log-Odds	Edcuation Model Log-Odds
Intercept	−0.074	4.012
	(0.846)	(2.224)
Non-Partisan Election	0.545★★★	0.413★★
	(0.103)	(0.157)
Appointment	0.701★★★	−0.094
	(0.146)	(0.204)
Retention Election	0.178	0.051
	(0.105)	(0.158)
Term Length	−0.010	−0.005
	(0.013)	(0.003)
Discretionary Jurisdiction	0.497★★	0.068
	(0.157)	(0.146)
Reversed Sentence	0.306	
	(0.372)	
Concurrence	1.052★★★	0.952★★★
	(0.046)	(0.101)
Ideological Extremeness	−0.008	0.102★
	(0.031)	(0.043)
Number of Seats	0.042	0.137★★
	(0.039)	(0.042)
Public Mood	−0.162	−0.025
	(0.718)	(1.121)
Professionalism	0.579	0.866★
	(0.304)	(0.350)
Simultaneous Voting	−0.206★	−0.092
	(0.096)	(0.100)
Maj. Opinion: Female Judge	−0.044	−0.131
	(0.081)	(0.110)
Maj. Opinion: African American Judge	−0.133	−0.273
	(0.121)	(0.214)
Authentic Language Use	1.062★	−0.823
	(0.503)	(0.657)
Analytic Language Use	−1.386	−6.551★★
	(0.715)	(2.239)
Percent Conservatives in State	−1.635★★	−0.304
	(0.499)	(0.844)
Frame: Legal Factors	−0.334★★	
	(0.120)	
Frame: Case Facts	−0.561★★★	
	(0.112)	

Indicators	Death Penalty Model Log-Odds	Edcuation Model Log-Odds
Frame: Jury Instructions	−0.614★★★	
	(0.153)	
Frame: Precedent	−0.325★	
	(0.163)	
Frame: Jury Challenges	−0.269★	
	(0.113)	
Frame: Procedural Issues	−0.562★★★	
	(0.121)	
Frame: Witnesses	−0.273★	
	(0.110)	
Frame: Questioning	−0.253	
	(0.133)	
Frame: Mental Illness	−0.094	
	(0.114)	
Frame: Ineffective Counsel	−0.537★★★	
	(0.095)	
Frame: Sentencing	−0.135	
	(0.108)	
Frame: Prosecution Error	−0.604★★★	
	(0.110)	
Frame: Physical Evidence	−0.497★★★	
	(0.113)	
Frame: Gen. Attorney	−0.561★★★	
	(0.108)	
Reversed Sentence★Public Mood	0.438	
	(0.990)	
Liberal Disposition		0.010
		(0.017)
Frame: Complaints		−0.253
		(0.148)
Frame: Funding		0.423★
		(0.164)
Frame: Employee Relations		0.092
		(0.141)
Frame: Injury Case		0.070
		(0.149)
Frame: Constitutional Requirements		0.361★
		(0.162)
Frame: Student Performance		0.241
		(0.166)
Liberal Disposition★Public Mood		−0.033
		(0.048)

(Continued)

TABLE B.3 (Continued)

Indicators	Death Penalty Model Log-Odds	Edcuation Model Log-Odds
Random Effects		
σ^2	1.00	1.00
τ_{00}	0.06_{JID} 0.04_{Year}	0.14_{JID} 0.03_{Year}
τ_{11}	$0.00_{\text{JID.stcode}}$ $0.00_{\text{Year.stcode}}$	$0.00_{\text{JID.stcode}}$ $0.00_{\text{Year.stcode}}$
ρ_{01}	1.00_{JID} -0.95_{Year}	-1.00_{JID} -1.00_{Year}
ICC	0.05_{JID} 0.04_{Year}	0.12_{JID} 0.03_{Year}
Observations	5206	1385
Marginal R^2/Conditional R^2	0.277/0.343	0.280/0.386
AIC	5309.201	1490.087

$*p < 0.05$ $**p < 0.01$ $***p < 0.001$

Source: Table Created by Authors

TABLE B.4 Impact of Dissent Decision on the Language Quality of Death Penalty Opinions on State Supreme Courts

Indicators	Cognitive Complexity Model Estimates	Reading Clarity Model Estimates
Intercept	−0.284	2.209*
	(0.147)	(0.929)
Non-Partisan Election	−0.030	1.446
	(0.126)	(0.790)
Appointment	−0.349**	5.970***
	(0.129)	(0.807)
Retention Election	−0.095	2.057**
	(0.104)	(0.618)
Term Length	−0.009	0.249**
	(0.012)	(0.080)
Frame: Legal Factors	0.006	0.232
	(0.025)	(0.136)
Frame: Case Facts	0.092***	0.570***
	(0.025)	(0.136)
Frame: Jury Instructions	0.176***	1.409***
	(0.035)	(0.194)
Frame: Precedent	0.141***	1.043***
	(0.035)	(0.186)

Indicators	Cognitive Complexity Model Estimates	Reading Clarity Model Estimates
Frame: Jury Challenges	0.128★★★	0.373★★
	(0.024)	(0.130)
Frame: Procedural Issues	0.043	0.656★★★
	(0.027)	(0.144)
Frame: Witnesses	0.012	0.472★★★
	(0.023)	(0.119)
Frame: Questioning	−0.005	0.675★★★
	(0.027)	(0.138)
Frame: Mental Illness	−0.050★	0.244★
	(0.022)	(0.115)
Frame: Ineffective Counsel	−0.006	0.275★
	(0.022)	(0.121)
Frame: Sentencing	−0.051★	0.150
	(0.021)	(0.112)
Frame: Prosecution Error	0.104 ★★★	0.540★★★
	(0.028)	(0.151)
Frame: Physical Evidence	0.046	0.578★★★
	(0.026)	(0.140)
Frame: Gen. Attorney	0.039	−0.092
	(0.026)	(0.140)
Discretionary Jurisdiction	0.010	−1.051★★★
	(0.036)	(0.241)
Reversed Sentence	−0.047★★★	−0.319★★★
	(0.014)	(0.077)
Concurrence	−0.058★	−0.088
	(0.023)	(0.142)
Ideological Extremeness	0.007	0.008
	(0.006)	(0.037)
Number of Seats	0.015	0.211★★★
	(0.008)	(0.052)
Percent Conservatives in State	0.069	1.359★
	(0.104)	(0.646)
Professionalism	0.010	−0.010
	(0.071)	(0.487)
Assign. Method: By Rotation	0.001	−0.739★★★
	(0.022)	(0.142)
Assign. Method: CJ if in majority	−0.001	−0.462★
	(0.032)	(0.225)
Assign. Method: CJ, for all cases	−0.066★	0.675★★★
	(0.029)	(0.191)
Assign. Method: Consensus of Majority	−0.001	−0.277
	(0.050)	(0.410)

(Continued)

TABLE B.4 (Continued)

Indicators	Cognitive Complexity Model Estimates	Reading Clarity Model Estimates
Cognitive Complexity: Dissent	−0.322★★★	0.135
	(0.030)	(0.162)
Ideological Distance: Majority	0.004★	−0.007
Author and Dissent	(0.002)	(0.010)
Reading Clarity	0.002	
	(0.005)	
Inverse Mills Ratio	−0.083★	−0.399★
	(0.032)	(0.199)
Non-Partisan Election★Term Length	−0.003	−0.212
	(0.017)	(0.111)
Appointment★Term Length	0.033★	−0.616★★★
	(0.015)	(0.093)
Retention Election★Term Length	0.006	−0.245★★
	(0.013)	(0.084)
Majority Opinion: Cognitive		0.105
Complexity		(0.141)
Random Effects		
σ^2	0.03	0.65
τ_{00}	0.00_{JID}	0.93_{JID}
	0.00_{Year}	0.09_{Year}
τ_{11}	$0.00_{\text{JID.stcode}}$	$0.00_{\text{JID.stcode}}$
	$0.00_{\text{Year.stcode}}$	$0.00_{\text{Year.stcode}}$
ρ_{01}	-0.77_{JID}	-1.00_{JID}
	-1.00_{Year}	-1.00_{Year}
ICC	0.16_{JID}	0.56_{JID}
	0.00_{Year}	0.05_{Year}
Observations	1395	1395
Marginal R^2/Conditional R^2	0.254/0.374	NA
AIC	−742.215	3800.761

$\star p < 0.05$ $\star\star p < 0.01$ $\star\star\star p < 0.001$

Source: Table Created by Authors

TABLE B.5 Impact of Dissent Decision on the Language Quality of Education Opinions on State Supreme Courts

Indicators	Cognitive Complexity Model Estimates	Reading Clarity Model Estimates
Intercept	−0.223	6.814★★★
	(0.385)	(1.789)
Non-Partisan Election	−0.419	−0.427
	(0.201)	(1.203)
Appointment	−0.105	−0.445
	(0.201)	(1.174)
Retention Election	−0.143	0.163
	(0.218)	(1.232)
Term Length	−0.013	−0.009
	(0.025)	(0.146)
Frame: Complaints	0.006	−0.009
	(0.048)	(0.181)
Frame: Funding	−0.107★	−0.361
	(0.053)	(0.202)
Frame: Employee Relations	−0.007	−0.275
	(0.044)	(0.161)
Frame: Injury Case	0.113★	0.088
	(0.044)	(0.172)
Frame: Constitutional Requirements	0.055	−0.199
	(0.052)	(0.199)
Frame: Student Performance	−0.065	−0.089
	(0.050)	(0.188)
Discretionary Jurisdiction	−0.026	0.003
	(0.051)	(0.275)
Liberal Disposition	−0.000	−0.001
	(0.001)	(0.002)
Concurrence	−0.046	−0.444
	(0.064)	(0.241)
Ideological Extremeness	−0.011	−0.050
	(0.013)	(0.053)
Number of Seats	0.038★	−0.064
	(0.018)	(0.093)
Percent Conservatives in State	0.252	−1.177
	(0.222)	(0.972)
Professionalism	−0.326★	0.059
	(0.132)	(0.696)
Assign. Method: By Rotation	−0.059	−0.122
	(0.034)	(0.184)
Assign. Method: CJ if in majority	0.030	−0.482
	(0.058)	(0.317)

(Continued)

TABLE B.5 (Continued)

Indicators	Cognitive Complexity Model Estimates	Reading Clarity Model Estimates
Assign. Method: CJ, for all cases	−0.015 (0.058)	−0.438 (0.290)
Assign. Method: Consensus of Majority	0.139 (0.107)	−0.433 (0.520)
Ideological Distance: Majority Author and Dissent	−0.004 (0.005)	−0.026 (0.018)
Reading Clarity	0.060★★★ (0.013)	
Inverse Mills Ratio	−0.120 (0.102)	−0.606 (0.386)
Non-Partisan Election★Term Length	0.044 (0.026)	−0.013 (0.154)
Appointment★Term Length	0.013 (0.025)	0.009 (0.146)
Retention Election★Term Length	0.020 (0.028)	−0.024 (0.156)
Majority Opinion: Cognitive Complexity		0.838★★★ (0.195)
Random Effects		
σ^2	0.04	0.55
τ_{00}	$0.00_{\text{JID:stcode}}$ 0.00_{stcode} 0.00_{Year} $0.00_{\text{Year.stcode}}$	$0.09_{\text{JID:stcode}}$ 0.12_{stcode} 0.05_{Year} $0.00_{\text{Year.stcode}}$
τ_{11}		
ρ_{01}	-1.00_{Year}	-0.89_{Year}
ICC	$0.09_{\text{JID:stcode}}$ 0.01_{stcode} 0.05_{Year}	$0.12_{\text{JID:stcode}}$ 0.15_{stcode} 0.06_{Year}
Observations	378	378
Marginal R^2/Conditional R^2	NA	0.145/0.419
AIC	124.761	1053.643

★$p < 0.05$ ★★$p < 0.01$ ★★★$p < 0.001$

Source: Table Created by Authors

Chapter 5

TABLE B.6 Language and Method of Retention Affects on the Likelihood of Writing Per Curiam Decisions on State Supreme Courts

Indicators	Death Penalty Model Log-Odds	Education Model Log-Odds
Intercept	3.939	−3.728
	(2.846)	(5.054)
Non-Partisan Election	−0.281	0.182
	(0.233)	(0.317)
Appointment	0.788★	−0.247
	(0.367)	(0.413)
Retention Election	−0.197	−0.772★
	(0.266)	(0.399)
Term Length	−0.208★★★	−0.005
	(0.051)	(0.005)
Discretionary Jurisdiction	−2.130★★★	0.084
	(0.284)	(0.326)
Reversed Sentence	0.096	
	(0.151)	
Concurrence	−0.222	−0.270
	(0.168)	(0.250)
Dissent	−0.282	−0.321
	(0.165)	(0.208)
Number of Seats	−0.058	−0.378★★★
	(0.078)	(0.088)
Professionalism	1.496★	2.656★★
	(0.734)	(0.852)
Assign. Method: By Rotation	−0.307	0.450★
	(0.184)	(0.191)
Assign. Method: CJ if in majority	−1.934★★★	−0.956
	(0.360)	(0.513)
Assign. Method: CJ, for all cases	−1.073★	−1.340★
	(0.470)	(0.568)
Assign. Method: Consensus of Majority	−2.207★★	−0.658
	(0.893)	(0.750)
Public Mood	3.235★	1.782
	(1.411)	(2.279)
Median Ideology of Court	0.518★★	0.938★★★
	(0.172)	(0.232)
Frame Consistency	−0.279	0.179
	(0.628)	(0.805)
Analytic Language Use	4.001	3.827
	(2.493)	(4.993)
Authentic Language Use	−0.369	0.406
	(1.235)	(1.267)

(Continued)

TABLE B.6 (Continued)

Indicators	Death Penalty Model Log-Odds	Education Model Log-Odds
Cognitive Complexity	0.814★	−0.030
	(0.398)	(0.379)
Reading Clarity	−2.511★★★	−0.823★
	(0.294)	(0.386)
Reading Clarity^2	0.147★★★	0.090★
	(0.018)	(0.046)
Cognitive Complexity^2	1.300	0.400
	(0.822)	(0.729)
Salient Frame	−0.422	−0.592
	(0.265)	(0.634)
Non-Partisan Election★Salient Frame	0.426	0.199
	(0.355)	(0.700)
Appointment★Salient Frame	−0.439	0.478
	(0.499)	(0.732)
Retention Election★Salient Frame	0.700	0.649
	(0.408)	(0.780)
Liberal Disposition		0.001
		(0.003)
Observations	4283	1408
Cox & Snell's R^2/Nagelkerke's R^2	0.081/0.212	0.052/0.103
AIC	1755.370	980.900

*$p < 0.05$ **$p < 0.01$ ***$p < 0.001$

Source: Table Created by Authors

Chapter 6

TABLE B.7 Language and Method of Retention Affects on the Likelihood of a Non-Unanimous Decision on State Supreme Courts

Indicators	Death Penalty Model Log-Odds	Education Model Log-Odds
Intercept	−9.538★★★	−4.369
	(1.342)	(3.321)
Non-Partisan Election	1.059★★	1.552
	(0.346)	(0.925)
Appointment	1.956★★★	−0.313
	(0.482)	(1.081)
Retention Election	0.255	−0.377
	(0.371)	(0.971)
Term Length	−0.081	0.012
	(0.058)	(0.014)

Indicators	Death Penalty Model Log-Odds	Education Model Log-Odds
Discretionary Jurisdiction	1.299★★ (0.463)	−1.047 (0.860)
Reversed Sentence	1.037★★★ (0.035)	
Number of Seats	0.412★★★ (0.122)	1.114★★★ (0.264)
Professionalism	2.545★ (1.034)	7.241★★ (2.247)
Assign. Method: By Rotation	0.167 (0.332)	−0.392 (0.668)
Assign. Method: CJ if in majority	−0.275 (0.487)	0.332 (1.099)
Assign. Method: CJ, for all cases	−0.362 (0.407)	−2.142★ (0.992)
Assign. Method: Consensus of Majority	0.285 (0.853)	1.906 (1.878)
Public Mood	−0.371 (0.792)	−11.157★★★ (2.859)
Female Judge	−0.033 (0.270)	−0.100 (0.611)
African American Judge	−0.377 (0.412)	−0.140 (1.148)
Prior Judicial Experience	−0.384 (0.241)	−0.065 (0.228)
Ideological Extremeness	−0.285★★★ (0.052)	−0.225 (0.187)
Ideological Distance from Median	0.357★★★ (0.053)	0.247 (0.195)
Salient Frame	0.132 (0.109)	−1.525★★★ (0.402)
Frame Consistency	1.648★★★ (0.192)	1.702★★★ (0.491)
Analytic Language Use	−0.721 (0.569)	−7.316★★★ (2.169)
Authentic Language Use	2.578★★★ (0.355)	−0.919 (0.637)
Cognitive Complexity	−0.307★ (0.123)	0.878★★★ (0.182)
Reading Clarity	0.771★★★ (0.073)	0.743★★★ (0.079)
Reading Clarity^2	−0.038★★★ (0.006)	−0.128★★★ (0.008)
Cognitive Complexity^2	−0.007 (0.218)	−0.101 (0.392)

(Continued)

TABLE B.7 (Continued)

Indicators	Death Penalty Model Log-Odds	Education Model Log-Odds
Salient Frame*Frame Consistency	−1.518***	5.746***
	(0.310)	(0.828)
Non-Partisan Election*Frame Salient	0.363***	−0.292
	(0.102)	(0.277)
Appointment*Frame Salient	0.372*	−0.335
	(0.154)	(0.299)
Retention Election*Frame Salient	0.681***	−0.919**
	(0.084)	(0.283)
Liberal Disposition		−0.009***
		(0.002)
Random Effects		
σ^2	3.29	3.29
τ_{00}	2.96_{JID}	31.38_{JID}
	0.48_{Year}	0.30_{Year}
τ_{11}	$0.00_{JID.stcode}$	$0.03_{JID.stcode}$
	$0.00_{Year.stcode}$	$0.00_{Year.stcode}$
ρ_{01}	1.00_{JID}	-0.75_{JID}
	-0.90_{Year}	0.00_{Year}
ICC	0.44_{JID}	0.90_{JID}
	0.07_{Year}	0.01_{Year}
Observations	4712	1384
Marginal R^2/Conditional R^2	0.120/0.570	0.121/0.917
AIC	32480.740	6981.884

*$p < 0.05$ **$p < 0.01$ ***$p < 0.001$

Source: Table Created by Authors

INDEX

Note: Page numbers in *italic* indicate figures or tables; in bold they indicate longer sections.

For Product Safety Concerns and Information please contact our EU
representative GPSR@taylorandfrancis.com
Taylor & Francis Verlag GmbH, Kaufingerstraße 24, 80331 München, Germany

9 781138 616844